Theology in the Mode of Monk: An Aesthetics of Barth and Cone on Revelation and Freedom

"This third volume of Raymond Carr's magisterial comparison of Karl Barth and James Cone retraces the meaning of the political for both these luminaries. Carr in a way unmatched by any interpreter of Barth and Cone lays side by side their notions of freedom and articulates their architecture both historically and theologically through the musicality of Monk. With these three volumes the ground has shifted and Karl Barth and James Cone may now be read together far more productively."

—**Willie Jennings**, professor of systematic theology and Africana studies, Yale Divinity School

"Raymond Carr is one of the few groundbreaking and path-blazing theologians of his generation! This magisterial trilogy on three of the towering spiritual giants of the past one hundred years gives us new terrain in our grim and dim times."

—**Cornel West**, professor of philosophy and Christian practice, Union Theological Seminary

"Thelonious Monk's unprecedented aesthetics allow Raymond Carr to innovate brilliantly a mode that creates the interpenetration of James H. Cone and Karl Barth as supplementation and correction in counterpoint. In this groundbreaking third volume, Carr, himself a theological jazz creator and trickster theoretician, deploys the Monkian melodies to engage sociopolitical reality."

—**Dwight N. Hopkins**, professor of theology, University of Chicago

"Raymond Carr draws on a Black liberative tradition and employs Monk's musical aesthetic for theological exploration. His trilogy, *Theology in the Mode of Monk*, invokes questions and invites readers to explore ideas and to challenge concepts of being."

—**Angela D. Sims**, president, Colgate Rochester Crozer Divinity School

"Raymond Carr undertakes an audacious attempt to construct 'irregular theology' in an aesthetic mode through which Karl Barth encounters James Cone. He interrogates and advances Barth's thinking of freedom (Mozartean) down a line that includes James Cone's spirituals and blues and Thelonious Monk's jazz. In Carr's groundbreaking proposal, Friedrich-Wilhelm

Marquardt's 'logos of society' finds significance in the Black experience of sociopolitical struggle. Do not miss this book!"

—**Paul S. Chung**, director, Karl Barth and Public Theology Center

"Raymond Carr is the *Conjunto Cat!* 'Conjunto' is Spanish for 'to join together' or a 'set' or a musical group. In *Theology in the Mode of Monk,* Carr has arranged a new polygonal bandstand on which appears a theological vision and practice whose main players are Karl Barth, James Cone, and Thelonious Monk! Watch out! Give a listen! Read deep! *Conjunto* can also mean totality, everybody! Come onstage by reading this book and join Raymond Carr's *conjunto.*"

—**Davíd Carrasco**, professor of the study of Latin America,
Harvard Divinity School

"Raymond Carr has emerged as one of the most creative minds in contemporary African American theology. His intensive engagement with James Cone and Karl Barth has already made a mark in the field but is now assured with the appearance of these remarkable volumes."

—**George Hunsinger**, professor of systematic theology,
Princeton Theological Seminary

"With great erudition and care, Raymond Carr cleverly utilizes the jazz aesthetic of Thelonious Monk to help explore the theological relationships between Karl Barth and James Cone. As he does so, we see the importance of Christ's faithfulness as our cantus firmus and hear an urgent call for the church to be prophetic as it hears the higher frequencies of God and the lower frequencies of the cries of the oppressed."

—**Gary W. Burnett**, senior fellow in New Testament, Belfast School of Theology

"*Theology in the Mode of Monk* is a masterpiece of theological aesthetics. Through Monk, Carr discloses obsolete philosophical systems before *and* after Karl Barth; and with James Cone signifyin(g) on Barth, he transforms deleterious theological, existential, and political systematics. Thus, this project attunes us to the sound(s) that arise from the cross of Christ—even as we improvise on that revolutionary melody and move to its rhythm(s)."

—**Johanne Stubbe Teglbjærg Kristensen**, associate professor of theology,
University of Copenhagen

Theology *in the* **Mode** *of* **Monk:**

An Aesthetics of Barth and Cone on Revelation and Freedom

VOLUME 3

Misterioso

Freedom for
Liberation in Creation

Raymond Carr

FOREWORD BY
Willie James Jennings

 CASCADE *Books* • Eugene, Oregon

THEOLOGY IN THE MODE OF MONK: AN AESTHETICS OF BARTH AND CONE ON REVELATION AND FREEDOM, VOLUME 3
Misterioso: Freedom for Liberation in Creation

Cascade Books
An Imprint of Wipf and Stock Publishers
199 W. 8th Ave., Suite 3
Eugene, OR 97401

www.wipfandstock.com

PAPERBACK ISBN: 978-1-6667-4525-2
HARDCOVER ISBN: 978-1-6667-4526-9
EBOOK ISBN: 978-1-6667-4527-6

Cataloguing-in-Publication data:

Names: Carr, Raymond.

Title: Theology in the mode of Monk, volume 3 : misterioso: freedom for liberation in creation / by Raymond Carr.

Description: Eugene, OR: Cascade Books, 2024 | Includes bibliographical references and index.

Identifiers: ISBN 978-1-6667-4525-2 (paperback) | ISBN 978-1-6667-4526-9 (hardcover) | ISBN 978-1-6667-4527-6 (ebook)

Subjects: LCSH: Karl Barth, 1886–1968. | James Cone, 1938–2018. | Thelonious Monk, 1917–1982. | Theological aesthetics. | Eschatology.

Classification: ML3556 .C366 2024 (paperback) | ML3556 (ebook)

VERSION NUMBER 11/18/24

Cover design by Damon Saddler
Illustrations by Edie A. Frederick

Dedicated to Dr. James Hal Cone (1938–2018),

Joi Carr,

and the people

of West Petersburg, Virginia,

who give me rhythm for life!

and all the precious souls who inspired me along the journey

who now rest with the ancestors . . .

Harvey Myrick

Elizabeth Myrick

Hampton Mason

Florence V. Mason

Melvin N. Mason

Sammie L. Martins

Charles H. Long

James A. Noel

Chris Spinks

and my precious mother,

Jean "Glut" Mason

Thelonious Monk—The High Priest[1]

Bebop is the music of revolt.[2]

They speak of freedom. But one has no right, under pretext of freeing yourself, to be illogical and incoherent by getting rid of structure and simply piling a lot of notes one on top of the other.[3]

Music is a servant before the face of God;
it has a priestly function.[4]

1. Epithet from Monk's album *The High Priest* (Prestige, 1968).
2. Scott DeVeaux, quoted in Van der Bliek, *Thelonious Monk Reader*, 267.
3. Fitterling, *Thelonious Monk*, 82, 84.
4. Van der Leeuw, *Sacred and Profane Beauty*, 262.

Contents

Naming the Mode of Transformation

They were transformed. Coltrane sounded one way and was transformed. So was [Charlie] Rouse. Every single musician that ever played with Thelonious was transformed. So why wouldn't I be transformed?[1]

Raymond Carr is after transformation. Christian theology, especially in the Western world, needs it. But transformed into what? That is the question that Raymond Carr seeks to answer with this magisterial three-volume work. Why does Christian theology need transformation? Because it has been much too slow and reluctant to follow its God, to allow thought to trace after the beautiful turnings, the round and round moving of the divine life. God moves. This is the inner reward we gain through the incarnation. When God's feet touched the soil, God was in rhythm, the very rhythm God created with the creation itself. This means that God birthed musicality. Birthing is the right word here, because music is the living child of the child of God. Musicality is the mode of being that God offers to aid us—help in a time of trouble—as we seek to discern the path to the abundant life God eagerly gives in Jesus Christ. This path leads to transformation not as an end point in our place and time, but as an art of life, a method for thriving. Musicality then companions us, walks alongside us in such a way as to constantly invite us to walk in and through it and thereby to be permeated by it—striding along, step by step, breathing in and out,

1. Thelonious Monk Jr., commenting on the impact of his father Thelonious Monk Sr. Cited in Kelley, *Thelonious Monk*, 424.

the sound, the rhythm, the chord progressions, the instruments, the voices and the voicing, the crescendos and decrescendos, the accelerando and ritardando, and of course, the silence, that beautiful sound.

Theology has lost sight of this God-given companion. I am not talking about losing sight of the relation of theology to the arts, or theological aesthetics, or a theology of music. All of which are important. But there is something more fundamentally urgent and compelling about taking note of this companion, for it is the musicality of theology itself without which theology is not moving. Without musicality theology just stands still like a statue that has become invisible through being constantly seen but rarely noticed. Psychologists call this inattentional blindness. People who are busy with simply trying to live life walk by it, drive by it, but they never see it, because they are moving, and it is standing still—still life. The most difficult task of any artist is to take what is no longer visible and make it visible freshly, but not in the same way. Indeed, great art takes the familiar and renders it queer—pulsating with newness that calls forth attention. Wait, you stand here, while it moves and moves again. Now you can move, and it will move as you move. That is art. That is music.

Raymond Carr takes on a herculean task—he takes what many people cannot see even though they observe it, and he renders it visible in a strange—beautifully strange, magnificently strange—way to allow it to move, allow it to return to its musicality. This is a work of repair. To say Carr is repairing theology would be too grandiose a claim, but we should say that he is repairing the visibility of two theologians by making them visible through each other. And he is doing this through another intellectual (should we call him a shadow theologian?), a musician of singular genius, extraordinary creative power, and prescient musical insight. Karl Barth, James Cone, and Thelonious Monk are each a mountain, existing on different parts of the planet, one might even say, on different planes of existence. Raymond Carr moves the mountains not simply next to each other, but he renders them nesting dolls, the one inside the other and then inside the other and then inside the other—movement indeed.

I must confess that I despair of both Barth studies and emerging Cone studies, not because I find either of these crucial theologians of diminished importance. They are even more critical for this moment than they were decades past. My despair is over their use. The last forty years in theological studies have imprisoned Barth's theology and life inside a tragic theological surrogacy. On the one side, he remains the manservant of white self-sufficient masculinist intellectual form. Writing or lecturing on Karl Barth in praise, critique, or support for a theological position has become a way to show mastery of a theological and/or philosophical tradition, or control of the European intellectual canon. Barth has been rendered a scholastic object in the Bordieuan sense of scholastic objectification, trapped inside the habitus of whiteness. This scholastic Barth functions like Aquinas functions within white masculinist intellectual form—a disembodied tool to build up or tear down, to make us all meaningful men (no matter what our gender), if we are willing to become self-sufficiently theologically learned. On the other side, Barth gives his back to be beaten—he is the symbol of all that is dangerous and destructive in theology—heterosexist, patriarchal, homophobic, misogynistic, patently Eurocentric, and of limited value for our moment. There are, of course, problems with Barth, but this aspect of his theological surrogacy turns him into a point of feared seduction or a roadblock that requires a detour around his work and therefore a theological formation that is *intentionally* geared against anything hinting of Barth. All of this has made it difficult to engage Karl Barth in any meaningful way without being drawn into his surrogacy. It has also made him unappealing to generations of scholars who shun both formations in whiteness and the hegemonies of our time.

James Cone has now become subject to a brilliant operation of evasion. The theological academy or, as Raymond Carr calls it, the academic industrial complex, has found a way to disarm Cone's profound critique of white Western theology by making him a spectacular theological object, capturing him in time, and then forming a detour around him—roping off his statue, requiring respectful silence as one passes by—and then carrying on as though he had never existed. Cone and his work are quickly becoming a museum statue—to be noted, observed, and then passed by as one moves on to the next theologian, or the next iteration of black religious thought. If on the one side of evasion, we find intellectuals who refuse to take seriously Cone's *black* theological vision, on the other side of evasion, we find intellectuals who refuse to take seriously Cone's black *theological* vision. Cone is diminished precisely through his invocation under these taxidermic conditions. Cone is a theological reckoning for Western theology that most theologians do not have the sensitivity—spiritual, moral, or intellectual—to recognize. Cone's work demands we contemplate the racial condition as a bedrock theological problem, inescapable, and if ignored—inexcusable.

Cone, however, is much more than an antiseptic against racism. He articulates a path to take seriously the black Christian subject as a turning point for theology in our moment. But who has heard our report? Raymond Carr has ears to hear, and he offers us some help to aid our hearing. Enter the great Thelonious Monk.

No one realized what Raymond Carr knows. Karl Barth and James Cone need Thelonious Monk. Thelonious Monk does not need them.

Indeed, Carr grasps the power of Monk as a companion who is fundamentally taking the lead here. Monk gave birth to a new moment, not simply in American jazz, but in modern music, and in so doing articulated a freedom inside musical and compositional form that others did not come close to imagining before him. Monk's music overwhelms us in its gathering power. On the one hand, his music summarizes the traditions of improvisation that came before him and existed around him, and on the other hand, his compositions draw together new possibilities for thinking in sound—dense offerings, multilayered in their elegant simplicity. Raymond Carr discerned what no other intellectual I know discerned—that the musicality that Monk conjured illumines the musicality that modern theology needs. It is a need born of the Spirit who would bring us into the melodic center of existence, the cantus firmus (as Carr puts it), of Jesus Christ. Carr brings us to the missing link that has been evident for decades, maybe even centuries, but it has remained elusive to pen down and make plain—theology longs for, even demands musicality. This musicality is not captured by an ableist conceit exclusive to only those who can hear music. It involves all the senses because it is rooted in the beating heart, the breathing body, and the sensing soul. Yes, that musicality grasps the auditory but more centrally it glories in the lyrical—constant movement with meaning.

Karl Barth and James Cone are together in ways that few if any people see. This is Carr's insight that he elaborates in an astounding way. There are legions of books on Barth, and a growing number of texts on Cone, but there is none that capture what it means to see Barth and Cone together with the depth, subtlety, and artistic dexterity of Raymond Carr. It will be clear to any reader of these volumes that Carr has been contemplating these thinkers for decades, but he has also been thinking deeply inside the artistic as well. Carr writes like a musician thinks, and he thinks theologically about musicality. This means that he is asking his readers to stretch their bodies across a flowing river, their feet touching Barth and their hands grasping Cone and Monk flowing through them and as an added helpful instructor Carr employs the great historian of religion and black phenomenologist, Charles Long. Carr reads Charles Long with as much depth and power as he reads Barth and Cone. This is singular genius, approaching Monk level. Enlisting Long into his project, however, is necessary because Raymond Carr is trying to articulate a new kind of theological practice that can only be recognized inside compositional logics, inside the freedom of musical form that is simultaneously structured through traditions of play and performance and structured improvisationally in the heat of the moment, the urgency of the situation, and the vicissitudes of daily existence. That is, Carr is placing theological practice inside of black practice that is black existence.

What does it mean to live through a song, or a drumbeat, or a bass guitar riff, or a chord progression, or lyrics that capture a stubborn dilemma? And who would find it necessary to do that? The answer to both questions is black folks and black life. This however is not a racial exclusivity—this is the way of all flesh enfolded in a world of trouble. The black dilemma is acute awareness through experience of being enfolded in a white world. But the black response is to bend open that world and establish a freedom that hopefully will not yield but grow. Bending open a racially enfolded world is where Charles Long finds the black religious subject. Carr is attuned to what Long saw and heard—the black sound, religious in character, being presented in music, in speech, in thought, and bodily practice that spied out a freedom to be had and held. That bending open for so many black folks was made possible by a God who became flesh and joined us in the bending. Indeed, this enfleshed God bent the world open permanently toward the divine life and offers what no other bender could offer—eternal freedom, beginning here and now and registered in the playing, dancing, and singing body.

Reverence is required before the divine *mysterium* found in Jesus of Nazareth that in some profound way is woven into the black *mysterium* found in black flesh. It is a weaving that cannot be easily captured in text but might be signified through sheets of sounds (much like the music of John Coltrane after his transformation through playing with Thelonious Monk). Yet here is the thing—Raymond Carr is attempting to weave text to sheets of sound to give witness to our existence centered in Jesus Christ. By theologizing inside Barth, inside Cone, inside Long, inside Monk, we gain from Carr this marvelous interweaving. Listen as he says, "Karl Barth improvised on the subjective experience of the *subject matter*, whereas James Cone improvised on the *subjective experience* of the subject matter." Barth articulated "the experience of *revelation*, Cone articulated the *experience* of revelation." "Barth should be thought of as seeking to establish a *theo*anthropology, as described in *The Humanity of God* whereas Cone established a clear theo*anthropology* as described in *The God of the Oppressed* where human dignity, in particular black affirmation, is found in the divine."

Experience, revelation—Carr is taking on the burden of working with these overused theological words, these wooden concepts, and bringing them not just to the Monk's epic musical archive, but baptizing them in Monk's method, Monk's musicality, Monk's mode. Carr works between the keys, registering neither the black ones nor the white ones, but in between. He works between revelation (and the massive conceptual edifice erected around it) and experience (and the equally massive theoretical structures that surround this concept). This is where it helps to listen to the Monk discography—"Epistrophy," "'Round Midnight," "Misterioso" (along with many other epic tunes)—in the order that Raymond is recommending. Each tune places you more deeply in between the keys, in between weary theological warhorses, in between unproductive readings of Barth and equally unproductive readings of Cone, in between theologies intoxicated with mind distorting conservativisms and mind-shrinking liberalisms. I need to be clear that what we have in these three volumes is no homage to Barth or Cone, or even Monk—no resting in place with them. Carr refreshes our readings of them, preparing us to hear through Monk what it means to think at the edge of that freshness and freedom. This work, however, is about movement, about musicality that is an antidote to theology's arthritic condition and as such it is only trying to set the movement in the right direction—more to come, more to hear, more to say, more to play.

For those who like me who have been in search of a theological lyricism—to articulate it, embody it, rejoice in it—we have great companions in Barth, Cone, Long, Monk, and now Raymond Carr. Together we are in search of a land the location of which we cannot nail down, but we can describe the landscape. It is both arid and lush, dry like a desert and watery, even swamp-like. It has mountains and valleys, foothills and dense woods, grasses and rock formations. It is permeated with the distinct sound of the blues broken into fragments, a line here, a riff there, echoing everywhere, layered in ugly beauty, but between the fragments is a powerful silence in which dances laughter and sayings, queries and jokes, tears and shouts, and of course prayers, many prayers. Rolling through the ground in this land, caressing our feet is the beat—polyphonic, multilayered, expressing multiple time signatures—moving from below to above and back again. The beat calls us to move in a movement that is thinking itself, thinking after the giver of music, the giver of life, that is, the triune God. This land lay before us. Now that we see it over the horizon, rushing toward us, we can imagine a change in theology—in the ways we write, speak, and think theologically with a musicality that sounds out freedom—as soon as our feet strike this Zion.

Willie James Jennings
Hamden, Connecticut

Prelude

When Wondering Why Monk?

Caveat lector! (Let the reader beware!) This is not a book on jazz. It is a project utilizing the musicality of Thelonious Sphere Monk (1917–82) as an agency of meaning—a medium to think theologically. To be more specific, Monk's aesthetic, stylistics, and musical thinking in general, with their initial location in the bebop revolution, serve as an aesthetic analogue for thinking about theology in the twenty-first century, a century mired in profound problems, stemming from external and internal colonialism, ethno-nationalism, militarism, racism, sexism, and other -isms, i.e., ideological problems, that plague the United States and its vaunted claims to freedom. Even now the nation is coming to terms with a radical form of political polarization, the fallout of a global pandemic, and the ever-present specter of wars and the naturalization of war.

Evoking black music to negotiate the contours of a perilous terrain is not a new endeavor, however. W. E. B. Du Bois's recognition of the problem of the twentieth century, "the color line," in *The Souls of Black Folk* immediately comes to mind; or Karl Barth's turn to hear the harmony of creation through the music of Wolfgang Amadeus Mozart; or James Cone's affirmation of black life in *The Spirituals and the Blues*; or Angela Davis's extension and sustaining of feminist consciousness in *Blues Legacies and Black Feminism.*[1] So just as I am indebted to the auditory structure that

1. *The Souls of Black Folks*, in Du Bois, *Writings*; *CD* III/3:297–302; Cone, *Spirituals and the Blues*; Davis, *Blues Legacies and Black Feminism*.

inspired Monk, others have aspired to develop integrative theories of music. To be sure, "black music has long helped literary critics understand black literature"[2] and other disciplines; therefore it should not come as a surprise that black music harbors the potential to assist in the task of explicating theology—especially in such perilous times. Students of the seminal, theological contributions of James Hal Cone will recognize the "inseparable connection between the Christian confession of faith and the struggle of poor people for justice, as the songs and sermons of Black Christians had suggested" and the attendant "need to demonstrate that connection in formal theological discourse."[3] Students of Karl Barth's theology, however, may be less resolute on this score, although Barth's relationship to music is unquestionable, and because I believe it is more substantive than formerly acknowledged, it seems appropriate to build theologically on this aesthetic dimension, recognizing that "music provides the broadest possible vista for the imagination."[4]

Hoping to affirm black humanity through shared dialogue—as we walk with Cone along the road designed to incorporate black religion into theology—I embrace the basic truth that black religion, a mode of being that includes creating a relationship to cultural components outside the black church, is at the heart of black theology.[5] Consequently, in this text Monk's musical language operates as a creative theopoetic for an aesthetics of liberation designed to explore the towering intellectual contributions of Karl Barth, the Swiss Protestant theologian, and James Cone, the father of black liberation theology.

Hermeneutically, Monk's attention to musical form has a functional effect on my thinking. His aesthetic approach influences the methodological and structural architecture of all three volumes, underscoring the inner material content that occasions the stylistics and shapes the multiple ways his mode of thinking functions as an aesthetic analogue that gives way to various symbols of freedom, including the signs and symptoms that arise from imagining Monk's music as a parable of the kingdom. Thus, Monk's musical aesthetic is more than mere metaphor for my hermeneutical efforts. His musicality contributes to the overall framing, interpreting, and explicating of the correspondence between Christ, the central theological content of the

2. Spencer, *Theological Music*, 96.

3. Wilmore and Cone, *Black Theology*, 611. See Cone's important work *Spirituals and the Blues*.

4. See Barth's dedication to Mozart in his book *Wolfgang Amadeus Mozart*. See also Stoltzfus, *Theology as Performance*, 107–66; and Colette, "Joy, Pleasure and Anguish," 96. For music as a "vista for the imagination," see Copland, *Music and Imagination*, 7.

5. Wilmore and Cone, *Black Theology*, 617–18.

Christian faith (*analogans*), and his relationship to the analogical extensions of faith (*analogata)* heard in the polyphony of experiences in general. Stated another way, Jesus Christ is the cantus firmus, a notion tied immediately to Monk's mode of composing, and the cantus firmus denotes the central reference point of the entire polyphony of creation.[6] In these theological aesthetics, then, the term *mode* or *modality* refers to Monk's unique musical idiom, which gestures insightfully as a history-making *way* or *mode* of communication that frames the conceptual tensions and resources that make Barth's and Cone's theological differences transparent and usable. Monk's music provides the way for me to revel in a type of unity-in-complexity and complexity-in-unity. I believe it is ultimately in a richer form of harmony that Monk discovered the sound that extended beyond what others call harmony. Indeed, I hope theologians will overhear new harmonics and rhythms in my efforts to improvise on the melodic center where Barth and Cone coalesce rather than focus on what has historically been described as a kind of dissonance between Barth and Cone—even if they fail to hear or admire my audacity in this regard.

The degree of selectivity implied by my focus on Thelonious Monk raises obvious questions and deserves an explanation. The leading question I am often asked—by theologians and jazz aficionados alike—is simply "Why Monk?" Why choose the enigmatic high priest of bop? Why choose a musician known more for his stylistics than his technique? Why choose a composer whose commitment to the religious world seems so ambiguous? Of course, more visceral questions are also implied, such as, why not Bud Powell or why not John Coltrane, perhaps his *Love Supreme*, or other beboppers, including those with the rhythmical gifts of Kenny Clarke or the harmonies and melodies of Charlie "Bird" Parker or Dizzy Gillespie?

In response to these latter, more facile questions, I hope to afford us an opportunity to peer into what Monk's aesthetic mode means for the field of theology. Understanding how Monk's music functions parabolically offers a key to respecting his particularity or individuation and an opportunity to learn from his rhythmic freedom that arises so audaciously in the bebop period, a revolutionary period, musically speaking, when black jazz artists channeled the radical mood and human mode of being that allowed them to conscientiously break with standing jazz conventions. I am interested in this type of conscientization.

6. Monk employed the "melody of a composition as the *cantus firmus* to be referred to constantly during a solo in the place of the more common practice during his day of creating new melodies that outline chord changes." Van der Bliek, *Thelonious Monk Reader*, 249.

Even before the bebop period, jazz as a genre had been accommodated by traditional practices, and bebop artists participated, sometimes unwittingly, in the new mood and mode of being in the world. Conversely, Monk not only mastered the tradition he inherited, but he is also described as "the only bebopper who never played bebop."[7] This angle, in my understanding, already sets him apart as a locus for meaning. Monk is thus a revolutionary functioning amid a revolution, and as *a revolutionary in a revolution* his music gestures to something more significant than revolutions, attesting to what I, for now, will identify only as a mystery, a revolution that revolutionizes a revolution.

Still . . . "Why Monk?"

Regarding the former questions, immediate answers that draw on Monk's narrative come to mind, beginning with his unparalleled and unique standing in the jazz genre. Monk's music is employed to articulate in theology an architectural structure based on an aural aesthetics that influences my thinking and disrupts aesthetic regimes inherited from the Western emphasis on images. This is an aural aesthetics. Second, Monk's name suggests, as Gabriel Solis notes, a kind of "countercultural hipness or nonconformism." In his mode of composing I recognize an aesthetic perception that resists homogeneity even as it ratifies an extensive kind of harmonious coherence.[8] Said differently, Monk's music breaks with conventional and universal claims even as it embraces a kind of universal coherence. A multiplicity of difference is allowed to hang together in Monk. It is no wonder that Monk's approach to music liberated drummers and other instruments (which were typically in the rhythm section) to freely engage the melody and not just be there to "keep time."

Knowing that normative or universal approaches can routinely undermine the rich diversity of human specificity and integrity, Monk's insistence that students of music "improvise on the melody" as a guiding philosophy opens the door to honoring the multidimensional experiences of being traditional and modern. So called opposites coexist in Monk's productions. This passion in Monk has influenced musicians, poets, artists, and academicians to such a degree that his name is often invoked as the moniker

7. Martin Williams reiterates this point: "Whatever his contributions to bop had been, Monk was not a bopper. He had been working on something else all along." In Van der Bliek, *Thelonious Monk Reader*, 212. Stanley Crouch says that Monk "brought about a movement within a movement." Crouch, *Considering Genius*, 88.

8. Solis, *Monk's Music*, 2.

for institutes, restaurants, blogs, Twitter feeds, etc. Even a routine Google search reveals Monk's influence with its wide range of references: the Thelonious Monk of the bass guitar, the Thelonious Monk of actors, the Thelonious Monk of DJs, the Thelonious Monk of the small screen, the Thelonious Monk of poetry and street wear. At one point, even a Belgian-styled abbey ale was named for Monk. Like these others, the tenor of his constructive, countercultural influence inspires me to (re)imagine theological thinking in the mode of Monk, leading us, hopefully, to a redemptive mode that can sustain the rich multiplicity heard in aesthetic life.[9]

Monk's music has arguably earned such an awe-inspiring agency that it is sometimes credited with creating a genre within jazz. *Free jazz* is arguably inspired by Monk.[10] Since America is a jazz-inflected nation (sometimes described as a "jazzocracy" rather than a democracy), a nation where various ideals collide, interact, and are exchanged, Monk's music—with its dissonances, angularities, shaped silences, diminished chords, rhythmic breaks, and profound simplistic conventions—serves as a fitting metaphor for exploring the subjective possibilities within this republic and its seemingly uninhibited, kaleidoscopic sensibilities which flow from East to West and back to the East. This American nation indeed embodies the African and the European, the aboriginal and the colonial, the metaphorical and the profound symbolic modes and meanings that coalesce and mutually reinforce each other, provoking dishonest agreement and honest disagreement among its residents. Monk's music, framed by his interest to know "how things struggle with their opposites—an intensity that expands possibility," suggests a parabolic way of reimagining our tensions and our various modes of being in America.[11]

Using jazz to illuminate a theopolitical context is not a new endeavor either. In this age of imagination, books utilizing jazz and other genres of music are regularly released to discuss theopolitical motifs.[12] The stylistics of

9. I make an early attempt to think of the redemptive mode as it influences aesthetic life in "Can Work Be Redeemed Through Play? (Or Why Is Playing Not an Option)," in J. G. Smith and Renslow, *Blessed Are Those*, 25–40.

10. For Monk as a precursor to free jazz, see Szwed, *Jazz 101*, 173. I will return to the discussion of free jazz in the "Head" below.

11. Komunyakaa, "It's Always Night," 52. Compare to Carr, "Wade in the Water Children," where I invert the Western movement by reframing the conversation from West to East.

12. For an extended list, see the bibliography in this book, but notice the following more recent examples, such as Davis, *Blues Legacies and Black Feminism*; Douglas, *Black Bodies and Black Church*; Pederson, *God, Creation*; Burnett, *Gospel According to the Blues*; Heltzel, *Resurrection City*; Eikelboom, *Rhythm*; and more recently Edwards, *Christ Is Time*; and Edgar, *Supreme Love*.

jazz improvisation are employed to raise questions about human knowledge in general, often deploying the art of improvisation to articulate intellectual freedom and to suggest imaginative and creative ways of theologizing. Hence, a more prescient question than "why Monk" may be to consider how Monk's mode of composing opens the door to the creative imagination and gestures constructively in our search for an alternative mode of thinking in contrast to that practiced, colonial mode that dominates the more abstract and discursive frameworks currently employed in modern religious thinking. Rather than highlighting technical ethnographic research and feigned objectivity as opposed to the lived experience of its subjects, Monk's music constantly leads me to ask what his stylistics connote for religion and theology. What possibilities are opened in our thinking when we consider the tonal range Monk employs in his bold harmonic sensibilities? What do his musical aesthetics mean hermeneutically for constructive theological thinking? And just what does Monk's music signal to tradition, religion, and theology when it encourages us to put the conventional to the test?

Like prior blues and jazz musicians, Monk's jazz conventions were developed to offer an imaginative framework in an era of transition and fragmentation. Even tribal and folk traditions are fragmented in America. We live in the age of the fragment. Thus Monk's response as a generative paradigm to fragmentation anticipates important questions for theology, questions such as "How should we engage and encounter one another where such diversity prevails?" This question and others speak ultimately to why I chose Monk, whose aesthetics allow for the interrelationship between affirmations and oppositions, between the fragment and the whole; and because his musical logic counterbalances even the tendency toward selectivity. Implied therefore in my efforts is the belief that jazz, especially Monk's jazz, can intimate some ecumenical foresight to attuned theological ears by offering an audible witness to assist in extending the range of our listening in the current social, cultural, and economic universe. Monk's musical prosody provides a framework for thinking through the (dis)continuities that are too often interpreted as disruptions between thinkers, like Barth and Cone, or disruptions in categories like revelation and experience, freedom and liberation, and our more modern problems that stem from our failure to honor the difference between discursive and aesthetic categories. Monk's music thus illuminates a way to transcend the limitations of difference and suggests an aesthetic vocabulary for thinking about how Barth and Cone, my two primary countermelodies in this project, supplement and correct one other in counterpoint.

We can sharpen our insight into questions about Monk by deepening our insight into what it means to identify America as a jazz-inflected nation.

As noted earlier, the music has the potential to furnish an aesthetic mode of religious apprehension to think about the nation and theology as they relate so profoundly to one another.[13] But we may begin by asking whether jazz should be used as an agency for meaning at all. Is the art form itself in some way compromised or diminished because we theologians attempt to "lay claim to it"? This question is important because music is routinely commodified in America and where it is not commodified, it is often excluded. Hence, it is important to speak of Monk's music with integrity. This means we ought to respect all the things jazz can be in the social imaginary. For example, Monk's jazz can be thought of *as jazz* and as something more than jazz.

Allow me to explain. When speaking analogically, jazz can be thought of as several things at the same time. One can think of it as *music* since jazz is a form of music indigenous to America, materializing, as it were, as part of American cultural expression and sounding forth from the creolization in America. Jazz is also an *art form*—and jazz musicians evidence their familiarity with this art through various instruments of choice. Jazz is *communal*. And various styles of jazz require different levels of engagement and participation, whether quartets, which were popular during the bebop period, or other forms and groupings such as big band or combo—even solos. At any rate, there emerges a kind of cooperative independence in such environments. Jazz is *improvisational*. To be sure, as Kenny Burrell once stated to me in a conversation, the fact that jazz is the flagship of improvisation arguably explains the reason the genre is not as marketable as other music genres. According to Burrell, the dynamic nature of jazz is not commodifiable in the same way as other artistic products. Notwithstanding this argument, jazz is *idiomatic*, and as a result when one hears various artists and their unique voicings, which are representative of peculiar tastes, limitations, and gifts, various forms of individuation arise. The list can go on, of course, including jazz as *performative*, jazz as *creative*, etc. Jazz is indeed all these things and more than these things, which I say only to point to the truth that jazz is also *theology*. It is theology while it remains all these other things without violating the integrity of what, as these other things, it happens to be. These descriptive ways then function as vehicles through which jazz as theology is conveyed.[14]

13. See Leonard, *Jazz*, for a view of jazz in relation to religion.

14. I owe this structured insight to the American lay theologian William Stringfellow, who expressed similar thoughts regarding the film *West Side Story*. His viewpoint demonstrates how the word of God is implicated in creation, and the literary structure I use draws freely on his. See Stringfellow, *Private and Public Faith*, 65.

A similar kind of conceptual turn occurs in the biblical narrative. The mythopoetic texts of Hebrew Scripture convey knowledge of God while retaining their integrity and value as ancient, mythopoetic texts that bear other meanings that give insight and reflect the cultural universe of their own sociocultural time and space. The ancient Mesopotamian world can thus be described as a *Weltanschauung* (worldview) or *intellectus* for their times. This partly explains why some theologians use the language of "the Word within the words." These thinkers are making a distinction between the word of the Bible and the world of God as attested in the Bible. The distinction drawn has a peculiar import. In terms of how jazz can function as an agency for meaning in this line of thinking, I attempt something similar in my use of Monk's jazz aesthetics, that is, to use his aesthetics as a way of witnessing to the reality of the Word.

From Mozart and the Spirituals and the Blues to Theology in the Mode of Monk

These conceptual turns and possibilities in jazz allow me to appreciate the mythic dimension in jazz in relation to American cultural aspirations. Monk's jazz or what I call "theology in Monk mode" conveys religious meaning, first, in terms of historical linear progression from classical music to blues and jazz, which reveals an immediate discursive and historical connection between Barth, Cone, and my own representative musical interests. Barth, for instance, idealized European classical music—especially Mozart. Being so fascinated with Mozart, his *Church Dogmatics*, especially in his emphasis on creation, resonate with aesthetic contrasts that arise out of Mozart's musical horizon. For instance, Barth was concerned fundamentally with the way Mozart "arranges the relationships among human voices."[15] His comments have led to the suggestion that even the motive structure of his dogmatics is shaped by Mozart's music. George Hunsinger, for instance, contends that Barth shares with Mozart "a certain taste for thematic interplay."[16]

Barth argued that Mozart composed "objectively." This objectivity allows contrasts, highlighting life and death, good and evil, joy and sorrow.[17]

15. Barth's reflections are in the *Church Dogmatics* and a small collection of writings with chapters culled from sections in his dogmatics called *Wolfgang Amadeus Mozart*. See K. Barth, *Wolfgang Amadeus Mozart*, 34–35.

16. Hunsinger, *How to Read Karl Barth*, 28.

17. For an extended development of the "objective" thinking of Barth, see Hunsinger, *How to Read Karl Barth*, 35–39; T. F. Torrance, who, despite his critique of Barth,

But Barth does not dogmatize what Colin Gunton calls "romantic portrayals of the sunny Mozart oblivious to pain and suffering."[18] On the contrary, even when Mozart hears the harmony of creation, according to Barth, he is aware that "the shadow also belongs [to creation], but in which the shadow is not darkness, deficiency is not defeat."[19] Mozart certainly knew of the shadow side of life, but Barth focused on the so-called "sunny side" as a primary point of interest. In other words, Mozart defied the chaos and discord of life.[20] For those who know Barth's theology, Barth unsurprisingly focused on the movement of Mozart's music as it progresses from the left to right, meaning *from light to darkness*. And even when "Barth's Mozart" moves in what looks like the other direction, that is, from real life to light, Barth interpreted "real life" from the prism or framework of the incarnation. This is what Barth means when he writes that "he [Mozart] moves from left to right, never the reverse," a fact that, no doubt, explains what Barth means by Mozart's triumphant 'charm.'[21] It is no wonder then that some theologians have accused Barth of a "triumph of grace."[22] Barth witnessed to the grace of life and its judgment on the chaos, whether one is speaking from creation to chaos (above to below) or from chaos to creation (below to above).

But is it possible to move from right to left? Can the darkness in its own mysterious and paradoxical way point to truth? Is not God the God of the light *and* the God of the darkness, the good and the evil (Isa 45:7)? Perhaps after perusing the relationship between Barth and Cone, we can offer better answers to these questions—or perhaps come up with better questions in light of the contemporary situation. Barth himself turned singularly to Mozart's music.[23] He expressed a profound interest in the way his turn to Mozart was analogous to his turn to Christ in what Barth eventually identified as a "christological concentration."[24] This concentrated centering of faith (and his theological agenda) focused on God's revelation as heard in the uniqueness of the person of Jesus Christ. It could be, as noted by one of Barth's former students, that "his practice of using the same composer's music to set a ground-tone for his work every morning should also

grounds even the "sacraments" of the church on the objective ground in the incarnation and atonement for rethinking worship: *Theology in Reconciliation*, 82–105.

18. Gunton, "Mozart the Theologian," 348.

19. *CD* III/3:298.

20. K. Barth, *Wolfgang Amadeus Mozart*, 33.

21. K. Barth, *Wolfgang Amadeus Mozart*, 33–34.

22. Here of course I am mindful of Berkouwer's classic critique found in Berkouwer, *Triumph of Grace*.

23. *CD* III/3:297.

24. Godsey, *Karl Barth 1886–1968*, 43.

be understood as a part of the ascetic discipline of a creative scholar, who had found this to be a useful aid in channeling and focusing his energies."[25] But this does not explain why Barth's preoccupation with this Catholic, Freemason musician dampened the melodies of all other musicians in his hearing.[26] I would like to imagine that what Barth heard was an *analogia relationis*, an analogy of the relationship between God and the creation that witnesses to the mysterious center. This melodic foundation is the ground tone for Barth's theological contributions.

James Cone was a child of the blues, however. The blues, with their deep sensitivity to problems of *a peculiar time*. The blues, with "unrefined" subjectivity, expressed in the logic of black aesthetic experience, transcend what Friedrich-Wilhelm Marquardt, the audacious interpreter of Barth, called the "logos of society." The genre of the blues beckons us to reinterpret society's logos from the standpoint of black redemption, beginning by recognizing how the "logos of *die Sache*," and God's profound concern for humanity, yes, black humanity, reinterprets the "logos of society."[27] Hence, in the hands of James Cone, the functionality and plaintive melodies of the blues witness to God's judgment on a society ruled by its own logos, its own *reality*, its own *space*; its own *freedom*.[28] In essence his interpretation of the blues correlates with the experience and consciousness of blacks in the sociopolitical soundscape in America—echoing its dissonances, angularities, and contradictions; thus the plaintive melodies of black life and experience resonate within the black cultural experience. As Cone writes, "Who could possibly understand these paradoxical affirmations but the people who live them?"[29]

If we bear in mind that Cone's turn to the blues represents a deliberate turn to black experience, his blues consciousness is latent at the beginning of his theological endeavors, perhaps unrealized in terms of his own theological identity, self-discovery, and agency. His metanoia-experience or conversion to blackness deepened and sustained his attentive turn (epistrophe) to the affirmation of black life. For Cone, the God of the exodus experience identified and journeyed with blacks. *Jesus* is heard in the blues. Jesus is *in* the blues. Jesus *is* the blues. Black life became a spiritual. Hear the inflection. Consequently, in view of the black deposit of faith, Cone maintained

25. R. Anderson, *American Scholar Recalls*, 408.

26. Solomon, *Mozart*, 117.

27. Marquardt, *Theologie und Sozialismus*, 202–3. While Marquardt did not have the blues in mind, the blues are to be regarded as parables of God's revolution.

28. See Cone, *Spirituals and the Blues*, 14.

29. Cone, *Spirituals and the Blues*, 5.

a singular focus on the "situation" as much as Barth focused on the christological concentration. Moreover, his studied concentration on this subject matter (for over fifty years) undoubtedly remains as one of James Cone's greatest contributions to the field of theology. Even his deliberate efforts to turn away from the grand theology of Karl Barth, reflect his profound concern and preoccupation with the lives of black people, and as we noted in *Epistrophy* (vol. 1, ch. 2), his critical engagement with five important black scholars—identified as counterpoints—propelled him even more deeply into black life and a blues aesthetic that provocatively gave momentum to his theology.

On a related note, the more facile and discursive insights above, moving from Mozart to the spirituals/blues and onward to theology in the mode of Monk, are enhanced when discussed in the context of classical objectivity (and the subjective) in music. Mozart, as is well known, is often acknowledged as a composer of unrivaled classical objectivity to such an extent that his works are thought to "transcend issues of personality, of self-revelation, of originality."[30] The philosopher Hegel and later Barth praised the "objective" in Mozart's music, reveling especially in his unique "sound." Barth wrote that "he does not reveal in his music any doctrine and certainly not himself."[31] This determination did not come without critics like Maynard Solomon, who argued that such interpretations amount to a trope of Mozart's so-called creative genius, especially one that separates Mozart *the individual* from his work. Still, for those who have come to understand Barth, it makes sense why no other trope of Mozart is as important to Barth as is the concern for a form of objectivity. Barth is an objective thinker through and through, even when acknowledging the subjective.[32] This penchant for objectivity emerged early in Barth's theology, but this is not an abstract vision of God that overemphasizes objectivity as an idol of some sort. Such a vision would be something akin to a form of objectivism. Barth, rather, was preoccupied with developing Christ as a critical center for his theology.[33] Barth should be understood as hearing Mozart in light of his theology and then as developing his theology in light of Mozart. This reveals how Mozart functioned parabolically. Barth heard the objectivity of the word of God in

30. Solomon, *Mozart*, 115–17.

31. K. Barth, *Wolfgang Amadeus Mozart*, 37.

32. Busch, *Great Passion*, 72–76. This penchant explains why Barth placed an emphasis on the objective side of revelation, that is, Jesus Christ. He states, "If I had made much of the Holy Spirit, I am afraid it would have led back to subjectivism, which is what I wanted to overcome." Godsey, *Karl Barth's Table Talk*, 27.

33. Barth used this language as early as 1914. See K. Barth and Thurneysen, *Revolutionary Theology*, 27, 49.

Mozart's witness, an ode to the *freedom* of God. As a result, Mozart's piety and personality, his religious propriety, and even his church tradition were all penultimate in relation to this ultimacy. This ultimacy placed everything else into perspective. As Barth writes, Mozart "was remarkably free from the mania for self-expression."[34]

According to the dean of jazz, Billy Taylor, jazz is American's classical music. In this respect, it indicates a logical step in the line from Karl Barth's *Mozart* and James Cone's *The Spirituals and the Blues.* Monk's way of composing breaks open the door to thinking of James Cone as a counterpoint to Barth's theological project. Monk's jazz aesthetic provides a *via cognoscendi*, a way of knowing, that juxtaposes Cone's blues world as a counterpoint with the world Barth analogized through Mozart. And because Monk expressed a deep sensitivity for the blues—with jazz representing the next logical step after the blues genre—his music resonates with the same "spirit of black emotion" found in the inflections of Cone's black theology.[35] The explication of this relationship informs the agenda I have in mind for theology. In other words, Monk's musical accents and inflections can be heard as an advancement of Barth and Cone, a subjective complement to the objective pronouncements Barth heard in Mozart—not merely because Monk promoted objectivity, through the normativity of melody, but rather because Monk attests to the possibilities surrounding the melody. Monk "could hear the music around the music."[36] This form of listening transcends the speculative forms of abstraction that have become the calling card of the modern world.

By acknowledging this form of aesthetic coinherence, Monk's jazz witnesses to the subjective in correspondence with the objective. His accents on angularities, silences, diminished chords, rhythmic breaks, and tremolos all symbolize the subjective possibilities that exist as a part of God's so-called objective music. Monk's way is another way that opens up other ways. One of Monk's fellow musicians who, using a bit of ribaldry, described Monk's musical aesthetics in the following colorful language: "I have traveled with musicians who can play all the white keys; and I have traveled with musicians who can play all the black keys, but I have never traveled with a m****f***** who can play between the cracks."[37] This playing between the cracks of the scale, which is often interpreted as playing "out of tune," characterizes the insight Monk brings to jazz and the illumination

34. *CD* III/3:298.

35. Cone, *Spirituals and the Blues*, 6.

36. The words of Nica Rothschild, "the Jazz Baroness," the patron of bebop. Rothschild, *Baroness*, 223.

37. Rothschild, *Baroness*, 156.

his composing offers as a an analogy for thinking theologically. Being "out of tune" might be a way to characterize all of the "unheard music" of the physical world that we miss with our so-called transparency. Joseph Sittler, the Lutheran theologian, captured what I think Monk's musical language helps us to hear:

> We sometimes suppose that people look upon the world and find it beautiful and then look for a language with which to adorn what they behold. I think that is true, but it also works the other way. Sometimes we are partly blinded toward this world, and then someone puts the beauty of which we had not been aware into a gorgeous line. Thereafter we behold it in a new way. We go not only from beholding to language, but we may go from the beauty of language to the enhancement of beholding.[38]

Third, as implied above, the "developmental logic" in Monk's reflective approach to jazz, applied hermeneutically, encourages a theological approach that decenters scientific and discursive methodological procedures that have become so deleteriously normative. This rational body of knowledge or, as Charles Long, the historian of religions, prefers to say, this *epistēmē* reinforces the priority of the aesthetics of whiteness by making use of methodological data to reinforce the priority of the American *epistēmē*.[39] This tragic deployment of the *epistēmē* marginalizes the creative possibilities within the black community. As a result, those with the power of definition, or in Long's words, "the power of cultural signification," shape the religious reality of black Americans. Like Long, I believe the best creative resources for deconstructing this tragic deployment arise from the shadow side of the Enlightenment. In responding from this angle, I hope to disrupt this influence, which is often employed reductively to discuss the relationship between theologians such as Karl Barth and James Cone.

In terms of his developmental logic, Monk often moderated his technique when composing to achieve a certain sound in his music. Monk prioritized the *sound* of a tune, letting the music determine the shape of his distinctive contributions. I would suggest that if the same mode of thinking that shapes his musical aesthetic is used to shape theological thought, then his stylistics function generatively as form of parabolic suggestiveness and can encourage theologians to move beyond strict limitations of readymade categories and techniques. In this aesthetic mode, parables supersede

38. Sittler, *Gravity and Grace*, 84.

39. Long uses *epistēmē* to refer to an "organized body of rational knowledge with its own proper object." Long, "New Look at American Religion," 124. Compare my brief discussion of the problem in Carr, "Wade in the Water Children," 65.

principles and precedents outstrip propositions in much the same way *Geschichte* (storied history) takes precedent over *Historie* (historical accounting). Of course, these things are not mutually exclusive, but the actualistic shape of this mode of thinking, especially as determined by the melody of a tune, provides us with a center whereby theologians can think to and from a common point of identity.

As for what this ultimately means for theological discourse, we must not forget that Monk's tendency to break convention caused many listeners to be slow in appreciating his style of jazz, believing "he lacked technique."[40] Without capitulating to such implicit bias, I will explore what Monk's jazz aesthetic, especially as it relates to how one identifies with revolutionary cultural moments, can illuminate in relation to the theological imagination while hoping we have ears to hear. Bebop, indeed, embodies profound connections to a peculiar cultural and historical impulse, being what Cornel West identified as "a revolt against the middle-class 'jazz of the museum' against swing and white musicians" whose style had become hegemonic.[41] Bebop in this respect signalizes a period where "coming of age" for black jazz artists and black people in general resonated with a cultural shift in mood. This revolutionary moment can offer what, in Barth's language, may amount to a "true word."

Using Monk's musical prosody, then, supports theologizing in a different key rather than simply mirroring the predominant patterns, religio-cultural norms, logics, and symbols, modeled in Western theology with its delimiting methodologies and stifling categories that are occasionally replicated in black theology and other contextual theologies.[42] Thinking with Monk has the potential to liberate us to engage in a kind of harmonious thinking that transcends the limitations of modern discursive thought. As a metaphor, the dialogical character of Monk's music—epitomized in silences, unpredictable uses of space, rhythmic displacements, and harmonic dissonances—encourages methodological insights that underline the continuity between Barth and Cone, a continuity that leaves room for contestation and difference. If we learn this lesson from Monk, I believe, along with Gabriel Solis, that the meta-communicative nature of black music, which permits artists to function *within* and *beyond* standard narratives, will benefit theologians. As Louis Armstrong points out, black musicians have "a language

40. Quoted in Hentoff, *Jazz Life*, 196.

41. West, *Prophetic Reflections*, 92.

42. See Charles Long, whose significant insights for doing theology out of the surplus of black experience are expressed in *Significations* and "New Look at American Religion," 118. As we saw in vol. 2, *'Round Midnight*, Long symbolizes a bridge to new rhythms in theology.

of their own."[43] This language exists beyond words and has the power to sustain our dialogue and cultural signification.

In what follows, I seek to be informed by this language and its surplus beyond the "semantical," believing that black music can make one of its strongest contributions to a theological hermeneutics and assist us in a faithful reflection on the subject matter (*die Sache*). As a point of fact, Solis places the black tradition of signifyin(g)—another important reason for why I chose Monk—on this communicative plane.[44] Indeed, this approach to theology harbors the potential to "testify" and gesture from human ambiguity toward the subject matter of Scripture; to gesture toward a God who is neither speech nor silence, neither above or below, neither on the right or the left, neither here nor there; to gesture toward a God who is simultaneously beyond and fully whole in *every* location, in *every* time, and in *every* space and thus irreducible to the binaries we create.

So how should we proceed?

Monk's Theological Discography: "Epistrophy," "'Round Midnight," and "Misterioso"

Although Monk clearly did not have theology in mind when developing his music, I frame the discussion in this project in three different ways. First, I use Monk's musical architecture to *structure* the body of this theological composition, setting forth parameters for the external framework as expressed in volume 1, even as it witnesses to the deeper reality expressed in volume 2. Second, in volume 2, Monk's music provides a way to conceptualize the internal *substance* or content of theology, embracing his way of composing as constitutive for coming to terms with the subject matter. This means that his penchant for "improvising on the melody" echoes the Chalcedonian mystery in its own way, which is then set forth in the coherence between the melody and the improvisation that embellishes and adorns it. Thus, in the mode of Monk means I play off of the inner material structure of faith as the internal ground of my theology. Third, in this volume, Monk is used as a secular parable or symbol to symbolize and *signify* the relationship between creativity and creation. In this way, the various aesthetica in creation are embraced and expanded in an inclusive direction. The trilogy closes here in volume 3 with a brief discussion of the academic industrial

43. Cited in Sehgal, *Jazzocracy*, 3.

44. See Solis, "Hearing Monk," 95–96.

complex, the primary working location of Barth and Cone, a locus that resides within what I term the harmony of redemption as I understand it.

To say more, this project is divided into four movements represented by three different songs in terms of its architectural structure: "Epistrophy," "'Round Midnight," and "Misterioso." Each book opens with a "head," a feature jazz artists employ as an orienting section for a tune. The head doubles as a "prologue." The head in each volume—symbolized by a hat—establishes the main theme of each motive. Moreover, because of the usefulness of Monk's song titles, identified here as Monk's theological discography, I adopt these three tunes because Monk often included them in a jazz set or quartet performance. These tunes also represent the primary loci Karl Barth used to frame his theology, that is, creation, reconciliation, and redemption. "'Round Midnight," for instance, represents the Christology in this trilogy.

"Epistrophy" in the first book indicates a "turning about" of historical and hermeneutical insights; the tune provides the theme for the first volume, where I discuss Cone's paradoxical beginnings in the context of white American "Barthian" interpretations (ch. 1); his arguments with black critics interpreted as counterpoints (ch. 2); womanist progressions (ch. 3) and the hermeneutical modalities that frame both Barth's and Cone's responses to their peculiar intellectual and sociopolitical contexts (ch. 4). "Epistrophy," arguably the first modern jazz song, has been called "the holy dawn of Jazz America," and it is particularly useful for initiating the new harmonics and theological rhythms that "dawn" in volume 1.[45]

The second volume utilizes the song "'Round Midnight" as its primary framing device. It is the most covered jazz song in history. The song furnishes the christological core of the project in three substantial chapters. These chapters are interrelated since Karl Barth, James Cone, and Charles Long represent my intellectual trinity just as James Cone used Martin Luther King Jr., Malcolm X, and James Baldwin to inform his theological thinking.[46] The concept of the "night" in "'Round Midnight" functions contrapuntally in that volume. It alludes to the judgment of God represented by the "night" of Barth's *Crisis Theology*, that "fell like a bomb in the playground of the theologians" during the metaphorical noon of German ascendency (ch. 1); and it also represents the "midnight in the social order" that characterizes the crisis that birthed Cone's black liberation theology at the apex of America's "savage sixties" (ch. 2). The fact of midnight in the social order recalls Martin Luther King Jr.'s brilliant assessment of the zeitgeist, the mood, and the

45. Hentoff, *Jazz Life*, 194. See also Smallenburg, "Monk, Bop," 36.

46. James Cone described his intellectual trinity in response to a question about my paper called "Theology in the Mode of Monk." See Cone, "Rev. Dr. James H. Cone."

hour in America that set the context for the ascendency, the coming "noon" of James Cone's black liberation theology.[47] Charles Long figuratively represents the bridge in that volume, standing between Barth and Cone (ch. 3). Other than Martin Luther King Jr., Long in fact is the only black person we have on record raising a question Barth acknowledged.[48]

Here in volume 3, which represents the third and fourth movements of the trilogy, I use "Misterioso," a tune whose clocklike rhythms permit us to situate Barth's and Cone's theologies in terms of their christological relationship to the freedom of God and the liberation of humanity, respectively. Aside from the literal allusion to the mystery of creation in the title of the song, "Misterioso" serves as a handy way to discuss Barth's understanding of the relationship between the *freedom of God* and human liberation in creation (ch. 1). Monk deploys rhythmic displacements and accentuates silence in the song, brilliantly and unpredictably highlighting dissonant notes throughout the song. Silence becomes a recognizable "tonal artifact," along with dissonance, playing a constructive role and giving shape to the song in much the same way human language and experience incorporate silence as a necessary part of speech and life in creation.[49] Another way to think of this silence is to imagine silence, as noted in the words of Wadada Leo Smith, the trumpeter and composer, "not as a moment of absence, or a space for resting, but as a vital field where musical ideas exist as a result of what was played before and afterward."[50] This also leads me to underline Cone's alternative accent on human liberation, identifying black oppression with God's freedom understood as a gospel of liberation (ch. 2).

Rounding out the architectural framework, *Theology in the Mode of Monk* closes with one final section that returns to the song "Epistrophy" (ch. 3). As I have also stated in the "head," before the final chapter, "Epistrophy" functioned as an outro for various jazz sets, segments, intermissions, and closings in Monk's early jazz performances. Fittingly, "Epistrophy (Reprise)" signals my own turnabout to the pneumatological vision I advance at the end of this trilogy (ch. 3). In this volume, I signify a new beginning with a turn to a "free, pneumatic counterpoint" as a new tonal center.[51] The chapter includes the beginning of an ethical critique of the *locus theologicus*

47. Said differently, the phrase "midnight in the social order: is a construct of Martin Luther King Jr., whose death contributed as an impetus for Cone's black theology.

48. Barth may have also met the educator, writer, and civil rights leader Anna Arnold Hedgeman through William Stringfellow, but evidence is still inconclusive.

49. Long, *Significations*, 65.

50. W. Smith, *Solo*, 1.

51. Although I may employ it differently, I thank Raymond K. Anderson, who coined this term. R. Anderson, *American Scholar Recalls*, 416.

of contemporary theology, that is, the modern American academy, seminaries, and divinity schools, representing the constellation of institutions I identify as the academic industrial complex (AIC).

Because Monk's compositions privilege musicality, that is, his attempt to play the sound he heard rather than to reify some aspect of technique, the melody of a song occupied the pride of position. He thus became known for encouraging his accompanists to "improvise on the melody." It is this penchant for the melody, i.e., a clear center—even when engaging in the act of "decentering"—that reveals the indispensable importance of the cantus firmus (the fixed melody) that he sets in relief.[52] This center gives meaning to all other melodies surrounding it, and this notion of the melody, interpreted as the parabolic center of the life of faith, augments my insight into what family kinship means when considering the theologies of Karl Barth and James Cone and their common relationship to the divine melody. Indeed, in this commonality, if we have ears to hear, we may find a new way of being in the world—a being in the mode of Monk.

52. See Bonhoeffer, *Letters and Papers*, 303–5. Dietrich Bonhoeffer, in the prison letters, found himself "pursued" by the idea of a cantus firmus, identifying it as a "musical reflection of [a] christological fact." As I will discuss below, Bonhoeffer connects this idea more to the potential for mutual love reflecting the christological center. In this project, however, I utilize the idea in a more nuanced way, impacting the way we think about the form, the inner material content, and ethical response to the gospel. As a sidenote, it was the music of Thelonious Monk, and not the theology of Dietrich Bonhoeffer, that introduced me to the cantus firmus. Still, as I note elsewhere, "Monk helped me discover Bonhoeffer musically and Bonhoeffer helped me discover Monk theologically. The same can be said of Karl Barth and James Cone." Carr, "Dancing Monk," n12. For Monk and melody, see M. Williams, "What Kind of Composer," 436–37; Hentoff, *Jazz Life*, 201–2; cf. Van der Bliek, *Thelonious Monk Reader*, 204.

Acknowledgments

This project, like the music staffs on the pages below, is a fragment, being part of a constructive journey in discovery. For me, it exists as an incomplete rendering of an elusive melody I am pursuing, and in this respect it is a testimony that has sounded forth in the presence of many friends, family, colleagues, and even involuntary interlocutors. I now offer my gratitude to all of you for the patience of your mind's eye and your listening ear. Hopefully, this fragmented melody will strike a chord with you, too, the reader.

Theology in the Mode of Monk first appeared as a fragment in discourse at the Graduate Theological Union (GTU), where Michael Dodds, my advisor; James A. Noel, of blessed memory; and Paul S. Chung graced me with a range of supportive insight born of their distinctive disciplines. Dodds with rigorous interpretations of Thomas Aquinas's concept of transcendence deepened my understanding of God's "otherness"; Noel introduced me to the history of religions school of thought where we interrogated the dazzling insights of Charles H. Long. Noel was a renaissance man with profound mystical sensibilities; and, finally, Chung, the underappreciated and brilliant legatee of the left-wing Barthian tradition, including the theological vision of Jan Lochman, introduced me to many in that tradition. These three committee members provided me with a unique soundscape for theological thinking.

After some time at the GTU, I tinkered with this elusive fragment in the context of a lengthy vocation at Pepperdine University, a premier "teaching institution," where I prioritized the demands of student learning over book writing, but not over contemplating a mode of thinking. The "Monk book," as some of my friends came to call it, played in and out of my mind like an unfinished melody, competing for my attention while I attended to the "polyphony of life" around me. Even as I became more attuned to the bittersweet music of life, music that included joy, the pain of vocational disappointments, the unexpected deaths of family and friends, I was never without the accompaniment of the "Monk book," which provided an outlet toward imagining a theology of playful freedom amid life's smiles and tears. This brings me to a very special dedication.

These three books would not have come to press without the support of Chris Spinks (1972–2024), a beloved editor in the Wipf and Stock family. He was the point person who believed so much in my work that he supported its turn to the more comprehensive project it is today. He knew more than the fragment on the page, however. He knew me. He *saw* me. In academic spaces sometimes that is what we need most. Chris conducted himself more like a supportive friend than an editor, but the truth is that I believe Chris made everybody feel like "a somebody." He lived in an endearing way, and he demonstrated a radical humanity—even in the face of his own death. Chris died after a courageous fourteen-month battle with brain cancer, but he lived in a way that redeemed what he touched in this establishment I call the academic industrial complex (AIC), a constellation of intersecting powers, including publishing houses, institutions, conferences, and agendas too numerous to name. Nevertheless, I know this. That part of this industry is a little bit better because of people like Chris Spinks. This project is dedicated to him and his radical witness to what it means to be human.

I would be remiss if I failed to offer gratitude to the Society for the Study of Black Religion (SSBR), the members of the Karl Barth Society (KBSNA), the Center for Barth Studies, the AAR Black Theology Unit, Fuller Theological Seminary, the Religion Forum at Queens University in Belfast, Ireland, King's College in London, the University of Cambridge, and the University of Oxford. These societies, gatherings, and institutions created space for me to vet many of the ideas in these books. The Karl Barth groups were initially the most important forums. In those meetings I came to terms with distinctions between right- and left-wing Barthians. George Hunsinger deserves mention for his unwavering support of my work, providing opportunities and encouragement for me to present before some of the most distinguished Barth scholars working in the field today. As I neared the end of this project, I benefited from the support of Harvard Divinity School due to the gracious invitation of Dean David N. Hempton. While serving at Harvard as a visiting professor and research associate at the Moses Mesoamerican Archive and Research Project, my distinguished colleague Davíd Carrasco deepened my insights into the thinking of Charles Long and the contributions of Toni Morrison, establishing an intersection that will have a significant impact in the forthcoming volume, *Signifying Monk* (Cascade), that follows this trilogy.

The Society for the Study of Black Religion (SSBR) and the Black Theology Unit have also been indispensable, not just to my thinking about theology but for my concrete engagement in theopraxis. The SSBR, without knowing it, provided community for me when I needed it most in the context of the academy. Moreover, the support of this group has helped me understand the intentionality of its founders, being a safe space where many of the most brilliant minds in the field of religion and theology rendezvous. This group engages in the study of religion comprehensively. Likewise, the Black Theology Unit gave me an opportunity to present in front of James H. Cone, who took an interest in my theology from the beginning. I remain deeply grateful for the opportunities we shared and his searching questions that still inform my thoughts.

To Melissa Pichette who, in spirited resourcefulness, never failed to acquire the articles or chapters I needed. She is the best-kept secret at Pepperdine University, being a talented research librarian and a friend who is quiet in spirit, but clear in judicious temperament. Every book in this project, including the ones I am still writing, is a testimony to her reliability. Pepperdine has a wonderful staff of librarians who still support me from a distance. To be sure, I owe a debt of gratitude to many colleagues, staffs, and students of several institutions: Pepperdine; the ENGAGE Youth Theology Initiative (2017–24) at Lipscomb University in Nashville, Tennessee; the life-giving group of students I named the "magnificent seven," who attended Phillips Theological Seminary where we studied the theology of James Cone; and the exceptional group of students at Harvard Divinity School where I lectured on "Theopoetics and the Religious Imagination" and James Cone's *The Cross and the Lynching Tree.*

Other colleagues well deserving of my gratitude include Robert A. Jackson Jr., Ronald W. Batchelder, Tracey E. Hucks, Constance M. Fulmer, Margaret E. Barfield, Richard T. Hughes, Gary W. Burnett, Robynn Cone, Angela Sims, Johanne Kristensen, Jeff McSwain, Tommy Amaker, Marlon Young, Keith David, Kenny Lattimore, Grady Lights, Darrick Purvis, Kenneth Gilmore Sr., Dwight N. Hopkins, Aaron Grizzell, Lee H. Butler Jr., Odolé Lana Martins, Cliff Frazier, Tabatha Jones Jolivet, Marcus and Nicole Brown, Marcus and Spring Cooke, Tanya Hart, Pernell Marsh, Damon McCaskill, Barbara Jean Wiggins, Charlie E. Taylor Jr., Chris Collins, Edward Adutwum, Mark J. Campbell, Randy "Ascot" Morgan, Eric and Sharita Wilson, Cedric "The Entertainer" Kyles, Claire and Kyle Frederick, Eric L. Williams, Cookye Rutledge, and Rev. Matthew V. Johnson. Several of my former students deserve special mention: Aljoharah "Juju" Alshaikh,

Latifa "Queen" Alsaud, Rawan Alsalim, Sofia Cena, Edward Adutwum, and Raymond "Ray Ray" Davison. These former students were important partners early and late in my work for various reasons, and they continue to inspire me today. I thank my colleagues Brandon Pierce, who read the manuscripts and made helpful editorial suggestions; Edie A. Frederick for her timely illustrations; and Damon Saddler for his magnificent cover design of Barth "above" and Cone "below" as seen through Monk.

I also wish to express gratitude to friends, including the team at Wipf and Stock. Since the beginning, Christian Amondson has always been a true brother and avid supporter of my work. I thank him for his efforts, along with Chris Spinks, to initiate this project, and I thank the extended editorial team at Wipf and Stock, especially Rodney Clapp, Stephanie Hough, and Rebecca Abbott, who finished the job with so much grace. This includes the blues philosopher Cornel West, who endorsed this project up front with the same generosity that adorns his brilliant contributions to intellectual life. I close with words of profound appreciation to Raymond and Cheryl Davison, who secured a location for me to concentrate on writing during my time away from the academy. The Davisons model such a wonderful form of melodic charm in a spirit of love and generosity.

Before I turn to say more about the dedication page of this book, I offer gratitude to three people who inspired me most. First, I thank Charles Houston Long (1926–2020), a mentor and friend. When I was revising this trilogy and doing more talking than writing, Dr. Long functioned as my most important interlocutor. Long was a brilliant teacher. He engaged my questions; he sharpened my thoughts with a lifetime of insight; he inspired and sometimes chastened me. Only those who knew the man can truly imagine the gift of having a person with his refined style, profound knowledge, and generous wisdom as an interlocutor. Second, I thank Willie James Jennings, who wrote the foreword for this project. Willie Jennings is more than a brilliant theologian. He is a friend and encourager who is gifted with a finely tuned sense of perception. Third, I must thank the inimitable Thelonious Sphere Monk (1917–82), whose musical genius and virtuosity have inspired my mode of thinking and unveiled the (inter)ruptive possibilities of the s/Spirit—the spirit of jazz and the Spirit of Life. I offer gratitude to Monk and to his family, who share his enduring legacy with the world.

This trilogy has its origins in my profound appreciation for the life and faithful witness of James Hal Cone (1938–2018). Cone's critical engagement with Karl Barth, which is so strikingly developed in an original and independent direction, commanded my attention, suggesting to me, not uncritically, that attending to Barth's theology is a worthy endeavor. Cone, who is also an exceptional interlocutor, intrigued me by what he discovered in

Barth, setting in relief what lay undiscovered. I am convinced that—because of the way he signified on Euro-American theological traditions and how he combined his learning with his profound love and affection for black folklife—his work will continue to inspire generations who are interested in systematic theology. His contributions to the field of theology are immeasurable. In my view, he is America's most important theologian. I thank him for his example of faith; his friendly theological embrace, which I came to know personally; and his efforts to write, as he stated, "for my people." I dedicate this project to him, my siblings (Melvin Mason, Shirley L. Thomas, Shawn Mason, and Charleston L. Taylor), and the people of West Petersburg, Virginia, who still give me rhythm for life.

I conclude with a special note to my love, Dr. Joi Carr. Words fail me when I try to capture the transformative experience of love and companionship shared with one who walks with you spiritually and intellectually, socially and vocationally. On those days when I interrupt our dinner to share an insight from James Cone or Karl Barth; or when I wake you up with the music of Thelonious Monk; or when we joyfully recall a sustaining memory about Charles Long or read a passage in the evening before bed, you are always such a gracious listener and ready interlocutor. Your lovely way of "being there" means the world to me. Your love is a resounding melody in my life, and this project is dedicated to you, for your *amor est vitae essentia.*

Abbreviations

AARAS	American Academy of Religion Academy Series
AThR	*Anglican Theological Review*
CD	*Church Dogmatics*. Karl Barth. Translated by Geoffrey W. Bromiley. 4 vols. Repr., Edinburgh: T&T Clark, 1980
ChrCent	*Christian Century*
HR	*History of Religions*
Int	*Interpretation*
JR	*Journal of Religion*
JRT	*Journal of Religious Thought*
KD	*Die kirchliche Dogmatik*. Karl Barth. 4 vols. Zurich: EVZ, 1932–67
PSB	*Princeton Seminary Bulletin*
SJT	*Scottish Journal of Theology*
ThTo	*Theology Today*
TJT	*Toronto Journal of Theology*
USQR	*Union Seminary Quarterly Review*
ZTK	*Zeitschrift für Theologie und Kirche*

MISTERIOSO

Freedom for Liberation in Creation

Truly, you are a God who hides himself, O God of Israel, the Savior. (Isa 45:15)

[An American theology of freedom] should also be marked by a freedom from fear of communism, Russia, inevitable nuclear warfare, and generally speaking, from all the aforementioned principalities and powers. Freedom for which you would stand would be freedom for—I like to say a single word—humanity. —Karl Barth[1]

There still is nothing more common than to confound the travail of liberation with the foundation of freedom.—Hannah Arendt[2]

Truth is divine action entering into our lives and creating the human action of liberation. Truth enables us to dance and live to the rhythm of freedom.—James H. Cone[3]

Rhythm entails movement, and movement implies space. —Raimon Panikkar[4]

1. K. Barth, *Karl Barth 1886–1968*, 79.
2. Arendt, *On Revolution*, 299.
3. Cone, *God of the Oppressed*, 28.
4. Panikkar, *Rhythm of Being*, 46.

HEAD

Affirming Freedom for Liberation

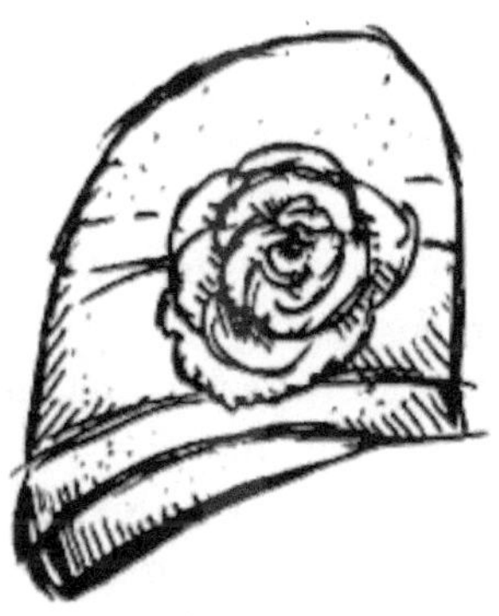

JAZZ IS A SYMBOL of freedom. Interpreted in its most robust sense, jazz, like other forms of black music, represents "one of the most powerful and distinctive expressions of America as informed by the African American presence."[1] Its symbolic value coincides with the African American struggle for survival and freedom that reached beyond the American situation into Europe, especially during World War II, where the Gestapo arrested and jailed jazz fans but failed to stop the spread of jazz.[2] Akin to other forms of black music, bebop arose out of the same kind of midnight of American experience and inspired even those beyond the borders of American life.

1. Long, *Ellipsis*, 202.
2. Litweiler, *Freedom Principle*, 240–41.

Although some musicians demurred, many practitioners of jazz recognized the music as a revolutionary force in American as well. Sonny Rollins, one of the most influential tenor saxophonists in America, summed up jazz as a "social force in this country . . . talking about freedom and people enjoying things for what they are and not having to worry about whether they were supposed to be white, black, and all this stuff."[3] Jazz in this respect embodied the same spirit of freedom found in the blues genre. With affirmations of black life it shaped the sociopolitical reality that informed human efforts to testify to freedom and liberation.[4]

Because I appeal to Monk's music analogically and symbolically throughout this project, his jazz, particularly for those who have ears to hear, builds on the relationship between the blues and jazz genres. It induces me to illuminate the alternation between *God's freedom* as articulated in Karl Barth's fascination with Mozart and *black liberation* as the frame of reference for James Cone's interpretations of the blues. When the two are read in counterpoint, they correspond, revealing an alternating accent on both God's freedom and human liberation, particularly when interpreted through Monk's aesthetic power which accentuates these abiding tensions. From the vantage of Monk's musical thinking this encourages a (de)*constructive* direction in theology.

A Monk-ish recombination arises from Monk's concern with proper form, that is, his penchant for playing on themes or standards, which includes his efforts to construct a way of playing things differently without rejecting previous traditions. Monk functioned therefore on the *inside* of musical tradition. This is where I would like to function as a theologian—on the inside of existing traditions. Stanley Crouch frames this emphasis and amplitude in Monk and opens the door to thinking about the implications of this insight:

> It is almost as though Monk understood more quickly than anyone else how the bebop style could be reduced to a mannered chord-running and rhythms that were far less varied than those of the musics that had preceded it. He seemed intent on forging a music that could make use of a variety of elements, including the call-and-response energy of New Orleans, the updated antiphonal relationships between soloists and rifts or thematic

3. Gitler, *Swing to Bop*, 303.

4. Rollins goes on to say, "Long before sports broke down its racial walls, jazz was bringing people together on both sides of the bandstand. 52nd Street, for all its shortcomings, was a place in which black and white musicians could interact in a way that led to natural bonds of friendship. . . . It was an expression of a new period, and a new era for black people in American society." Gitler, *Swing to Bop*, 304.

> backgrounds heard in Ellington and Basie, the percussive nature of the Afro-American piano tradition, and Jelly Roll Morton's dictum that a jazz pianist should sound like a *jazz band.* And all of this telescoped through the syncopations, polyrhythms, and flirtations with the tempo of the Afro-American dance tradition.[5]

It is as though Monk knew the melodic theme had the richness and ability to ground compositionally all the variations and oppositions together, that is, "the call-and-response energy," the "antiphonal relationships," the "syncopations," the rhythmic displacements. Indeed, because of his radical concentration on the melody, even the silences maintained musical shape in Monk's aesthetic, characterizing the kind of freedom that emerges from his music. It is no wonder the piano soloist had the potential to sound like a jazz band.[6]

When considered in a wider context, songs like "Misterioso," with its bluesy-sounding "walking sixths," demonstrate Monk's aesthetic genius for freely inventing harmonics and rhythmically playing around with the beat. In keeping with other tunes, it reveals how he has a way of "making use of all the unused space around jazz."[7] Monk even refashioned the form of this particular tune, composing and playing "Misterioso" without a head arrangement (quite unlike the other two songs I use in this project). Theologically, what I hear echoed in this free principle in Monk's "Misterioso" is what Barth calls the polyphonic "testimony to the work and word of God." As Barth goes on to say, "Everything that can be heard there [in Scripture] is differentiated—not only the voices of the Old and New Testaments as such, but also the many voices that reverberate throughout both."[8] But I would venture even further than this. The voices of the witnesses extend beyond primary witnesses of the text, including the many voices and other immanent possibilities. The historical strivings of earthly freedoms as expressed in all of their varieties in culture and the literary genres witness to the polyphony of life with God. "For the spirit searches *everything*, even the depths of God" (1 Cor 2:10). While we should avoid overemphasizing the influence of Eastern or Western culture, we should also resist theological interpretations of the Bible that appeal ironically to the communicative

5. Crouch, *Considering Genius*, 86. Emphasis in original.

6. For a brief insightful discussion of silence in Monk's musical understanding, see Komunyakaa, "It's Always Night."

7. Van der Bliek, *Thelonious Monk Reader*, 28. See also 214 for a brief discussion of the blues theme in "Misterioso."

8. K. Barth, *Evangelical Theology*, 33.

action of God in order to circumscribe the multidimensional dynamism, the beauty and mystery of the depths of God that can be attested to in culture.

The mystery of God then is not a turn away from the world. In its proper sense the *mystery of* God is not an enigma or form of perplexity; it is rather the open secret of God, who shares a peculiar "treasure of wisdom and knowledge hidden in Christ," who is the interpretive key to understanding the world (Col 2:2–3).[9] Although he was not thinking about theology, a turn from mystery to meaning explains in some respects why Monk knew he was doing something new, seeking to say things differently and offering new ways of syncopating in order to articulate a certain kind of truth about America. As I suggested in the volume called *'Round Midnight*, Monk's well-known penchant for playing on/off the melody or standard is not only central to understanding his accent on compositional form as the key to his improvising. It provides the melodic ground for Monk's expansion into alternative forms and countermelodies, which I use here to help us (re)imagine the relationship between freedom and liberation.

In this line of thinking we encounter a strong counterpoint between Karl Barth and James Cone. Monk's aesthetic freedom is determined by the very rules he inverted. Thus when he draws on his predecessors' penchant for the melody—unlike many bebop artists whose interpretations were designed to display virtuosity and digital dexterity on an instrument—Monk established a rich and mysterious ground since his modus operandi was to favor the melody without completely obscuring the original tune.[10] John Szwed adds that Monk was "improvising on melodies, taking parts of the tune and using them to recompose it. He sometimes played older pop tunes relatively straight, in stride fashion, but with bop harmonies and chord voicings; even there his approach was so crafted that every note was set in relief against its harmonic and rhythmic background."[11] This preference for the melody probably contributed to his apparent distaste for free jazz, which does not mean he had no interest in freedom or the relationship between jazz and freedom. He, rather, once famously said, "Jazz and freedom go hand and hand. That explains it. There isn't any more to add to it. If I do add to it; [the meaning] gets complicated."[12] Monk's freedom, then, accentuated form, and the form accented his freedom. Accordingly, regarding his take

9. See Thornton, *Revelation and the Modern World*, 30–31.

10. Here I draw on the insights of Scott DeVeaux in Van der Bliek, *Thelonious Monk Reader*, 268–69. Ian Carr also argues that Monk like Ellington "improvises more on the melody than on the harmonic sequence of a tune." Van der Bliek, *Thelonious Monk Reader*, 204.

11. Szwed, *Jazz 101*, 172.

12. See Kelley, "Monk's Dance," 3.

on freedom we must reiterate that the freedom he advocated in relation to the form is a freedom that reshapes and reforms tradition. As Stanley Crouch points out, "Monk has totally rethought the tradition." In doing so, "he taught musicians *and* listeners *and* critics how to *think*."[13] I hope the same can be said for his influence on theological thinking.

This mode of thinking appears in Monk's audacity to freely engage the past, including the religious and the secular. After traveling with an evangelist, dabbling in country blues, and training amateurs and budding professionals, it makes sense that Monk would shun elitist emphases on virtuosity, choosing by contrast the spare, calculated, and controlled notes that would eventually characterize his music. He distilled thematic and traditional materials in jazz and made songs out of the tokens and fragments and motives in the music of his day. As a result, tradition itself became his way of expressing freedom. Here, again, the melody makes a song into a song, and his preference for melody explains his self-discipline when composing in contrast to other self-centered uses of structure.[14] To put it differently, Monk did not exploit the form. He actually *used* it, signifyin(g) on the form, and allowing it to condition his harmonic and rhythmic sensibilities. As is clear from some of Monk's greatest songs like "Blue Monk" and "Misterioso," his predilection for the melody or form does not mean he ignored the vibrant harmonies or the *swing effect* in music, which is often heard in his nonbinary rhythms. Rather, he was a master of swing, composing songs with rhythmic patterns, sometimes on and sometimes off the beat, but always swinging.

Monk's peculiar freedom emerges more clearly when we scrutinize his use of musical space and time, which marked the horizontal dimensions of his music. The rhythmic movement in Monk accentuates the gaps, the junctures, and the intervals that signal the need for a relative openness to possibilities; and when listening carefully we can actually hear space, a musical allusion to the radically open sociopolitical and economic world order that can accommodate our tensions and contradictions, our possibilities and contingencies. The way Monk (re)composed a melody in songs like "Misterioso" transcends any dialects that would unwittingly reduce such an aesthetic mode (or even our God talk) to a form of consistency that is ultimately determined by Western modes of music (or logic). This tension-ridden sense in Monk is evident in his songs (and even their titles), such as "Brilliant Corners" and "Ugly Beauty." It is heard in the harmonic structure and rhythmic break in "Lulu's Back in Town" and in the dissonance in "You

13. Crouch, *Considering Genius*, 87–88. Emphasis in original.

14. Fitterling, *Thelonious Monk*, 82–84.

Are Too Beautiful" where Monk's harmonics symbolize the very realism that exists, yes, beyond his music.

"You Are Too Beautiful," for example, uses dissonance to encourage listeners to come to terms with the realism in life, and its accentuated silences force you to recognize that there is more in the song than what meets the ear. It is as if Monk's music allows us to peer into eternity through time. Litweiler rightfully counsels that Monk is not the naïve innocent as some thought: "Monk was not deluded by attitudes like optimism or pessimism; the hard strain of realism runs through his forms, rhythms, and harmonies."[15] Paradoxically, the organic unity Monk cherishes in his music is, again, the foundation for a world of possibilities and contingencies where the melody itself functions as a (de)*constructive* center that (inter)rupts the classical constraints of colonial logic(s) even as it offers a new constructive soundscape for our thinking.

Considering the brilliance of Monk's disharmonious harmony, the role rhythm played in Monk's aesthetics may come as a surprise. His aesthetic imagination antedates those who contend that the rhythm of a song can frame the other elements, including the harmony, melody, and timbre. Monk had long used rhythm to highlight harmony by choosing dramatic time signatures to outline dissonant notes.[16] This means his music was characterized by its musical flow, with the rhythm being a key marker for responding to his aesthetics in general. Even his use of rhythmic displacement coincides with his feel for the timing of a song and our timing for life. To put it simply, Monk was the consummate master of the "jazz beat," creating unique intervals with his use of musical space and time; so much so that "his expansion and contraction of rhythm . . . make a good case for calling him a precursor of free jazz," which for the most part jettisons conventional patterns and structures.[17] Monk, however, criticized free jazz artists for their emphasis on musical freedom without structure, stating that "they speak of freedom. But one has no right, under the pretext of freeing yourself, to be illogical or incoherent by getting rid of structure and simply piling a lot of notes one on top of the other."[18]

Though Monk expressed no appreciable interest in free jazz, which became an innovation during his day and on into the atomic age, it is not surprising that many still argue that he inspired free jazz, alluding to the

15. Litweiler, *Freedom Principle*, 232.

16. See Monson, *Saying Something*, 28; cf. Hentoff, *Jazz Life*, 181. For Monk's background in Kansas City swing, see Fitterling, *Thelonious Monk*, 105–9.

17. Szwed, *Jazz 101*, 173.

18. Fitterling, *Thelonious Monk*, 82–84.

ingenious way he placed notes on different parts of the beat, setting space around the beat in such bold relief so that even the silence within his songs manifested itself as part of the rhythm of the music. This is the case with Monk's brilliant rendition of "Blessed Assurance." It is as if the silence is a reminder for us to leave room for our differences, our contingencies, and our need for contemplation as part of the rhythm of life. Monk's rhythmic confidence is even evident in his free, spontaneous response to many of his own songs during his performances. To be sure, if Monk danced, according to Charlie Rouse, it meant "that the thing was swinging."[19] Thus Monk's rhythms reveal his sense of swing, not only demonstrating what it means for a song to swing, but also modeling what many believe to be a quintessential hallmark of African American music and life—its *rhythm*.

As mentioned in chapter 1, Monk's imaginative freedom for exploring previous genres symbolized an aspect of freedom that Karl Barth prized, that is, the freedom to "always to be open . . . thinking and speaking [or playing] in responsibility and openness on all sides, backwards and forwards, toward both past and future, and with what [Barth] might call a total personal modesty."[20] It is no surprise that when asked which jazz artists had influenced him, Monk responded with a laugh and said, "I've been influenced by all jazz musicians before me. All of them influenced me."[21] In this subtle answer there is much to learn from Monk's rhythmic impulse and his unburdened, reimagined (re)compositions of prior tunes. And while a refined harmonic sense is one of his great gifts he brought to the melody, his rhythmic sense corresponds with the melodic line and creates space for the harmonies by setting them in relief. Rhythm represents the tension in which Monk lived. Rhythm is the being and doing of jazz, but it is also, for those who live by faith, the movement where we affirm experience in the Spirit. Cone viewed the rhythmic sense of black people as significant in his theological reclamation of the spirituals, stating that "one must feel one's way into the power of black music, responding both to its rhythm and the faith in experience it affirms."[22] This intuition is, of course, not limited to the spirituals. It resides in the blues and jazz and it percolates more subtly in

19. Kelley, *Thelonious Monk*, 232. See my "Imagination Lost."

20. K. Barth, *Final Testimonies*, 34. Here I am reminded of the response of my colleague who missed a dimension of depth in Barth by equating intellectual modesty with humility, that is, by missing the point that the *Sache* (subject matter) of Scripture sets one in question. See Carr, "Merton and Barth in Dialogue," 182–83.

21. Monk, "Interview de Thelonious Monk," 0:34–0:42.

22. Cone, *Spirituals and the Blues*, 4.

various forms of hip-hop.[23] Black folk do not simply create the rhythms of the music we make. We live them.

Randy Weston, a master pianist, identifies this sense of rhythm with the whole universe, suggesting that a deeper connection to the earth and its natural rhythms gives way to improvisations whereby human beings responsibly, creatively, and ethically participate within the rhythms of creation.[24] Weston, who was especially impressed by Monk, viewed him as somewhat akin to a Sufi master who brought magic back to music, stating that "'Misterioso,' the title of one of his songs[,] explains perfectly what he did with the music," playing between the standard notes and playing the piano as if it was another instrument altogether, stretching the imagination through his free, spontaneous, and creative musical gift, which opened up endless possibilities "that brought the mystery back into the music."[25] Ultimately, in Weston's worldview, this musical freedom transcends European forms and echoes a creativity found in African traditional music and African American musical aesthetics, a creativity among those who were oppressed and had to experience the truth of the world's negativity and "transform and create *an-other* reality."[26] Thus Monk's freedom, as Robin Kelley notes, reverberates from the collective memory of a people, and therefore it is "more than breaking the strictures of functional harmony and standard time. His grandparents were freedom's first generation and they did everything they could to make a good life for themselves under a hopeful democracy."[27] From this point of view Monk's freedom should be interpreted as corresponding to the aspirations of previous generations, which echo the life rhythms that spring from the eternal rhythms of revelation.

Freedom for black folk, consequently, is more than the mere resonance of humanity lived in view of a joyful emancipation—the supposed freedom offered to blacks by American society. Black freedom transcends American notions of emancipation. Charles Long, the historian of religions, described the transcending nature of black freedom succinctly, writing that "their freedom is a meaning of freedom which has come from a people who have known that freedom is more than property rights; freedom is more than legal contracts."[28] Freedom is not even determined ultimately by Monk's

23. Cone himself thought that hip-hop carried the witness we hear in the spirituals. Cone, "James Cone on *Cross*."

24. Weston, "Interview."

25. Weston, *African Rhythms*, 60–62; cf. Kelley, *Africa Speaks, America Answers*, 50–51.

26. Long, "Perspectives for a Study," 59.

27. See Kelley, "Monk's Dance," 3.

28. Long, "Signs of Wholeness," 3.

transcendence of standard forms, for in such a negative freedom there is a *more than*; hence, despite the breaking of boundaries of harmonic, melodic, and rhythmic conventions, Monk's freedom can actually be interpreted as a kind of "testimonio," akin to the testimony of the spirituals and blues, that is, a freedom that in its constructive development gestures and testifies to a space, time, and reality beyond any routinized "American" conventions. It is even more than provincial Christian meanings. As Long contends, "[Black] music not only speaks of the condition of Africans in the United States, it takes on social, psychological, and economic meanings within the wider culture of African Americans," being a mode of communication and site for "powerful and distinctive expressions of America as informed by the African American presence."[29]

I would go so far as to suggest that Monk's relationship to his music bequeathed Monk with a peculiar sense of the temporal. In contrast to Laurent de Wilde, the jazz pianist and author, who argued that "when he sat down at the piano, who could ever be more *time-free*?,"[30] I want to make a different case for Monk's relationship to time. When thinking in the aesthetic mode in his music, especially as it relates to rhythm and time, I prefer to imagine its ultimate meanings in the rhythms of our wider reality, suggesting that his music gave him a kind of rhythm for life. His life shaped his music, and music shaped his life.[31] Monk therefore was not time free, he was *time full*. As Harold Trulear points out, "The rhythms point to the walking beat of African-American culture."[32] So Monk was *time full*, in engaging the past and inspiring the future. He drew rhythms from previous genres of jazz, such as swing and stride and, simultaneously, parodied (including the harmonic, melodic, and rhythmic clichés) earlier contributions to jazz.

Following this way of thinking we can imagine how melody influences the freedom to create (improvisation) and how Monk's musicality witnesses analogically to a way for theologians to (re)imagine a more radical ground for freedom, i.e., a freedom tethered to and governed by the constituent melodic foundation of the subject matter. In other words, it is a freedom in correspondence to, or *in rhythm with*, the melody of Christ, the cantus firmus. Monk's dependence on the melody functions as a metaphor not just to articulate Barth's and Cone's relationship to revelation. It extends to the constructive relationship between freedom and liberation, giving rise to an

29. Long, *Ellipsis*, 202.

30. Wilde, *Monk*, 211. Emphasis in original.

31. See Kelley, "Monk's Dance," 6–7, for a discussion of how Monk's masculinity was evident in his music.

32. Spencer, "Theology of American Popular Music," 80.

aesthetic mode of religious discourse, a *via cognoscendi* (a way of thinking), to channel the rhythmic tensions between Barth and Cone, alternating between conformity and displacement. To be sure, in this section Monk's way of thinking provides a symbolic gesture toward a mode of discourse that honors the mystery of what it means to hear and respond to the cantus firmus. This mystery plays out in the way our principals emphasize their various viewpoints externally.

Barth, for example, chose to "underline the sovereignty of God over against man [humanity]. . . . [Humanity thus] disappears for a moment, but then re-appears."[33] Likewise when Cone underlines the liberation of humanity over against emphasis on God, God seems to disappear for a moment, but then reappears. The respective emphases are dialectical, harboring important hermeneutical implications. Steven Somers contends that Monk had a propensity for displacement *and* conformity (*Aufhebung*), a fact that produced a "wide variety of accentuation happening on various levels."[34] But I would argue that the extension of Barth's and Cone's theologies encourage us to play in the tension between one side and the other, a consequential realm for human ethics.

Without belaboring the point, what I am after can be expressed in the following way. Barth should be thought of as seeking to establish a *theo*anthropology, epitomized in mature works like *The Humanity of God* where he sounds the call of God's descent into human reality; whereas Cone established a clear theo*anthropology* as described in the *God of the Oppressed* where human dignity, in particular, black affirmation, is found in the divine. It is in the counterpoint between Barth's and Cone's respective emphases on freedom and liberation that the polyphony of human response can be found. If we improvise on the same melodic foundation and acknowledge two different accents to provide equilibrium and contrast, then we can revel in the rhythmic tension in the mode of Monk, a tension heard in the following pedagogical slogan: "Barth affirms a *freedom* for liberation, and Cone affirms a freedom for *liberation*." Underlining this rhythmic tension encourages us to honor their respective contributions to an ethical harmonization that ultimately finds its meaning in the mystery of the divine melody.

33. See R. Anderson, *Karl Barth's Table Talk*, 116.

34. Somers, "Rhythm of Thelonious Monk," 44.

1

Karl Barth's *Freedom* for Liberation

*Theo*anthropology and the Internal Ground of Liberation

They speak of freedom. But one has no right, under the pretext of freeing yourself, to be illogical or incoherent by getting rid of structure and simply piling a lot of notes one on top of the other. —*Thelonious Monk*[1]

That lady [the Statue of Liberty] needs a little or perhaps, a good bit of demythologization. Nevertheless, maybe she may also be seen and interpreted and understood as a symbol of a true theology, not of liberty, but of freedom.—*Karl Barth*[2]

Negroes and Whites sat peacefully together, worshiped, heard the Word of God, sang, and prayed together. White men and black men!—a fact, an external structure of the cosmos—and in this case, we may say a remarkable proof of the existence of God. —*Karl Barth*[3]

1. Fitterling, *Thelonious Monk*, 82–84.
2. K. Barth, *Karl Barth 1886–1968*, 79.
3. K. Barth, *Gespräche*, 463.

The cause of freedom is not the cause of a race or a sect, a party or a class—it is the cause of humankind, the very birthright of humanity.—Anna Julia Cooper[4]

Jazz is freedom.—Thelonious Monk

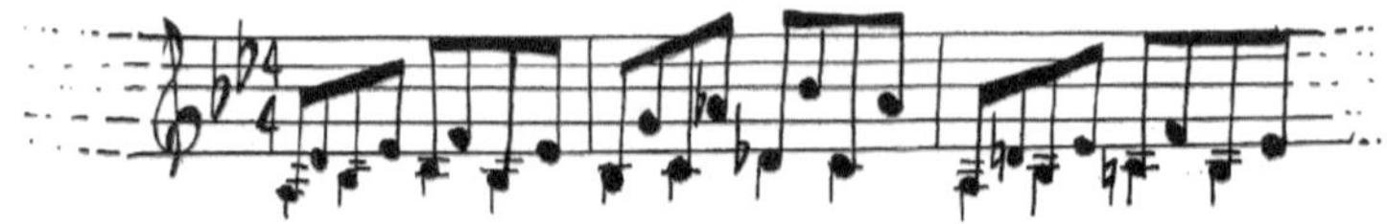

JAMES CONE'S ARGUMENT THAT Karl Barth had a defective Christology attacked the very core of "Barthian" theology. It did not attack the core as it is interpreted in the left-wing Barthian tradition, however. These more radical "Barthians" believed Barth expressed one of his strongest themes in the christological concentration on the freedom of God *for* the world. The being of God *for us* furnished the meaning for what God means in the left-wing tradition where theologians promote "God as the one in Christ who changes everything." This leitmotif, lifted from volume 2, paragraph 28 of Barth's *Church Dogmatics*, witnesses to a free God whose love is anchored in the fact that "*God is*." Barth expressed this point succinctly, writing, "They [human beings] should and must live with the fact that not only sheds new light on, but materially changes all things and everything in all things—the fact that God is."[5]

This material fact of God's mode of being, according to Marquardt, is a "real transforming fact." And while it is important to interrogate Barth's christological development, we should never overlook its relationship to the rhythms of human freedom (or liberation) arising as the motive force, the cautioning word, and the challenge Christology presents.[6] Precisely because Barth "improvised on the *melody*," faith and its corresponding deeds can be harmonized in Barth's view of ethics. Stated differently, faith in the faithfulness of Christ (the divine center) occasions the mysterious ground for the endless variations, the relativities, the ambiguities and contingencies that

4. Cooper, *Voice*, 106.

5. *CD* II/1:258.

6. For examples, consider F.-W. Marquardt (God's revolution), Eberhard Jüngel (christological anthropology), Jan Lochman (concentration on Christ), and Paul Chung (symptom-seeking approach) or my position as a kind of Monkian cantus firmus along with Barth, Bonhoeffer, and Lochman. See Marquardt, "Idols Totters"; Chung, *Karl Barth*, 467; Jüngel, *God as the Mystery*; Lochman, "Theology of Christological Concentration"; and Carr, "Dancing Monk."

make up the improvisational rhythms of faith as a witness in the common life of the world.

We can delineate this connection by scrutinizing the constructive tension between the revelation of "the God who loves in freedom" and the liberation of a people who freely love.[7] For when these two notions are theologically inverted, acknowledging that Barth also conceptualized from his experience, we are left with the question of how he disciplined the analogies (*analogatum*) that arise from personal experiences. We can also open a door to thinking about how Cone's emphasis on black experience, the opposite side of the dilemma, can be employed to strengthen Barth's vision. To be sure, answers to this question help us see how Barth's emphasis on the freedom of God corresponds to Cone's emphasis on human liberation and how this correlation reveals a deeper relationship between these two theologians.

The God Who Loves in Freedom

To pursue this matter further in this chapter, I again appeal to left-wing Barthian contributions to illuminate the frequently overlooked political dimension of divine freedom in Barth and its impact on creatural life. I certainly do not limit myself to the left-wing tradition here, choosing to work beyond the impasse of so-called left- and right-wing Barthian traditions.[8] As Cone may put it, I find ingredients in these traditions to do my own dance, and inexorably the turn to Monk's harmonic inventions and rhythmic impulses helps to analogize and parabolically imagine the spontaneous interplay between the God of freedom and human liberation, especially since Monk demonstrated an "expert command of tension." Indeed, as I have considered the relationship between these two "Christocentric" theologians, I remain mindful of Monk's use of harmonic clusters, which consists of opposing tensions that shape my harmonious thinking.[9]

Furthermore, what set Monk apart from many of his contemporaries is the uniqueness of his *sound*. Wadada Leo Smith describes it best, writing that Monk "does not use full two-hand chords—he finds the most relevant

7. For a brief discussion of this dialectic in the context of idolatry appeal, see Carr, "Theological Response," 127–28.

8. I take a cautionary approach to these distinctions, knowing that such alternatives between left- and right-wing Barthianism can lead to the polemicizing of the difference between dynamistic and ontological visions of God. Markus Barth and participants at the Leuenberg Conference in 1972 leveled this criticism. Put simply, however, I am in search for ways such differences can contribute theologically when one affirms and adopts such emphases in their best light. Cf. M. Barth, "Current Discussions," 91–93.

9. Hentoff, *Jazz Life*, 182.

notes in those chords and uses those."[10] In this respect, like Monk, I try to remain true to the genius of Barth and Cone without slavishly following a particular tradition like the left-wing Barthian tradition, although my own vision for theology is deeply shaped by that tradition. Nor do I seek to identify the exact period of the shifts in the thinking of Barth or Cone. I leave that work, and the arguments that surround it, to the brilliant work of Bruce McCormack, J. Kameron Carter, and others.

The differences between Barth's accent on the freedom of God and Cone's turn to the liberation of humanity must also be heard in relation to the fixed melody of Christ—the divine cantus firmus—who dwells at the center. And despite the protest of those who think otherwise, I am already insinuating a rapprochement between Barth's *God who loves in freedom* and Cone's black Christ, *the Liberator of the oppressed*. As a point of fact, God's freedom and human liberation are reflective of the two great prongs of Reformation thought, which means, in accordance with Barth's way of thinking, that any turn to practical theology or ethics (or as some liberation theologians may prefer to say, "orthopraxis") is already bound up with the radical movement of God. Barth, following the apostle Paul, alludes to this in his commentary on Romans, making it clear that in our ethics (or practices) we speak of the "varied refractions of the uncreated light."[11] This suggests that Christ's salvation for the world is bound up with the rhythm of our human responses to God's salvific melody.[12] If rhythm is to save the world, it will occur because it is grounded in the melody of Christ. Any saving of the world from our vantage is found only in our witness to having been saved by Christ (1 Tim 4:16). Of course, this is not a narrow exclusive note of salvation that closes Christian faith off from other religious ways.[13]

Barth demonstrated a profound awareness of the role dogmatics played for thinking about ethical questions, believing theology should "keep precisely to the rhythm of its own relevant concerns, and thus consider well what are the *real* needs of the day by which its own programme should be directed." When this approach is taken, dogmatics, can make a stronger contribution to politics—in Barth's case specifically to German liberation. This fundamental viewpoint led Barth to commit himself to

10. W. Smith, *Solo*, 6.

11. K. Barth, *Epistle to the Romans*, 426–27.

12. This sequence is written in response to Kabir Sehgal, the jazz bassist and political consultant, who argues that "rhythm saves the world." Sehgal, *Jazzocracy*, 107.

13. See Paul Chung's important exposition of Barth's radical christological vision in Chung, *Karl Barth*; and James Cone's clarification of his Christology in the preface to the 1997 edition of *God of the Oppressed*; and Cone, *For My People*, 205–6.

dogmatics during the conflict of the Second World War.[14] Perhaps one of the primary reasons Barth is viewed as a theologian of freedom is linked to the prophetic role he played in response to the ascendency of nationalism in Germany. Indeed, consider the liberative character of his theology in relation to both neo-Protestantism and Catholicism;[15] the epistemological break he initiated in relation to the historico-critical method;[16] and finally, as I will explicate below, his efforts to position theology and ethics (noting a distinction but not separation between theology and the sciences) on its proper foundation, i.e., the subject matter (*Sache*), the melody of Christ.[17] Thus when read charitably, Barth clearly related dogmatics to human freedom from the very beginning. Even his developmental logic coincides with the sociopolitical situations that occurred over an extended period of time, and it was in this shifting terrain that he argued for dogmatics as a more significant contribution to German liberation:

> I believe in fact that, quite apart from its ethical applications, a better Church dogmatics might well be finally a more significant and solid contribution even to such questions and tasks as that of German liberation than most of the well-meaning stuff which even so many theologians think in dilettante fashion that they can and should supply in relation to these questions and tasks.[18]

This passage suggests that Barth valued a concrete complementarity between dogmatics and ethics. During the war his writing of dogmatics also centered his focus on theology "as if nothing had happened," a statement that does not mean he engaged in a kind of world-effacing resignation or quietist neutrality. It means, rather, that he refused to construe the task of theology abstractly, that is, outside the scope of human life. His response to Brunner, for instance, corroborates my assessment that the task of theology coincides, for Barth, with the concern for humanity in crisis. So, when writing a rejoinder to Brunner's criticism, Barth wrote: "It is a legend without historical foundation that in 1933 I recommended 'passive resistance' when I urged the Germans to fulfil their duties of Christian witness 'as though

14. *CD* I/1:xvi. Emphasis in original. Cf. K. Barth, *Against the Stream*.

15. See Küng, *Justification*, xxv. Although Barth's critique of the Catholic Church as the "antichrist" was demonstrated as being too strong, his theology nevertheless played a distinguishing role as a via media between neo-Protestantism and Roman Catholicism. Barth regretted the polemical nature of his early theology and wished fundamentalism had been included in his critique. Godsey, *Karl Barth's Table Talk*, 40–41.

16. See Barth's debate with Adolf Harnack in Rumscheidt, *Revelation and Theology*.

17. See *CD* I/1:11. For one example of Barth being understood as a theologian of freedom, see Green, *Karl Barth*.

18. *CD* I/1:xvi.

nothing had happened,' ignoring Adolf Hitler's alleged divine revelation." On the contrary, Barth surmised that if his advice to engage in Christian witness had been followed, their standing against National Socialism would have been a "political factor of the first order."[19] Correspondingly, this demonstrates that, for Barth, when Christology and sociopolitical reality are radically interconnected, theory and praxis; dogmatics and ethics; and freedom and liberation are in rhythm with one another. This would be "radical" in the true meaning of the word, i.e., to get at the root of the situation or the "first order" of things.

In this way, the objective and subjective dimensions of faith are interrelated and interdependent. The pertinent question is *how* are they related? To think about this in the "mode of Monk" we should consider not only to what degree the connection between dogmatics and ethics reveals continuity between Barth and Cone—despite Cone's criticisms of Barth's theology—but we should bring them into a greater conceptual correspondence and play within the tensions that exist in their differences, that is, in between the cracks. This would be a Monk-ish kind of freedom. Another way to think of this is to explore Barth's view of the freedom of God and his emphasis on liberation of humanity and interrogate what it reveals about the way Cone, in his initial contributions, critically incorporated Barth's theology. Following the lead of Marquardt, I think the left-wing Barthian tradition, despite its limitations, contains significant unattended insights into the development of Barth's theology.

The Freedom of God in "Left-Wing Barthian" Tradition

Cone's criticism of Barth's theology as christologically defective derogates the fundamental contribution of left-wing Barthian interpretations as seen in the writings of Friedrich-Wilhelm Marquardt, Helmut Gollwitzer, Jan Lochman, and more recently Paul S. Chung, who all underscore Barth's dogmatic mode of addressing the historical, cultural, and sociopolitical context of human freedom.[20] This context, to attuned ears, has profound importance since it mitigates against interpreting Barth's theology as abstract and focused on ontology and metaphysics. The left-wing Barthian tradition, sometimes referred to as the "Berliner's Barth," emphasizes the

19. K. Barth, *Against the Stream*, 118.

20. While Lochman's existence in the left-wing tradition can be questioned, the way he employs ideas from the tradition warrants his inclusion. Marquardt himself justifiably found the labels "right-wing Barthian" and "left-wing Barthian" somewhat misleading. The fact that they are already considered *on the left* exposes the political nature of the problem.

political dimensions of the triune God who, being radically free for the world, sounds a melody that has radically transformed the material world. Marquardt is unequivocal on this point, writing that "those who think that it [*Church Dogmatics*] establishes a theological ontology of transcendence are wrong."[21] He contends that it was the hearing of the word of God in a revolutionary situation that provoked Barth to theologize in the first place. Barth thus conceived of God in relation to sociopolitical reality, and from this vantage point Barth's theology is "socially reflected," even as it qualifies history.[22] The question that should be pondered is *what makes American theologians so suspicious of this insight?*

While Marquardt's interpretation is the subject of many disagreements, especially for those who fail to hear the theological "changes" in his thought, by attending to the period of the two editions of *The Epistle to the Romans*, he painstakingly demonstrated how Barth's expositions of his early theology—which were aimed at the performance of faith—reorient human activities away from ontological and metaphysical motives to more eschatological orientations.[23] So, in addition to the social dimensions, his turn to the biblical text as represented in the continuity between the first and second editions of *Romans* is key for understanding Marquardt and others.

Although Marquardt's argument is more audacious and provocative than Eduard Thurneysen's more balanced interpretation, they both corroborate the idea that it was when Barth turned to the Bible that he found the deeper ground he was seeking. Still, Marquardt interprets Barth's reading of the Bible as having profound political dimensions since Barth's reading was already shaped by his context and the intellectual horizon that arose from his immediate experience in the socialistic praxis of religious socialism. According to Marquardt, the Bible itself, as articulated in Barth's first edition of *Romans*, sets the tone for how Barth did theology. The specious mythology that Barth first clarified his concepts and then wrote theology overlooks Barth's attention to the problems in his social situation. In sum, theology for Barth means interpreting the Scriptures.

We can also frame this problem if we read Barth as subjecting the gaze of the interpreter to the subject matter of Scripture. He thus placed the biblical subject matter in the position of the conscientious interpreter. In this way, modern consciousness stands in a position of being already

21. Hunsinger, *Karl Barth and Radical Politics*, 68.

22. Hunsinger, *Karl Barth and Radical Politics*, 65.

23. This should not be heard as a rejection of a properly understood ontology. Barth in an interview with Hans A. Fischer-Barnicol on May 5, 1964, argued that "Jesus Christ dares to make an eminently ontological statement about being human." K. Barth, *Barth in Conversation*, 3:103.

criticized since the world of the Bible is "aimed at the central position that consciousness occupies in every modern theology, expelling it from its key function in the construction of theology and filling the vacated place with the exposition of scripture."[24] Certainly we can moderate Marquardt here, but the dislodging of any hegemonic role that a form of subjectivism may play in the modern interpreter's world is central to (re)envisioning modern theology. Moreover, it is an insightful way of characterizing the central problem of Barth's situation.

The primary reason for Barth's criticism of consciousness is not merely the role normative consciousness plays for the theologian in relation to the subject matter of theology. The removal of the individual consciousness actually enabled Barth to move biblical proclamation into its proper location, again, a subtle shift—which is often maligned as a type of biblicism or *Offenbarungpositivismus* (revelation positivism)—where "*the Bible becomes the consciousness of the theologian.*"[25] The strange new world within the Bible thus "projects itself into our old ordinary world," leading us "into a new world, into the world of God."[26] This new world would become the habitation of new ways of being and new rhythms that both remain in tension with and transcend the preestablished rhythms of the old world.

Moreover, the displacement of modern consciousness, especially as seen in historicism, permits the process of *doing* theology to proceed with the exegesis of Scripture in the primary position throughout the process, permitting Barth to further offset the "domineering position of the modern consciousness" with "the new world of the Bible."[27] In Barth's thinking these two foci encounter one another, and in the end it is the world of the biblical text, the world of God, that exposes *(aufhebt)* the relativity, brokenness, or limitations of the consciousness it encounters. Contextually, according to Marquardt, this encounter resonates from a sociopolitical confrontation tied to Barth's leftist political concerns rather than an epistemological orientation.[28] These reverberations culminated in Barth's ethics where he argued that the churches should keep to the left of other movements.

Barth's so-called "leftist" approach echoed the biblical text and its rhythm with God on the "side of the victims," providing a countermovement on behalf of humanity, especially the weak and marginalized.[29] His

24. Marquardt, "Idol Totters," 176.

25. Marquardt, "Idol Totters," 176. Emphasis in original.

26. K. Barth, *Word of God*, 37.

27. Marquardt, "Idol Totters," 176–77.

28. Marquardt, "Idol Totters," 177. The insertion of the term *aufheben* is my own.

29. *CD* III/4:544. See also *CD* II/1:386, where Barth argues that "in the relations

approach, furthermore, directly attacks any natural theology intertwined with a type of bourgeois consciousness that understands itself as a substitute for Christian revelation. According to Dieter Schellong, natural theology essentially conscripts the revelation of God and sanctions human commitment to the nation and the state.[30] Such theology interprets the accomplishment of God's will as humankind's own possibility, and humanity therefore becomes the master of revelation. These ideological viewpoints occur when nationality, race, or class replaces the "new world in the Bible." Moreover, and most dangerously, such viewpoints displace the sovereignty and freedom of God. It is no wonder then that Barth could see "natural theology" functioning precipitously as a means to an end with its culmination in the events of the year 1933, a fateful year in which Barth considered the "transformation of the Christian Church into the temple of the German nature—and history—myth."[31]

By contrast, it is in the encounter with the biblical world that one comes in contact with the sovereignty of God and the "right divine thoughts about [humanity]."[32] Marquardt interprets such insights as having a peculiar significance for the proletarians who as outsiders are no longer confined by their condition but by the God who conditions. This is what is meant by a *freedom* for liberation. Because human reality has been changed by the God of freedom, it becomes radically open to free human actions and interventions, i.e., human liberation. Human acts find their significance and their destination in God, "the heavenly Father! But the heavenly Father even upon *earth*, and upon earth really the *heavenly* Father."[33] The implications of this insight for theology in a new millennium are significant and will be addressed in what this means for the academic industrial complex (see ch. 3). Arguably, this orientation is evident in Barth's understanding of human freedom as it corresponds to Scripture where he attempts to avoid Catholic authoritarianism on one hand and Protestant liberalism on the other

and events in the life of His [God's] people, God always takes His [God's] stand unconditionally and passionately on this side and on this side alone: against the lofty and on behalf of the lowly; against those who already enjoy right and privilege and on behalf of those who are denied it and deprived of it . . . and we cannot hear it and believe it without feeling a sense of responsibility in the direction indicated."

30. See Schellong, "Bourgeois World-View," 77.

31. *CD* II/1:173.

32. K. Barth, *Word of God*, 43.

33. K. Barth, *Word of God*, 41–48 (esp. 48). Emphasis in original. Cf. Marquardt, "Idol Totters," 177.

by acknowledging that both are two sides of the same coin and must be modified by a type of correspondence and rhythm with the being of God in analogy.[34]

Christologically, Marquardt's interpretation of Barth suggests a conception of God that is not simply addressed to the soul. It transcends provincial attempts to mythologize or romanticize human life. Barth, of course, conceptualized this most clearly in the Tambach lecture called "The Christian in Society" where his position on the lordship of God in Christ has a perduring significance for his view of God, and where the uniqueness of God's lordship, characterized by Barth as "lordship in freedom," has profound political connotations.[35] But even before it is articulated in this more radical sense, it must first be heard from the standpoint of Christ, even if it is Christ in us. With this acknowledgment, we can surmise that the political dimension does not occur "independently of his will and intention," but in relation to "Christian service." Correspondingly, the lordship of God for Barth relates to all domains of life. This includes political administrations, which are neither outside of God's lordship nor outside of the call to do Christian service within the world.[36]

Further, when considering Barth's insight into the freedom of God, we must conceptualize God as a God of freedom in correspondence with human liberation or praxis. As noted in the epigraph at the beginning of this chapter, Barth resisted using terms like "liberty," preferring instead the term "freedom." He said as much when visiting America in 1962, using the Stature of Liberty as an example of the problem: "That lady [the Statue of Liberty] needs a little or perhaps, a good bit of demythologization. Nevertheless, maybe she may also be seen and interpreted and understood as a symbol of a true theology, not of liberty, but of freedom."[37] Obviously for Barth freedom had a dimension of depth not found in the term "liberty" with its problematic relationship to American civil liberties.

Although his position is grounded in God's freedom, it is nevertheless freedom for *liberation*. Barth, especially in the *Church Dogmatics*, underscored this viewpoint in his theology without direct allusions to his interlocutors. His oblique viewpoints were determined more or less by the context and crucible of his experiences. As pointed out in *'Round Midnight*, volume 2, chapter 1 of this trilogy, under the influence of Ragaz and others,

34. *CD* II/1:232–33.

35. K. Barth, *Word of God*, 272–327. His view of lordship related to the freedom of God is in *CD* II/1:301. For a more accessible discussion, see K. Barth, "Theologians Answer Student Questions," 154.

36. K. Barth, "Theologians Answer Student Questions," 154.

37. K. Barth, *Karl Barth 1886–1968*, 79.

Barth already in 1915 argued that he could not do theology as if he could "remain suspended in the clouds above the present evil world but rather it had to be demonstrated here and now that faith in the Greatest does not exclude but includes within it work and suffering in the realm of the imperfect."[38] With this argument, Barth anticipated the attack of theologians such as Reinhold Niebuhr who presumed that his emphasis on divine grace was "a way of escape from, rather than a source of engagement with, the anxieties, perplexities, sins and pretensions of human existence." Niebuhr actually failed to note Barth's emphasis on the freedom of God in relation to all human experiences. Niebuhr, moreover, argued that freedom over traditions and law "cannot mean emancipation from the tortuous and difficult task of achieving tolerable justice," but his position represented a straw man that Barth never argued against.[39]

Niebuhr essentially misinterpreted how Barth related divine action to human freedom and human efforts to witness to God's justice. Stated differently, Niebuhr sidestepped how, for Barth, human freedom, read here as liberation, resided in rhythm (or in correspondence) with divine actions and how the crux of the issue revolved around the *third dimension*, "the word of God, the Holy Spirit, God's free choice, God's grace and judgment, the Creation, the Reconciliation, the Kingdom, the sanctification, the Congregation; and all these not as principles to be interpreted . . . but as the indication of *events*, of concrete, once-for-all, unique divine *actions*, of the majestic mysteries of God that cannot be resolved into any pragmatism."[40] Human freedom is thus characterized at its root by the mystery seen in the eschatological dimension that demands improvisational and dynamic transactions between the absolute divine freedom and relative human liberation.

The relationship between the freedom of God and human liberation is fundamental to apprehending Barth's theological ethics. In keeping with his way of sequencing the priority between revelation and freedom, human participants are grasped or, as Barth would write, "*made* a direct participant in this freedom."[41] Or as Eberhard Jüngel succinctly states, "anthropologically faith is the emergence of freedom."[42] Human freedom transpires from the freedom of God. It is established by God, that is, God vis-à-vis humanity. And despite Jüngel's emphasis, Barth's insight into the freedom of God matures over time.

38. K. Barth and Thurneysen, *Revolutionary Theology*, 28.

39. Niebuhr, "We Are Men," 1140.

40. K. Barth, "Continental vs. Anglo-Saxon Theology," 203. Emphasis in original.

41. K. Barth, *Evangelical Theology*, 76. Emphasis in original.

42. Jüngel, *God as the Mystery*, 164.

Barth knew at the beginning, however, that he could not proceed theologically without utilizing concepts; but being troubled by the *intellectus* of the modern world, he sensed a need to push back against conceptual predications about God and ironically found himself "fighting against all *concepts* of God, for *God-self* and against the human imaginations of *God* that are at play in all concepts of God."[43] Thus in Barth's final speeches, particularly in America, he stressed the freedom of God *for* humanity who cooperates with the free grace of God, and he coined the term *theoanthropology.* As a consequence, Barth's overall development of freedom can be described as prolonged attempts to articulate the interconnection between the ultimate freedom of God and the contingent freedom of humanity. Arguably from the time of his Marburg education, the freedom of God remained as a permanent motif of Barth's personal evolution, born of his ever-deepening, aporetic elucidation or improvisational response to the subject matter (*Sache*).

The Freedom of God in God's Self-Giving

The left-wing school of Barthian thought also has significant implications for Cone's appropriation and critique of Barth because Cone shifts away from Barth in order to transcend parochial readings, which he believes embody a form of "Christological exclusivity."[44] This interpretation of Barth, however, minimizes the importance of the freedom of God in God's revelation. Barth not only emphasized revelation to acknowledge God as the initiator and the one who gives Godself, but he conceptualized revelation to underscore God's *freedom* in self-giving. Theologically, the freedom of God then functions to transcend ontological, historical, and biblical categories; and, moreover, to transcend parochial christological categories that would limit God to Jesus in an exclusive sense.

It is clear, for Barth, that God's relationship to the world unfolds out of the freedom of God for the world. He established this position while accentuating the acts of God, or God's so-called actualism, in relation to God's self-disclosure or self-giving. As a counter to my earlier position, this does not reduce God to a process of knowing God, such as *esse sequitur operari*, a point at which I misread Barth, rather than arguing that "the knowledge of being follows the knowledge of activity," a position sometimes read as a

43. Marquardt, "Idol Totters," 174–75. Emphasis in original. Marquardt discusses an early view of God as overcoming concepts. Also see Chung, *Karl Barth*, 114–90. For discussion of theoanthropology, see K. Barth, *Evangelical Theology*, 12.

44. Cone, *God of the Oppressed*, xiv.

reversal in Barth.[45] I would suggest, however, that the knowledge of God is born of God's own initiative in self-revelation, an important nuance that encourages us to construe the freedom of God with God being the subject of God's own revealing. God gives Godself to be known and this self-giving grounds human freedom, pragmatically, so that "over against any intellectual impulse which erupts in the compulsion to act, it liberates the courage to serve its own understanding in thought and action."[46] Barth's approach has other important implications.

First, regarding ontology Barth avoids any idea of God as a type of localized ontology within God. He, ironically, avoids this problem by relying on the *aseitas Dei*, i.e., the aseity of God. God establishes the relationship with creation, not by maintaining a distinction, but in the way God exercises the distinction. As a result, God's freedom is both unconditioned and conditioned. It is unconditioned in that external conditions cannot determine God's freedom. So, God is consequently not negatively interpreted over-against creation. This freedom, then, is unconditioned and free *for* creation. As Barth writes, "He is the ground without grounds."[47] God's freedom is thus self-grounded in terms of God's relation to creation as seen in the acts of God. This freedom is conditioned by the fact that the triune God freely chooses (decides) to participate with that which is other than Godself. God's revelation of Godself is therefore a form of self-communication in freedom in which the profound sharing of Godself occurs. This self-communication occurs "*suo modo, sua libertate, sua misericordia*" (in its own way, in its own freedom, in its own mercy).[48]

Barth therefore avoids localizing God ontologically by using the self-communication of God as seen in God's unique way of speaking to discipline his view of ontology. For this reason he grounds his understanding of aseity in the act of God rather than a concept of aseity that gestures towards an "empty freedom," or "impulsive freedom," or some kind of ontological independence that is articulated in an abstract sense. For Barth "God is *a se*."[49] As Helmut Gollwitzer acknowledges, the "*ontological difference* between God and all non-divine, i.e., creaturely, being must be stringently

45. *CD* II/1:82–83.

46. Jüngel, *God's Being*, 132. See also Marquardt, *Theologie und Sozialismus*, 19–21; cf. Gollwitzer, *Existence of God*, 132; and Paul Chung's explication of this thematic problem in *Karl Barth*, 396–97. In my thinking, the judicious reader will hear an attempt to transcend the alternative between Marquardt's social view of God and Jüngel's so-called ontological localization of God.

47. *CD* I/1:307.

48. *CD* I/1:158.

49. *CD* I/1:157.

maintained—and yet *not* be supplemented by an ontology of God."[50] In contrast to those who read Barth's theology as a type of ontological localizing of God, a view that could be accommodated to reinforce the status quo of bourgeois culture, Marquardt reoriented the perception of Barth's view of transcendence, identifying it as the reverse image of society. As a result, God's ontology is not something otherworldly, "beyond and aloof." God, according to Marquardt, is "in connection with the Wholly Other of the new man [humanity], the new world, and the new age."[51] Barth's vision of God and understanding of humanity is thoroughly eschatological. It is a radical *freedom* for human liberation.

Second, the harmonics of God's revelation are determined by God. As a matter of fact, he elaborated the freedom of God to underscore how the divine is revealed. God must be *God* in revelation for human beings to be genuinely free. This does not mean that dogmatics will not at times use the language of ontology and other concepts. Jüngel is in fact correct when he argues that "God's revelation is the criterion of all ontological statements in theology."[52] God is not revealed where God is not free! What is revealed in such cases is something less than God, and despite any understanding of a hermeneutical/dialectical approach in theology, God transcends the dialectic itself. Barth is explicit in his position on the freedom of God: "[God] *is* and *remains free*: else he were not God."[53] This position reiterates Barth's earlier position in the first edition of *Romans* where he writes, "Denn Gott ist und bleibt *frei*" (God is and remains *free*). In the earlier Romans commentary Barth italicized the term "free," whereas in his later lecture on theological ethics he emphasized God's action, i.e., "is" and "remains free."[54] Of course, here I am concerned with the freedom of God. Nevertheless, God remains *free* because "God is and remains the Subject of [God's] word."[55] This emphasis sanctions the distinction between the freedom of God in revelation and the means of revelation.

50. Gollwitzer, *Existence of God*, 133. Emphasis in original.

51. Hunsinger, *Karl Barth and Radical Politics*, 66–68.

52. Jüngel, *God's Being*, 77.

53. K. Barth, *Word of God*, 178. Emphasis in original.

54. See K. Barth, *Römerbrief*, 427. Emphasis in original. Cf. K. Barth, *Epistle to the Romans*, 126, 470.

55. Even in his false start at dogmatics Barth maintained this distinction. Cf. K. Barth, *Lehre vom Worte Gottes*, 64.

The Freedom of God in Revelation

To further "affirm God's *freedom* for liberation," Barth, as noted above, had to also distinguish revelation from the means of revelation, a distinction that included more than an emphasis on the way he developed the relationship between revelation and the Bible. According to Eberhard Busch, "God's revelation can never become a revealedness we can control as if God's hiddenness were merely a passing phase or a partial truth . . . allowing us, after all, to possess God."[56] Barth therefore sought to maintain the mystery of God in revelation over against the means of revelation. This mystery is important for acknowledging the way human acts of liberation witness to God. Busch is therefore correct in his assessment. It is indeed fascinating that this motive in Barth's agenda arose as a problem as early as his student writings, viz, "Faith in a Personal God," where Barth wrestled with the absoluteness of God; but this agenda takes on a more peculiar ring in his first cycle of dogmatics called *Göttingen Dogmatics* where he sharpened the distinction between God's freedom in revelation and the means of revelation.[57] The point is that for Barth God is fully *God* in revelation. But God is also hidden in God's revealedness, and God's hiddenness is "not alongside or behind revelation but in it."[58] This points to the mystery of God's participation in revelation.

Revelation is therefore "fully self-grounded," and "self-contained," which basically establishes Barth's argument that "lordship means freedom." As such "it is thus, as One who is free, as the only One who is free, that God has lordship in the Bible."[59] So, along with the Reformers, Barth maintained God's freedom in revelation as the highest authentication of Scripture and not vice versa. This peculiar ground of Scripture is the reason Barth emphasized God as the "Subject" of God's revealing.[60] God's free relationship to Scripture, moreover, provides the criterion for understanding the relationship between revelation, Scripture, and the polyphony of "true words" that witness to God "outside the walls of the church" (*extra muros ecclesia*). The test for these "true words" redounds to the inner material relation between God the revealing subject (cantus firmus) and secular words outside the walls of the church (polyphony).

56. Busch, "God Is God," 111.

57. K. Barth, *Göttingen Dogmatics*, 95. Cf. *CD* I/1:321–22. A *motive* in music is essentially the smallest structural unit possessing thematic identity. See glossary.

58. K. Barth, *Göttingen Dogmatics*, 93.

59. *CD* I/1:306–7.

60. *CD* I/1:114.

As a result, God's revelation is neither polymorphous nor "a revelatory event among many."[61] Revelation, moreover, is not a mere truth nor is it an objective reality. It is *the* truth and *the* objective reality because it is *Dei loquentis persona* (God's speaking person). According to Barth, "God's Word means the speaking God." God's Word is not "anticipated or repeated."[62] Certainly interpreters are free to raise questions as to why such an absolute portrayal of God is necessary, but such a view of God's revelation invests revelation with a peculiar character, that is, a mode of being *characterized* by the freedom of God. This view also protects the mystery of God from the human tendency to constrain God in light of human acts. In this way, Barth consistently affirms a *freedom* for liberation.

This freedom of God in revelation also precludes us from restricting God's aseity to a form of divine insulation where God is perceived as self-possessed, as if engaged in a form of celestial navel-gazing. Barth developed God's self-giving (or this reiteration of God's freedom in revelation) as the history of a God who loves in freedom. In this respect, God's love for humanity is unconditioned in relation to any other reality. Consequently, one can argue that no other reality deserves humanity's loyalty as does the love of God. Eberhard Jüngel describes this freedom of God as a form of self-determination.[63] God determines God's self-giving in revelation as a way to speak of God's freedom in revelation. Another way to speak of this freedom is perhaps in Jan Lochman's term, *proseity*, which refers to God's proexistence.[64] God has God's life from God's own self, but it is a life that is utterly and unequivocally concerned with humanity as seen in the Trinitarian history of God turned toward humanity.

Such a distinction is important for several reasons. First, it allows Barth to radically and concretely turn to what he sees as the subject matter of Scripture, i.e., Jesus Christ. To be sure, witnessing to the freedom of God in Christ is no parochial turning to a form of Christomonism (a narrow exclusive view of Christ cut off from the world). On the contrary, Barth read Scripture not in terms of Christomonism, but in terms of a christological

61. Cf. Cone, *God of the Oppressed*, xiv. After much consideration, I am not fully convinced Cone's argument over against exclusive views of revelation is a material argument as opposed to a political one aimed at those who would unwittingly absolutize their vision of Jesus.

62. *CD* I/1:136–37.

63. See Jüngel, *God as the Mystery*, 36.

64. Lochman, "Trinity and Human Life," 179. Lochman's term is used with a caveat when speaking of God's preexistence; it should be understood not as a "'proexistence', which characterizes him [God]," but rather a preexistence characterized by God's being for us.

concentration. Barth's christological concentration permitted him to say things more "freely, openly, and comprehensively."[65] Lochman neatly distinguishes christological concentration from Christomonism, describing the latter "as the tendency to reduce the rich diversity of biblical themes solely to the name 'Jesus Christ' and then to turn to the world and relate the name of Christ to the richness of human history in a primarily defensive and exclusive way."[66] Furthermore, according to Barth, it was his turn to Christology that led him to be more preoccupied with *Geistesgeschichte* (history of ideas).[67] It was consequently his focus on Christ that led to a more radical openness to the history of ideas and presumably to *Geistesfreiheit* (freedom of thought or conscience).

Second, God's freedom in revelation coincided with Barth's later emphasis on theology as a form of theoanthropology.[68] Although Barth did not use terms like "theoanthropological unity" in his early theology, he did attempt to understand the relationship between revelation and the various forms of revelation, notably in his early theology, especially the relationship between Scripture and proclamation. During this early period, he was primarily concerned with finding the proper foundation for preaching. As Alexander McKelway reiterates concerning the *Göttingen Dogmatics*, "when Barth turns from revelation to the doctrine of God, he continues to keep the preacher in mind."[69] Christ, in the long history of Barth's theology, is not an exclusive modality that rejects the life of humanity; and theology is neither monistic nor dualistic for Barth. It is "unionistic," meaning that in theology one witnesses to the union between God and humanity:

> Christomonism would mean that Christ alone is real and that all other men are only apparently real. But that would be in contradiction with what the name of Jesus Christ means, namely, union between God and [humanity]. This union between God and [humanity] has not been made only in Jesus Christ but in him as our representative for the benefit of all [human beings]. Jesus Christ as God's servant is true God and true man, but at the same time also our servant and the servant of all [human beings].[70]

65. K. Barth, *Karl Barth 1886–1968*, 43–44.

66. Lochman, *Reconciliation and Liberation*, 33.

67. K. Barth, *Karl Barth 1886–1968*, 44.

68. K. Barth, *Evangelical Theology*, 12.

69. McKelway, Review of *Göttingen Dogmatics*, 416.

70. K. Barth, "Theological Dialogue," 172. I corrected retrograde language to sharpen the distinction between the role of Christ as the "real man" and Barth's use of "men" as representative of humanity. As is clear, on some occasions I avoid correcting retrograde language for various reasons tied to meaning and tone.

Because of his christological concentration Barth can interpret the word of God in terms of Christ's universal lordship. Revelation, religion, and the world are not mutually exclusive, false alternatives from one other. The freedom of God in God's revelation is radically related to the world so as to call for a "theo-anthropological unity."[71] The point of Barth's development in the first volume of the *Church Dogmatics* is to consider the written word and proclamation in light of revelation, but the relationship between revelation, Scripture, and preaching only points to the vocation of the church within the common life of the world. Revelation is by no means limited to the church's self-understanding and determination within the world. Such a restriction would be a limitation of the freedom of God in God's revelation. This leads to a consideration of the relationship between the freedom of God for the world, which further affirms Barth's affirmation of *freedom* for liberation.

The Freedom of God for the World

In thinking of God's freedom *for* the world, it is important to first acknowledge that Barth construed revelation as being profoundly related *to* the world. As early as 1926 in his Amsterdam lecture called "Church and Culture," Barth proposed a way of considering natural theology (*theologia naturalis*) in light of revelation (*theologia revelata*). Despite the fact that he was and remained a stalwart critic of natural theology, he valued the effectiveness of Christ's lordship as witnessed in creation. God's claim on humanity was not delimited by the fallenness of the world. God's love for humanity consisted in the "affirmation of [human] life in communion with [God]."[72] Arguably, no other aspect of Barth's theology pointed more to Christ's universal lordship than the fact that creation itself is the external ground of the covenant. The world is the "arena of God's actions," according to Hordern's astute analysis of Barth.[73] Barth's concern with a "more natural" natural theology has implications for nation, culture, and even race.[74]

71. For a rich development of this concept as it relates to religious pluralism, see Chung, "Karl Barth and Inter-Religious Dialogue," 244–45.

72. K. Barth, *Theology and Church*, 342–43.

73. Hordern, "Barth as Political Thinker," 412.

74. See Carter, *Race*, 161. Carter's engaging argument does not attend to Barth's discussion of culture, which anticipated Cone's liberative thrust, and although Barth did not focus on race per se, God's grace completes nature and God's promise gives human culture its true rhythm. Barth argues, for example, that "the dogmatician, too, must think and speak in a particular age and should thus be a man [person] of his age. . . . The problem of culture is the problem of being human . . . and dogmatics can be seen as wholly set within the framework of the problem of culture." *CD* I/1:283–84.

This new and different look at the world through revelation should first be interpreted in terms of the freedom of the word of God. Already in the first volume of the *Church Dogmatics*, Barth distinguished the word of God from the church that proclaims the word of God; thus the word of God is, as noted above, not determined by the limitations of churches. The whole world in fact has the potential to attest to the glory of God: "what God can do" is distinct from what the church is commissioned to do.[75] With this interpretation of the freedom of the word of God, Barth developed his view of the word of God that speaks *extra muros ecclesiae* (outside the walls of the church), which includes, of course, culture.

In view of the freedom of God, Barth highlighted the radical political dimensions of God's relationship to the world. The transcendence or freedom of God is not only beyond the creature, but "free enough partially or completely to transform its being or to take from it again as God first gave to it."[76] The freedom of God is thus portrayed in a way that highlights the incapacity of humanity to know or limit God, but also the capacity of God to lift up humanity. At the same time, therefore, God opens up the possibilities for humanity, because God is for the world in a particular way. "*The fact that God can* do these things is God's freedom in immanence."[77] Such a view therefore mitigates against God being universally ascertainable by humanity, but it sets in relief God's concern for humanity. In other words, God is not a supreme being accessible to humanity; nor is God one whom humanity has the capacity to know; therefore, the revelation of God is an act of God's own self-determination—a grace-inflected choice made in relation to human beings in the world.[78]

In God's self-determining choice for humanity, the freedom of God for the world is first heard. God's being for the world is heard in the musicality of the incarnation, which gives rise both to the Trinitarian interpretation of God's freedom and the acts of God in God's creating, reconciling, and redeeming work within history. The freedom of God is a freedom determined by God's love for the world. As Jüngel points out, "God determines God's self."[79] And in this Trinitarian determination the history of the divine being is clearly seen in *God's coming* for the world, a movement that is not

75. *CD* I/1:54.

76. *KD* II/1:352; cf. *CD* II/1:313.

77. *KD* II/1:353; cf. *CD* II/1:314. Emphasis added.

78. *CD* I/1:158–59.

79. Jüngel, *God as the Mystery*, 36.

without radical consequences for the world, being the encounter with a God who radically reorients the human situation in light of God's own acts. This logic of God gives way to new rhythms, disrupting the established human situation.

This transformation of the human situation is a significant emphasis within Marquardt's interpretation of Barth. Marquardt argued that Barth apprehended God as the one who alters the situation for all human beings at all times (*die Veranderung der Situation der Menschen aller Zeiten*). With this emphasis, Marquardt acknowledged Barth's shift from God as *der Ganz Andere* (the Wholly Other) to an emphasis on God as the basis for the transformation of the human situation (*Realgrund der Veränderung ihrer Situation*).[80] Barth as a matter of fact made an effort to critique his earlier vision of God as the wholly other (*der Ganz Andere*) as seen in the second edition of *Der Römerbrief*.[81]

He realized his improper emphasis on the "wholly other God" could promote a vision of a detached deistic view of God, a *Deus otiosus*. Rather, for Barth, it is God the Son who journeys into the far country for humanity and not a god who is "absolute, high and exalted, far removed from any lowliness and quite alien to it." Marquardt's emphasis simply echoes Barth's interpretation of God's relation to the world as the one who changes reality, revealing God in terms of God's impact on sociopolitical reality. This same God is the One who loves the world in freedom. This interpretation furthermore allowed for the freedom of God to be interpreted in light of the lordship of Christ where one is called into the ethics that reflect God's being in freedom, i.e., a calling into "the freedom of the children of God, into a following of the freedom and the work in which God Himself is God."[82]

Marquardt, nevertheless, focused on the freedom of God as it is elaborated in a phrase in Barth's exposition of the doctrine of God entitled "The Being of God in Act." God is the fact by which all live, which means "they should and must live with the fact that not only sheds new light on but materially changes, all things and everything in all things—the fact that God is."[83] Herbert Hartwell, among others, criticized Marquardt for using this phrase, identifying it simply as a marginal phrase. However, Marquardt in my view has isolated the significance of important interpretive themes in Barth's thinking, and he reinforces this in the way he later explicated the dogmatics. The movement of God in Christ—epitomized in his death and

80. *KD* IV/1:348–49.

81. *CD* IV/1:191; *KD* 4/1:209.

82. *CD* IV/1:191.

83. *CD* II/1:258.

resurrection—alters human history. This viewpoint gives radical political impetus to the rhythm of human freedom, and it offers a liberating word that radically distinguishes the church from other viewpoints.

As a corrective to Helmut Gollwitzer, who argued that this change "is no magic formula which changes everything with one blow," and secondarily that this change consisted in the fact that it "creates the readiness for change, that it liberates to this readiness," I want to suggest that Barth's realism here is grounded in his threefold view of time where the freedom of Christ reaches into the present, being irreducible to a promissory emphasis on human readiness for the future.[84] I further suggest that if we align more with James Cone, we can imagine Christ as being free for the world and the children of God who live in the rhythms of his freedom in the present realities of the world.

From this perspective, the liberating word, on one hand, irrupts any narrow form of revelation positivism (*Offungbarungspositivismus*); and on the other, it disrupts any liberal emphasis on human preparedness. Barth simply does not conceptualize the freedom of God as a reductive principle or datum that can be read into the being of God; nor does he pursue a historicist frame of thought where original autographs (such as Scripture) convey and subsequently capture the freedom of God. To the contrary, humankind is confronted by the freedom of God in an eventful manner in every new situation. Christ himself is radically free because Christ is the reiteration of the Father through the Holy Spirit. This viewpoint opens radically to the possibilities of black theology in a way that honors liberative efforts by those who live in the rhythms and power of the Holy Spirit. Moreover, in light of this more radical interpretation of Barth, Cone's critical insistence on Jesus the Liberator—as not being central in Barth's Christology—is set in relief by the urgency of Barth's situation.

The Freedom of God for the Liberation of Humanity

One can be tempted to criticize any painstaking discussion of the freedom of God in revelation; but a correlation between divine freedom and human liberation is impossible without an emphasis on the proper sequence between God and humanity. Freedom "is not an ultimate or absolute value by itself."[85] Theological freedom, as interpreted by Barth, does not stand alone abstractly in the form of a generic concept. It finds meaning and specificity

84. Hunsinger, *Karl Barth and Radical Politics*, 110.

85. W. Norris Clarke, SJ, "Freedom as Value," in Johann, *Freedom and Value*, 1. See also 17–18.

in an encounter with God. Barth was quite fond of the Latin phrase *Latet periculum in generalibus*, which means that generalities are dangerous.[86] Barth therefore sought to define the freedom of God in terms of the object of faith (*Gegenstand*) itself and not some generic notion of freedom. He noted that "when we say that God is free, the accent does not fall on 'free' but on 'God.'"[87] Hence, the meaning of freedom is disciplined, ordered, or sequenced, as interpreted by "the fact that God is, which changes everything and everyone."[88] This is an "irreversible sequence," where in Jesus Christ human liberation finds its affirmation in the condescension of God, being "wholly enclosed in the freedom of God."[89] It follows then that the relationship between the freedom of God and the freedom or liberation of humanity is determined by freedom as it is fulfilled *in revelation.*

Human Freedom as Fulfilled in Revelation

A primary question that naturally arises from Barth's theological construction is whether the correspondence between God's freedom and human liberation allows for self-determination and responsible human decisions in relation to God's freedom. Before considering any substantial answer, one would be remiss without offering criticism of the presumption within such a question, i.e., that God's revelation and human freedom are somehow mutually exclusive. Indeed, Barth addressed this false dichotomy. He writes, "Revelation itself is the gift and work of freedom."[90] The revelation of God recognized as a gift and heard in faith has its origin in the freedom of God. God frees humanity from its own powerlessness.[91] Following this line of thought, one is not merely freed *from* bondage, which includes the law and the panoply of institutions, ideologies, and ideas. God exceeds this narrow construction of freedom by liberating one to be *for God* in a peculiar way—beyond any simple *freedom from* things in the world.

86. See Busch, "Deciding Moments," 61.

87. *CD* II/1:320.

88. This is not only Marquardt's construction and emphasis, but Eberhard Busch's. Busch also isolates this phrase in Barth's thought, a theme reflective of Barth's teaching in general, although Hartwell describes it pejoratively as a "marginal phrase (in small print)." Busch, "God Is God," 112; Hartwell, Review of *Theologie und Sozialismus*, 63–72.

89. K. Barth, *Humanity of God*, 48–49.

90. K. Barth, *Final Testimonies*, 37.

91. *CD* I/1:456.

A simple freedom from the world would in fact open the door to all types of possibilities and choices for humanity, which would basically leave human beings as some type of "Hercules at a crossroads."[92] As a result Barth frames the possibility of choosing for or against God as an impossibility; it is a form of powerlessness. Seeing the danger in the former kind of freedom, Barth concentrated on real human freedom as "freedom for God, for the 'glorious liberty' of the children of God (Rom. 8:21), the *analogia fidei* (the analogy of faith) of the divine freedom, which alone really deserves to be called freedom."[93] Freedom, then, takes on a peculiar mode of being in the world, a rhythm or correspondence with God's freedom. Said differently, human freedom is characterized by God's freedom in the way rhythm is characterized by the melody for Monk's way of improvising.

This view nevertheless leaves open to question Barth's understanding of human decisions and the space necessary for so-called "natural freedom" to take place. First, in claiming our human freedom, the history of God in Christ "begins with a voluntary decision of God and continues in a corresponding voluntary decision of humanity."[94] Such a relationship reveals God's true desire for human beings and the fulfillment of human freedom, i.e., *theoanthropology*. This rhythm with God critiques freedom when framed as some type of naked autonomy or license. More importantly, God's freedom places a judgment on institutions, ideologies, and images that would claim the freedom of a person for themselves or those which are operationalized to claim the freedom of an(other). Barth's concern stresses the divine sphere in terms of its movement *von Gott her* (from God to us) and cuts across human spheres, revolutionizing them. In this sense, God's freedom and human freedom are not in opposition to one another but in harmony.

Second, human self-determination is not incompatible with God's determination because they are not a type of "coexistence on the same level." As mentioned above, God determines human beings for God. Hence, on the one hand, human self-determination does not displace the determination of God, nor does it become a synthesis or harmony in the sense of some type of semi-pelagianism. On the other hand, God's determination does not eliminate a person's self-determination, i.e., resigning humans to a type of evasion or quietism in face of God's freedom.[95] According to Barth, the

92. See K. Barth, *Humanity of God*, 76; and Barth's ethics for more background on this metaphor regarding morality: K. Barth, *Ethics*, 74; cf. Godsey, *Karl Barth's Table Talk*, 37.

93. *CD* I/1:457.

94. *CD* II/1:28.

95. *CD* I/1:200.

word of God is "strong" in its summons of a human being and determines one's existence, allowing one to determine oneself.[96] It matures human freedom and lifts it up into a new harmony. Barth developed this argument in his *Church Dogmatics* by juxtaposing the self-determining of God with the self-determining of humanity under the category of "acknowledgment."

In this view, Christ, the cantus firmus, comes to human beings in judgment and grace, establishing the melodic center, characterizing the context, and compelling the attitude for true acknowledgment to occur improvisationally.[97] Human self-determination and God's determination are not mutually exclusive or discordant but reestablished with one another. The freedom of God and freedom of humanity are not independent, static, or arbitrary, but harmonious, established in a dynamic interrelationship "with Christ dancing the lead." Some American theologians have been influenced by this vision in kinship with Barth. Thomas Merton, for instance, described it as a partnership or participation, a "mutual commitment between the limited and contingent freedom of man [humanity] and the ultimate unlimited freedom of God."[98] From this vantage point, human freedom is truly affirmed when it corresponds or finds its rhythm in witness to God, and by implication human freedom is not based on a philosophical concept of free will but on revelation and an attendant and responsive human will to this concord created by God.

This rhythmic tension leads me to the third and final part of human freedom as it relates to its fulfillment in revelation; that is, the dialectic between human freedom, understood from the vantage of the freedom of God in revelation, and the modern emphasis on what is often called "free will." I must reiterate that to focus on free will—as an explanation of what freedom means—does not expound human freedom from a theological vantage point. Human freedom has its melodic foundation in Jesus Christ; for through God in Christ the "creature is taken up into the sphere of divine lordship."[99] Through Christ the whole creation is enabled to participate in the being of God. This participation, however, does not arise from the essence of the creature itself; it is not the creature's own "free will" allowing for participation, but rather the permission of God. God in love seeks and

96. *CD* I/1:203.

97. See *CD* I/1:205–8.

98. See Merton, *Opening the Bible*, 77–78. I appeal to Merton at this point because his view of freedom has a striking similarity to Barth's view. Merton appeals to Barth, although I resonate with Barth's suspicion of the language of "partnership."

99. *CD* II/1:670.

draws the creature unto God "in order that He [God] may be God with it and not without out it."[100]

But this acknowledgment of God does not undermine human freedom. It completes it. It gives human liberation its rhythm. Thus freedom and liberation find harmony in the generosity of God. According to Barth the creature is taken into service. Barth even argued that "[in] our incapable capacity, we are permitted and commanded to do something which if it came from our own free choice would be madness, but which in the freedom and obedience of revelation is the good sense of God."[101] This mystery is the freedom of God operationalized in such a way so as to provoke a free improvisational response, a liberation grounded in the freedom of God. The commandment, then, must be interpreted as the law *in the form of* the gospel. This law is the law of freedom at work in humanity. Daniel Migliore echoes Barth when he describes *freedom as a gift* that points to "the transcendent source of liberation and helps to guard the struggle for freedom against every absolutization of methods and achievements."[102] In my view, this includes the achievements of institutions and human beings. Admittedly, Barth wonders if it is the so-called achievement of humanity that is in view "above all else," even from the beginning.[103] If such is the case, it stands to reason that the false freedom of the human will—the ego or the autonomy that wants to escape from any harmony with God—is the first bondage from which humanity is in need of liberation. Thus, the gospel offers a *freedom* for liberation. Moreover, perhaps this is the reason that Barth argues that human decisions represent the loss of freedom—"with but a single exception," *the choice for God*, viz, the choice that paradoxically establishes human freedom.[104]

Human Freedom as an Event of Revelation

Based on the fulfillment of human freedom in revelation, human freedom is accordingly an event. As I have reiterated throughout this chapter, it is rooted first of all in God's freedom: "The archetype form of God's gift of grace lies in the incarnation of His word, the unity of God and man [humanity] in Jesus Christ."[105] God's freedom for humanity is therefore seen

100. *CD* II/1:671.

101. *CD* II/1:199.

102. Migliore, *Called to Freedom*, 95.

103. K. Barth, *Final Testimonies*, 37.

104. K. Barth, "Reformation as Decision," 159.

105. *CD* II/1:354.

in the melody of Christ, the word becoming flesh. For Barth, God's radical transcendence—evidenced in the positive movement of God towards humanity—creates a harmonizing fellowship, a spontaneous interplay, relativizing our differences and providing space for the call-and-response, alternation, that allows human beings to actualize human freedom. Following this sequencing, any notion of an "infinite qualitative distinction" between God and humanity is already overcome *by God*, and the freedom of God is no longer contrasted with humanity or creation. God's freedom, as a "non-contrastive freedom," has its positive content in the movement of God in history, especially in the incarnation (the revelation of God).[106]

Moreover, in the musicality of the incarnation, divine freedom (transcendence) "cannot be exhaustively defined as God's opposition to the reality distinct from Himself [God's own self]." On the contrary, divine freedom occurs through the exercise of God's own freedom. God "enters into and faithfully maintains communion with this reality other than himself [God] in His [God's] activity as Creator, Reconciler and Redeemer."[107] The freedom of humanity therefore receives its character from God's turning toward humankind in fellowship. History, and by extrapolation, *freedom* or human liberation, derives its ultimate positive and constructive value from what Jan Milič Lochman identified as Barth's emphasis on the *liberating event* of God: "the biblical message of freedom starts not from a concept of freedom but with liberation as an *event*, freedom as a gift."[108] For Barth, "[God's] operation is history."[109] We might add that it is nowhere as clearly seen as it is in the incarnation; since the divine melody of the incarnation unionizes God and humanity. Any discussion of human freedom is therefore oriented by this event, leading Barth to identify authentic theology as "unionistic."[110] In other words, the incarnation reveals the real encounter between God and humanity, and human freedom improvises on the melody of this divine musicality.

This unionistic theology means that history is a predicate of revelation. The sequence is never reversed, because the history of God is not a history that we can, as human beings, freely place ourselves behind in order to domesticate God. Human freedom responds to God's freedom, in

106. The language "non-contrastive transcendence" is borrowed from Kathryn Tanner to emphasize a radical freedom or transcendence in God that differentiates God from a direct contrast with the creation itself, but at the same time it precludes any separation of God from the world. See Tanner, *God and Creation*, 82–83.

107. *CD* II/1:303.

108. Lochman, *Reconciliation and Liberation*, 120. Emphasis in original.

109. *CD* II/1:600. Barth is articulating a covenantal view of the history of God with humanity for all time.

110. K. Barth, "Theological Dialogue," 172.

counterpoint, but it is human freedom, nonetheless. Barth is careful here, arguing that "divine freedom was not initiated in and by this act of human freedom. Nor is it accomplished and somehow encompassed in it. Rather, God's freedom is and remains above and beyond human freedom."[111] Human acts of liberation will as a result always be stamped by the mystery of their provisional character.

Using several terms to distinguish between these two forms of freedom, Barth has a protracted discussion about God's history. He initially used the term *Urgeschichte*, which means "primal history." Although Barth would later regret the usage of this terminology, it allowed him to speak properly of history as a predicate of revelation. Jesus Christ fulfills time. History is thus "limited and determined by the history of fulfilled time."[112] This concretized perceptivity of history has a peculiar implication for how we interpret the freedom of historical events as they relate to the experience of freedom in the mode I am suggesting in this book.

The unique history of Jesus Christ means that we can witness to a particular "realm of freedom" as different from "freedom in history" or "natural freedom"; however, the two will nevertheless coexist in a dialectical relationship.[113] Natural freedom is thus explicable from the standpoint of Christian freedom, i.e., the realm of freedom.[114] Human freedom is therefore criticized and elucidated in relation to God's freedom. Barth even argued that "human freedom never ceases to be the event wherein the free God gives and man [humanity] receives this gift."[115] This position is demanded because it envisions Christ's history (or *Heilsgeschichte*) as more than sui generis; for it is of no genus whatsoever, but rather "a history of salvation and revelation."[116]

111. K. Barth, *Humanity of God*, 74.

112. *CD* I/2:58–59.

113. For a similar development to Barth's, see Moltmann, *Religion, Revolution, and the Future*, 66–69; *CD* II/2:567–71.

114. Here I use the term "realm of freedom" to move beyond the concept of "*Christian*" freedom, which has been burdened with the freight of Christianity understood ideologically as the "Christian religion." Dialectical theologians, including Barth, argued against such a Christianization of faith. We can presume that in speaking of "Christian freedom" Barth had in mind Christianity as a "religion of revelation," i.e., religion bound up with the revelation of God. In this respect one can compare Barth's provocative statement that "the religion of revelation is indeed bound up with the revelation of God: but the revelation of God is not bound up with the religion of revelation." See *CD* I/2:329. Barth may also be speaking exclusively of theological ethics rather than offering a more extensive view of freedom within creation. See the bridge in volume 2, *'Round Midnight*, where I employ Charles Long to offer an alternative to Barth's view of religion.

115. K. Barth, *Humanity of God*, 75.

116. K. Barth, "Theological Dialogue," 175.

This "realm of freedom" as seen in Christ's history gives form to human freedom *for liberation* in much the way the melodic form gives shape to Monk's improvising, providing for its freedom, its variations, its possibilities.

It follows from this argument that the mysteriously free movement of God in history characterizes human freedom as a gift, because the incarnation is an unrepeatable event. It is *the* fixed melody. The incarnation therefore has real meaning for history, but it is the meaning that revelation itself ascribes to it. According to Barth, there is no "identity," "extension," or "parity" with revelation.[117] There is only the possibility of correspondence or, as I prefer to say, rhythm. Therefore, although natural freedom does not reverse the relationship between God and the human will, it can be posited as an act of will in counterpoint to God's freedom. The pertinent question is whether it is really an act of *free* will. How should one interpret human freedom as it relates to the "realm of freedom," i.e., the freedom of God and the freedom bestowed by God on humanity? I would suggest that one way to construe this relationship is to argue in Barth's fashion that *human freedom is bound up with God's freedom, but God's freedom is not bound up or delimited by human freedom.* Put another way, the free person revels in God's freedom, which provides the melody for the rhythm of human liberation.

Human Freedom in History

Since human freedom for Barth is inextricably related to Jesus the Liberator, the fact that *God is* includes humanity. God chooses humanity to be in covenant with God. Following Barth, the God of the Bible refuses to be God without humanity. There is in fact a self-determination in God that includes humanity. If, as Barth argued, "this is not an accidental historical fact but in its historical uniqueness is the revelation of the divine will . . . then God's freedom is essentially not freedom *from*, but freedom *to* and *for*." In Christ the Liberator, therefore, one sees the movement of God; one hears the musicality of God. It is this "history which leads to the ultimate salvation of humanity." Humanity therefore participates in God's history, and the God who loves in freedom participates in human history. Central for understanding the biblical God is to see God historically "appropriating human nature into the unity of His [God's] own being."[118]

This dance between God and humanity is pivotal for understanding human freedom, "for in becoming man in Jesus Christ God has claimed for

117. *CD* IV/3.2:729. See also *CD* I/2:59.

118. K. Barth, *Humanity of God*, 72, 75.

Himself [God] our human freedom."[119] And when Barth argued that God's justice as revealed in the covenant "confronts all human attempts to create justice, order, peace, and so on with this superior justice,"[120] he framed God's freedom in a way that critiques and claims human freedom. In the early stages of his *Church Dogmatics*, he posited that because God is Lord, God is free over against the creature's "original sin."[121] Barth established this point by using the virgin birth to critique, not the natural element in human sexuality, but the sinful element in humanity. More importantly, he used the virgin birth to demonstrate that the act of outstripping human freedom occurred from God's side. Thus, when confronting the human person, God negates any arbitrary notion of freedom arising from humanity.[122] Human freedom is thus determined by this act of God in Christ, rather than something that human beings accomplish independently. Freedom is accomplished by God's action in history and God's action upon the creature. This dialogical relationship explains why Barth used the metaphor "Hercules at the crossroads" to make the point that God does not leave human beings in the situation of a false choice, a specious form of freedom.

Human freedom, historically understood, is set within the "aim and goal" of a future already determined by God. This history of God in Christ is the ground of the alteration of the human situation, the transformation of life. In other words, Christ—through obedience—revolutionized the historical sphere and makes a claim on humanity.[123] And because of Christ's act of obedience and God's subsequent claim on human freedom, one has to seriously question any shift away from this christological concentration to an emphasis on Jesus as simply "an important revelatory event among many."[124] Moreover, when Jesus is simply considered as one revelatory event among others, human choices are reopened to a number of vague possibilities.[125] In such cases, we must consider how to avoid confusing or conflating human goodness or human acts of liberation with divine righteousness

119. *CD* II/2:565.

120. K. Barth, "Theological Dialogue," 176.

121. *CD* I/2:190–91.

122. *CD* I/2:191.

123. *CD* II/2:571.

124. Cone, *God of the Oppressed*, xiv. This reading of Cone and the subsequent interpretation should be read as a correction to my earlier one-sided interpretation of Cone in the first take on this material. See Carr, "Barth and Cone in Dialogue," 253.

125. K. Barth, "Gift of Freedom," 77. I should note here that I am not making a general argument that would give way to a type of Christomonism or religious absolutism, but rather a specific argument about the nature of human liberation.

revealed in Jesus Christ.[126] Can we truly actualize human freedom if divine freedom is dismissed?

Still, in fairness to Cone's intentions, the christological concentration resists any narrow exclusivist readings of revelation that separate God from the polyphony of human history, including the richness of "blue notes" which arise from black theology. Indeed, I am reminded by the aesthetics of Thelonious Monk and the words of Dietrich Bonhoeffer that "where the *cantus firmus* is clear and plain, the counterpoint can be developed to its limits."[127]

Human Freedom as a Theological Category in the Rhythm of "God's Lordship"

With Barth's starting point of faith, Christian freedom occurs within the orbit of the freedom of God in Jesus Christ as the fulfillment and eventful history of God. The efficaciousness of Christ transcends the subjectivity of faith, however. Barth explained this development protologically: "God's word was already in effect even before we believed." Drawing on the established melody of the older Lutheran tradition, which emphasized the *efficacia verbi extra usum* (efficacy of the word apart from its use), Barth based his case for the real ground tone of freedom on the priority of the word. Human beings who have faith live by the real object who is the subject (*Gegenstand*) of Scripture.[128] As noted earlier human beings are, therefore, lifted up by God through the power of the Spirit. The creature is incorporated (*hineingenommenwerden*) into the sphere of God's lordship.[129] Consequently, it is through God's power that the hearer of the word of God "is drawn thereby into the sphere of the real power of this lordship."[130] For Barth the whole creation is "enabled to participate in the being of God."[131] In this way it is the action of God that identifies human liberation as a theological category. Freedom is thus not simply conceptual, terminological, or abstract. Like the deeper conceptual meaning of Monk's rhythmical harmonics in relation to the melody, human freedom is given its shape by the movement of the

126. *CD* II/2:565.

127. Bonhoeffer, *Letters and Papers*, 303–4.

128. *CD* I/1:154. See also *KD* I/1:159. Barth uses the term *Gegenstand* to denote an object that is not objectified. This object encounters human beings, a point accented in Barth's doctrine of God where the discussion revolves around "Man [Humanity] before God." *CD* II/1:3–31.

129. *CD* II/1:670; *KD* II/1:756.

130. *CD* I/1:153.

131. *CD* II/1:670.

Triune God who comes to us in freedom.[132] God, as H.-J. Kraus argues, "breaks through all the closeness of history." Moreover, in God's peculiar freedom, "the promise of freedom comes to all the world and to all human beings involved in it."[133]

This fact of humanity's liberation by the power of God should alter and (re)characterize how human freedom is conceptualized. Human freedom does not participate in a sphere unto itself. It finds its rhythm in relation to God's liberation, which has already been accomplished in Christ. For this reason the "sovereign freedom of the Creator"—to use Barth's dear friend Pierre Maury's description of God—establishes human freedom: "God's freedom is the sovereign liberty of the Creator, which our liberty may neither dispute nor judge."[134] Thus the call of God's freedom implicated its respondents more deeply into the rhythm of God's lordship. Maury's insight is important because Barth's theology followed in this "fundamental direction."[135] Maury furthermore underscored the *theological* rather than the *anthropological* accent in the doctrine of election to promote the freedom and mercy of *the God who predestined* rather than focusing on the *ones who are predestined.*[136] This sequencing is, again, important because God freely chooses to be bound to creation and gives character to human history.[137] To shift contexts as an example, history is not "determined by the oppugnancy slaves felt toward the world."[138] History is the predicate of the word of God. Correspondingly, human decisions are truly radical when characterized by the movement that gives life a particular mode of being, a liberated rhythm, "an unambiguous and irreversible movement." It is the decision of faith of one who is bound to God.[139]

Humanity is thus captivated or taken up in the decision for God—in the movement of God. As the Shrove Tuesday song makes clear, *"Christ*

132. The discussion of the *coming of God* is an important thematic discussion in left-wing Barthian contexts, and it discloses the crux of the argument between the so-called left-/right-wing Barthian positions. Paul S. Chung is one of the strongest proponents of this view, writing that "God's being in becoming cannot be properly understood without deliberation of God's coming." Here Chung gestures toward the sociopolitical implications of Barth's Trinitarian doctrine. Chung, "Engaging Karl Barth's Missional Church," 2.

133. Kraus, *Reich Gottes*, 102.

134. Maury, *Predestination and Other Papers*, 36.

135. Maury, *Predestination and Other Papers*, 16.

136. Maury, *Predestination and Other Papers*, 37.

137. *CD* II/2:155.

138. I am inverting the order found in William Turner's "Musicality of Black Preaching," 26.

139. K. Barth, "Reformation as Decision," 160–61.

dances the lead and all his rhythm heed."[140] Humanity is no longer subject to the tyranny of decisions, i.e., "to overhaul, correct, or simply replace them with new decisions." Barth goes further, contending "that man in all of his decisions—with the exception of a single one—grasps one of his own possibilities and goes to bat himself for this one chosen possibility and so fetters himself on the basis of his decision."[141] Following Barth's lead, then, the category of human freedom is not understood as simply a possibility for God. It is "the great saving possibility of God for [human freedom]."[142] God's freedom stands in relation to humanity's condition, conceptuality, commitments, and circumstances. In this mode of being, one approaches the word of God and faces the world with a variety of conceptions, but as Bonganjalo Goba, the South African theologian, makes clear, we come to the word of God "broken, hungry, poor, shattered by the sheer circumstances surrounding our lives."[143] By acknowledging God in such brokenness we are "liberated from a fixation on [ourselves] and believers are 'the first released captives of creation.'"[144] This *freedom* for liberation is a theological concept because freedom transpired in Jesus Christ who is the eternal center, the mysterious melody of divine love, sounding in this historical sphere toward humanity.[145]

God's self-revelation "as the Lord who loves in freedom" produces human beings who become the "first released captives." In this glorious confrontation, revelation not only "clarifies one's existence," as Cone wrote, it offers profound insight into what is meant by freedom, justice, order, and peace.[146] Barth's primary argument, especially the relationship between church and our political responsibility, evidences itself in the improvised relationships as seen in a style of life that is deeply implicated in the world—implicated in a new situation created by God.[147] This position clearly tran-

140. Shrove Tuesday song, quoted in Leeuw, *Sacred and Profane Beauty*, 30. Emphasis added. "Jesus, he must dance the lead, / And the Virgin Mary; / All must pay his rhythm heed; / To reach God's sanctuary."

141. K. Barth, "Reformation as Decision," 160–61. Again, I am mindful of the problematic language here.

142. K. Barth, "Reformation as Decision," 162–63.

143. Goba, *Agenda for Black Theology*, 9.

144. Jüngel, *God as the Mystery*, 391. I am quoting Jüngel. Jüngel draws on the work of J. G. Herder, a text I did not have in my possession.

145. *CD* II/2:571; *CD* II/1:672.

146. For a discussion of revelation tied to Barth's formula of "God is God," see Busch, "God Is God," 113.

147. See as an example K. Barth, *Church and State*, 8–9. Early in this text Barth offers a critique of the Reformers' attempts to separate the church into some type of sacred sphere.

scends the arguments of the Reformers whose advocacy for two separate realms failed to demonstrate the profound relatedness of justification *and* justice, freedom *and* liberation, and God's melody *and* the polyphony as witnessed in rhythms of human liberation. To be sure, in making this argument Barth pursued a more vital connection between God's freedom and human liberation, between justification and justice, between the commands of God and the corresponding rhythms in human life. This is what I mean by Barth's *freedom* for liberation.

Eberhard Jüngel also created an apt phrase to capture Barth's approach to theological freedom. He suggested that "the Christian faith is to be made understandable as a life based on the experience of *liberating freedom*."[148] This liberating freedom or shall I say "*freedom* for liberation" is shaped by the dynamic movement of God. For in Christ human beings participate in liberation, because of God's liberating freedom. In this freedom we enter a transformed situation, and as members of the new creation we are implicated in a new order governed by God's liberating freedom for justice and peace. So, as we turn about to James Cone, we will see in this next chapter the corollary of God's liberating freedom in Christ as "God enters human affairs and takes sides with the oppressed."[149] In sum, if I may play off of Jüngel, I would suggest that, in Barth, Christian faith is made understandable through liberating *freedom*, and, in Cone, Christian faith is made understandable through *liberating* freedom. And in this common rhythmic tension, we who have been born into the divine rhythm of freedom and liberation witness to the lively hope of God's revolutionary situation born of the resurrection of Jesus Christ from the dead (1 Pet 1:3).

Listening Guide

Thelonious Monk, "Misterioso," 2001,
https://www.youtube.com/watch?v=coEGhvEAT8o

Thelonious Monk, "Misterioso," 2012,
https://www.youtube.com/watch?v=30HjXTZO33g

148. See the foreword in Jüngel, *God as the Mystery*, xi.

149. Cone, *Black Theology and Black Power*, 36.

Thelonious Monk, "You Are Too Beautiful," 2014,
https://www.youtube.com/watch?v=oFZy2Jk7IVw
(The reader should listen first to the Richard Rodgers Classic to gain an appreciation for Monk's signification.)

Thelonious Monk, "Ugly Beauty," 1968,
https://www.youtube.com/watch?v=oWArkytksIU

Thelonious Monk, "Lulu's Back in Town," 2003,
https://www.youtube.com/watch?v=N-8G70306-o

Thelonious Monk, "Locomotive," 1966,
https://www.youtube.com/watch?v=NCmP2tmcSMg

Miles Davis, "Bag's Groove," 2007,
ttps://www.youtube.com/watch?v=lF74qucsaWY

II

James Cone's Freedom for *Liberation*

Theo*anthropology* and the External Ground of Freedom

The freedom of the Word cannot be separated from the liberty of men.—Karl Barth[1]

For such a time as this, the urgent question is not necessarily where is God in the midst of this entrenched pervasive evil. Rather, a serious concern is how to experience God.—Angela Sims[2]

The Church, then, is those people who have received God's revelation as liberation and who accept the risks of striving for freedom.—James H. Cone[3]

Black theology is the theological arm of Black power, and Black power is the political arm of Black theology.—James H. Cone[4]

1. K. Barth and Thurneysen, *Come, Holy Spirit*, 227. For a brief discussion of freedom in Karl Barth quoting the Gospel of John, see K. Barth, *Final Testimonies*, 37.

2. Sims, *Lynched*, 125.

3. Cone, "Violence," 167.

4. Cone, "Black Power, Black Theology," 209.

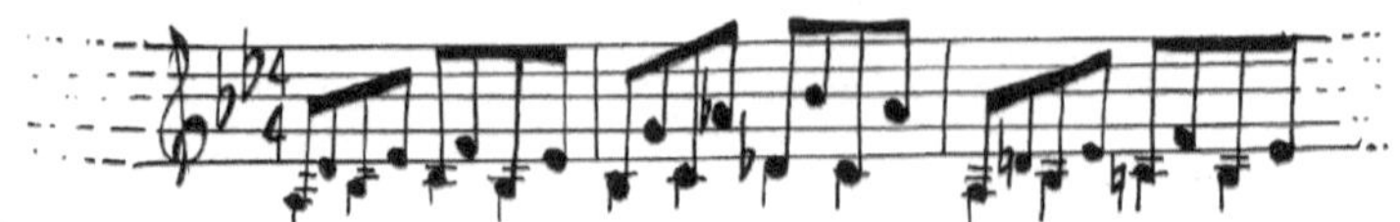

Black liberation theology occurred within a distinctive contextual setting, a setting shaped by black suffering and transcended by black song. Even from the beginning of his improvisational turn to the melody of the black Christ, black liberation stood at the center of James Cone's theological vision. Cone viewed liberation as "consistent with divine revelation" in contrast to any eschatological approach that would unwittingly postpone divine liberation to the future for black people.[5] Liberation was, for Cone, a *present happening* in the worship itself that found its rhythm concretely in the streets of black communities. Any theology "derived from the black experience must reflect the rhythm and the mood, the passion and ecstasy, the joy and the sorrow of a people in a struggle to free themselves from the shackles of oppression."[6] Black liberation came out of this "independent black version of the gospel." Thus, as pointed out in *Epistrophy*, chapter 2 (entitled "Four in One"), Cone heavily accented the note of liberation.[7] He arrived at this conclusion because he recognized that black folk traditions needed to hear the harmonious relationship between Christian faith, the civil rights movement, and the Black Power movement as developments that participate within the larger freedom movement. Although these movements extended beyond the historic black church, this concrete combination of social events catalyzed Cone's understanding of black liberation theology.[8]

Any attempt to develop a theology that combines the strengths of Cone and Barth must come to terms with the prophetic, including the polemical and *constructive* elements in Cone's understanding of liberation. To be sure, if Barth can be viewed as focusing on the objective movement of the divine subject, then Cone can properly be described as accenting the subjective response to the divine object (as the true Subject). Cone said it best, writing that "liberation is not an object but the *project* of freedom wherein the oppressed realize that their fight for freedom is a divine right of creation."[9] The melodic foundation of this subjective response is "the Spirit of the Lord

5. Cone, *Spirituals and the Blues*, 35, 137.

6. Cone, *Speaking the Truth*, 12, 18–19.

7. Cone: *Black Theology and Black Power*, 35–38; *Black Theology of Liberation*, 1–10; *Spirituals and the Blues*, 32–43; *God of the Oppressed*, 127–225.

8. Cone, "Conversation," 19.

9. Cone, *God of the Oppressed*, 127.

Jesus [who] bestows upon the oppressed the courage and power to resist humiliation and exploitation."[10] Properly understood, then, Cone is accenting the subjective movement even as he remains in the rhythm of the God of the oppressed. He was not preoccupied with knowledge about God. He wanted to know what God was doing in the world. *What is Jesus doing* is what Cone asked. He did not ask, *What would Jesus do?*[11] This actualist understanding of faith sets the tone for the black style of life.

Using Barth's construct, this means we recognize in Cone's "irregular" theological agenda an area of interest that warrants recalling the pedagogical slogan I introduced in the previous chapter, that is, "Barth's theological vision accents divine *freedom* for liberation, whereas Cone's theological vision accents divine freedom for *liberation*." While this formulation serves as an important aid, we must remember that Barth's eschatological orientation does not preclude human liberation nor does Cone's more concrete liberative interventions rebuff the freedom of God. What attracts me in this chapter is Cone's rhythmic creativity in response to the dialectic resident in Barth's christological accent, governed by the black revelatory experience in America, i.e., his freedom for *liberation*. To say this in the language of jazz, Cone "*improvised* on the melody of Christ," which means that his theological accent fell on human liberation as it is known in the rhythms of black experience in continuity with the gospel of the historical black church. This black human liberation has no rhythm and temper of its own. It is tethered to the freedom of God and gives way to an ecstasy characterized by "shouts of praise and bodily rhythm[s]" in black worship—rhythms heard "in sermon, song, prayer, and testimony which all testify to another realm of experience which they believe will be the decisive statement about their humanity."[12]

To appreciate Cone's development of this liberation theme, we must reach back into the effective history of blacks in America, or as Charles Long may argue, "crawl back into the past" and "go back into the water for a reorientation."[13] The significance of Long's admonishment here should not be minimized, since Cone's theological development was originally couched within the larger context of the freedom movement in America and, more specifically, the Black Power movement. Returning to the historical, episodic events represents the return to the river in which Cone himself waded at the beginning of his theological development. Whether we agree with Cone's revision of contemporary American theology or not, his beginning

10. Cone, "One Lord," 37–38.

11. Cone, *Black Theology and Black Power*, 139.

12. Cone, "One Lord," 39.

13. Long, *Ellipsis*, 206. See Carr, "Wade in the Water Children."

had its *locus theologicus* in the mood of this revolutionary period where blacks were seeking a new order of things. Black theology, subsequently, made an urgent appeal for black liberation in the context of both an existing societal injustice and an existing justice (or liberation) movement.

With the rise of the Black Power movement, which was proposed as an answer to the civil rights movement, the meaning of blackness was transposed in an affirmative history-making turn that conveyed, even as black people were experiencing midnight in America, the message that there was (is and will be) another power or reality resident within their historical experience. This power provided light in the darkness, an illumination that reveals the night as far gone and the day that is at hand (Rom 13:11–12). The symbol of *blackness* or *night* or *darkness*, therefore, especially when interpreted solely as evil, fails to capture the meaning it conveyed for black folk. Indeed, literal readings of blackness miss the experience that changed the rhythms of what blackness signified in America. The *Spirit of the black Christ* itself provided a new orientation that occasioned the black rhythms of liberation. Cone, at the height of his improvisational powers, stated it thus: "I encountered the presence of the divine Spirit, and my soul was moved and filled with an aspiration for freedom." This freedom arose from the black church that introduced him to the real "essence of life as expressed in the rhythm and feelings of black people in Bearden, Arkansas"; and he was soon introduced to a world that did not know his reality nor the "Black Spirit of God who descended upon that community when folks there gathered for worship and praise."[14] This is the God who brought enlightenment through the light of the mystery of faith to a people in darkness, a God who encountered the oppressed and inverted the meaning of darkness.

This light in the darkness, or as Howard Thurman may prefer to say, this *luminous darkness*, established anew the creative rhythms of black existence in America: "It was a black life-style, a movement and a beat to the rhythm of freedom in the souls and bodies of black slaves. It was a hum, a moan, and a hope for freedom."[15] Black liberation is a lived experience. It is not sought within whiteness nor is it wedded to a white beat. It is lived in the peculiar rhythmic freedom that, in the words of Charles Long, was "fired in the crucible of oppression."[16] Liberation is thus found in the ground tones of the struggle to be free and its witness to the freedom of God. Liberation is basically the praxis of freedom. This aesthetic orientation, born of *blackness* and *liberation*, moved beyond Barth's failure to "set forth the political

14. Cone, *God of the Oppressed*, 1–3.

15. Cone, *Spirituals and the Blues*, 86.

16. Long, *Significations*, 210.

implications of the divine-human encounter with sufficient clarity."[17] Cone is intentional here. Even if Barth had his eye on political problems, which I believe he did, his emphasis on the transcendence of God, at least in the mind of his interpreters, trivialized the political import of his analysis.[18]

Cone's argument is fair. He demonstrates a remarkable freedom to raise questions about Barth's methodological obtuseness and the Swiss theologian's general failure to elucidate the political problem, but his critique does not change Barth's sociopolitical context on the other side of the dialectic. Barth should rather be heard as a respondent to his own situation and as a countermelody to Cone. When heard in this groove, i.e., with stress on the freedom of God, we hear a theology designed to "underline the sovereignty of God over against [humanity]," an agenda that creates the impression we noted earlier that humanity "disappears for a moment, but then reappears."[19] For this reason, I am convinced Barth's development of a more radical *theo*anthropology could have appeared in his unfinished theology of redemption where, potentially, he may have accented the Spirit of God to secure human participation within the covenantal history (*Geschichte*) of God. This emphasis on the harmony of redemption corrects his then-obligatory one-sidedness and sharpens his engagement over and against the powers that be. In any event, Barth's so-called failure to develop this aspect of his theology should not be left unattended.[20]

Although Cone, as noted earlier, had no deep interest in repristinating or in even correcting Barth, in agreement with Wilmore his black theology should be heard as a response to Barth's challenge to develop a theology of freedom.[21] In touching on this vital problem and highlighting the theme of liberation, Cone offered a brilliant counterpoint to Barth, and his extended liberative response is attuned critically to the freedom of God in Christ. Even more, though he emphatically distinguishes his theology from Barth's and did not deliberately pursue harmony between God's freedom and human liberation, his attempt to resolve an imbalance has gifted us with a somewhat dissonant note that shifts the emphasis to human liberation, "stretching the form" and revealing a type of syncopation with Barth—even as he offered a critical polemic against whiteness. In Cone we undoubtedly

17. Cone, *God of the Oppressed*, 133.

18. Cone, *God of the Oppressed*, 133. For Barth's sharp critique of those who misunderstand what he means by transcendence, see K. Barth, *Karl Barth 1886–1968*, 48–49.

19. These are Barth's words in R. Anderson, *Karl Barth's Table Talk*, 116.

20. For a deeper discussion of this point, see Carr, "Thelonious Monk." Here I use Barth's portmanteau "theoanthropology" in two ways to stress Barth's accent on God, *theo*anthropology, *and* Cone's accent on humanity, i.e., theo*anthropology*.

21. Wilmore and Cone, *Black Theology*, 4.

find the black Spirit of God and a new beat with new rhythms for liberation. For this reason, I interpret Cone's theology as affirming a "freedom for *liberation*" that corresponds to Barth's "*freedom* for liberation," a corrective turn or furtive counterpoint designed to embrace the *others* in response to Barth's so-called overemphasis on *otherness*. As Aaron Copland, the American composer, surmised when discussing what it means to swing a beat, "you cannot stay off the beat unless you know where the beat is";[22] I surmise that James Cone knew where the beat was; and for this reason he offered a wonderful counterpoint playing off and signifyin(g) on the beat of "Barthian" rhythms.

The Liberating God of the Oppressed

Because of his attention to Euro-American theology in the academy, James Cone learned what Barth's theology represented for his theological vision. Acutely aware of the provisional nature of all God talk, especially if one centralized any source outside of Jesus Christ, Cone developed black theology as a purposive theological discipline in the academy.[23] Whether he acknowledged it or not, Cone's approach echoed to some extent the motif of the trickster, the antihero of black folk literature who creates a new "direction through indirection."[24] Thus, much like a jazz artist, who, after the mastery of technique, signifies creatively on previous melodies, Cone exercised his theological imagination in a way that played off the dominant themes in white theology. White theologians thus became his instruments. As he once put it at a conference, "I played Barth like B. B. King played his guitar!" And with this orientation Cone reminds us that his penchant for signifyin(g) is most formidable and uncompromising when speaking in the rhythms of black liberation, which became more refined over time. To be sure, the theme of black liberation during the revolutionary period of the sixties set Cone's soul on fire.

22. Copland, *Music and Imagination*, 87.

23. See Cone, *Black Theology and Black Power*, 34–35. As a caveat, although Cone established black theology as a discipline in the academy, he argued that "black theology is not an academic theology," meaning it is not a theology of the "dominant classes and racial majorities." See *For My People*, 117.

24. Abrahams, *Deep Down in the Jungle*, 66–67. I am not arguing that Cone is personally a trickster, but that his theology contains a trickster aesthetic through which he signifies on Euro-American sources.

Black Liberation and the God of the Oppressed

The notion of the liberating God did not materialize in a vacuum, however. To say that God is the Liberator of the oppressed black, especially in the context of the radical immanence of God, means that Cone recognized God's freedom as a qualifying reality for black life. It also means that God's freedom is a freedom *for liberation* (or a liberating freedom). In this turn of phrase, we can hear what Jan Lochman, the Czech theologian, called God's "proexistence." God *for* us! The God who freely turns to humanity sets humanity free. God is immanently transcendent and transcendentally immanent. It should come as no surprise then that in his efforts to accent liberation, Cone on one hand drew from the resources of his formal education, including Barth, Rudolf Bultmann, Paul Tillich, Wolfhart Pannenberg, Reinhold Niebuhr, and many other European existentialist and non-European sources.[25] This preparation characterized the theological academy of his day. Over and above this, American theologians had an inordinate dependence on Europe, and Cone, as he acknowledged, had an "inordinate methodological dependence upon the neo-orthodox theology of Barth."[26]

On the other hand, his theology was not limited to his formal training in the academy. As Cone reiterates in his memoirs, "Black liberation theology came out of black culture and religion, and it celebrated a new freedom to talk about God and Jesus in a jazz mode, a blues style, and with the sound of the spirituals."[27] The social background for his engagement was the freedom movement in general and the civil rights and Black Power movements more specifically. And while this milieu provided Cone with a unique sociopolitical setting, a distinct mood, and black aesthetic resources, it also presented him with another more enigmatic part of the legacy of the civil rights movement, that is, the existing problem between liberation and freedom. As Cone indicates in *Said I Wasn't Gonna Tell Nobody*, "Freedom and liberation were used interchangeably in the civil rights movement, with the younger Black Power people preferring the term liberation."[28] The term "freedom," somewhat clichéd in America, found a new emphasis in the ground tone that was set by the revolutionary mood. The call for Black Power inspired Cone to link that revolutionary mood to the Christian tradition and God's liberating work in the exodus, the Hebrew prophets, and

25. See the discussion of Cone's passage through Barth, Tillich, and a Heideggerian-like ontology in Carter, *Race*, 171–72.

26. Cone, *Black Theology and Black Power*, 88. For his dependence on Barth, consult the preface to Cone, *Black Theology of Liberation*, xii, xviii.

27. Cone, *Said I Wasn't*, 64.

28. Cone, *Said I Wasn't*, 69.

Jesus's history as seen in the New Testament (NT). Both terms, freedom and liberation, were used in the stories, sermons, songs, and sayings; and both terms accented black self-determination and agency. This liberating ethic was resident in the mood and experiences of black Americans, helping to establish the critical negation of the diseased social imagination and to illuminate the profound religious relevance of liberation for social, political, and economic justice.[29]

If there is one thing that distinguished black theology from white or Euro-American theology, it was that black theology harbored an improvisational vigor, stemming from black liberation as its critical point of departure. This is the element that radicalized Cone's theological development, leading him to ask questions that were not asked in the modern academy. Black liberation was not just Jesus's essential work; it was also the new thing. Therefore, the identification with black experience corresponded to the black Christ and to new rhythms of being, or as Cone suggested, Black Power was a "transition in the black community from nonbeing to being."[30] Black theology also represented an attempt to understand that power in light of the Christian gospel. Cone framed the importance of this relationship when he said, "Black theology is the theological arm of Black power, and Black power is the political arm of Black theology."[31]

Cone's inspired interpretation of Black Power and its encounter with Christ underscored a peculiar truth about the kingdom of God: "The Kingdom strikes at the very center of [humanity's] desire to define . . . [human existence] in light of his own interest at the price of his brother's enslavement."[32] And perhaps, picking up on the mood during his day, Cone went so far to suggest that the whole "age is of liberation," and in his customary style he drew on one of the programmatic passages in the NT (Luke 7:22) in order to correlate the suffering in black ghettos and criticize those who would disregard such a significant hermeneutical criterion.[33] Following this line, the christological problem or problem of revelation takes on unrivaled significance in the wake of what Cone identified as Barth's "relentless, devastating attack on natural theology."[34] Perhaps more than any other

29. Cone, *Said I Wasn't*, 68–69.

30. Cone, *Black Theology and Black Power*, 134.

31. Cone, "Black Power, Black Theology," 209.

32. Cone, *Black Theology and Black Power*, 35–36.

33. Cone's emphasis on the black struggle as the point of departure is the mainstay in his books. It is also the distinguishing feature that sets him apart from his black critics. See Hopkins, *Black Theology USA*, 41–46.

34. Cone, *Black Theology and Black Power*, 34. See also Cone: *Black Theology of Liberation*, 42–45; *God of the Oppressed*, 5.

theologian at the time, Cone remained profoundly aware of the specter of Barth's theology, embracing the ethos of the Copernican shift it made and its influence on the mood and tonal color of the development of black theology. He worked inside the tradition and, ironically, even embraced Barth's ideological critique. But despite Barth's usefulness, Cone identified limitations in how Barth unfolded the liberative capacity in his theology. Barth, of course, was aware of the poor and weak and oppressed, but for Cone he did not take the liberation of the oppressed seriously enough.

> On this point Karl Barth was right. Unfortunately Barth did not explicate this Christological point with sufficient clarity, because his theology was determined too much by the theological tradition of Augustine and Calvin and too little by Scripture. While Barth's christological starting point enabled him to move closer to the biblical message than most of his contemporaries, his understanding of theology was not derived from the biblical view of Jesus Christ as the Liberator of the oppressed. Because Jesus the Liberator is not central in Barth's Christology, his view of theology is also defective at this point.[35]

Black Liberation and the Bible

The charge that Barth failed to appeal to Scripture properly is not the first time Cone suggested that Barth has to some degree been overdetermined by tradition and philosophy. As I stated in volume 2, *'Round Midnight* ("James Cone's Noon at Midnight"), he first charged Barth with having a troublesome relationship to Scripture in his master's thesis where he argued that Barth did not take seriously the NT idea of Satan. Still, to fully transcend Barth's neoorthodoxy on the one hand and the problems stemming from liberal theology on the other, Cone developed interpretive strategies and a distinctive approach toward Scripture. His efforts to dialectically relate Scripture to the meaning and sources of black liberation reveal one of the most significant hermeneutical advancements for understanding the Bible in the twentieth century. It furthermore stands as the first time that the biblical emphasis on freedom became foundational for black identity in a systematic theology.

This development is certainly the case in Cone's second book, *A Black Theology of Liberation*, where Cone offered a brief systematic theology based on the black freedom struggle. The immediate context of that

35. Cone, *Speaking the Truth*, 6–7.

history—which includes sit-ins, freedom rides, marches in "Bombingham," Selma, and protests of the Vietnam War—informs the black experience, black history, and black culture, which Cone used to interpret Scripture as the revelation of God. Black history and culture are resourced and employed as a healthy form of *eisegesis* (reading into the text), leading Cone to scrutinize Christian traditions that do not contribute to black liberation. To be sure, he wisely approached these negligent canonical traditions with a hermeneutics of suspicion.[36]

Cone surmised that completely breaking away from the influence of whiteness is an impossible task—especially white definitions of the self, white values, and metrics—if blacks did not have other ways of defining themselves. He thus had to find a way to engage biblical history and authority, because although biblical interpretation can be liberating, it can also be dangerously misleading. This means blacks had to read theology and facilitate human liberation without falling back on false notions of authority that are grounded in European or Anglo-American traditional readings of Scripture. Consequently, in his efforts to use black experience for liberative readings of Scripture, Cone had to resist the habit of accepting refined notions of doctrine previously formulated by whites. He underscores this point in *God of the Oppressed*, even as he accuses several former generations of having this problem.

The Constantinian church, for example, was not just characterized by the problem of civil religion born out of a comity between the church and state. That church failed ethically because Christian theologians in the main failed to recognize the biblical God as the God of the oppressed. This included Luther, Calvin, Wesley, and other religious leaders in the church. For Cone, "they were wrong ethically because they were wrong *theologically*. They were wrong theologically because they failed to listen to the Bible—with sufficient openness and through the eyes of the victims of political oppression."[37] The modern tendency to dismiss their failure as a sign of their being "people of their time" amounts to a form of escapism, because it masks their capitulation to the ethics of the status quo. Hence, these theologians, according to Cone, never came to terms with reading Scripture as a vision of God as the Liberator of the oppressed. This form of conscientization required other reading strategies. As the religious historian James Noel points out, "such a project entails critiquing antagonistic theologies and reading strategies functioning to legitimate the status quo by obfuscating the issues of power and domination hidden in particular theological modes

36. Cone, *Black Theology of Liberation*, 35.

37. Cone, *God of the Oppressed*, 183.

of discourse." This includes interrogating any element within the biblical text, especially when it "condones slavery, racism, sexism, homophobia, and anti-Semitism."[38]

Using biblical imagery as part of religious understanding without limiting it to traditional biblical usage could potentially draw out notions of freedom that are then expropriated with new meanings of freedom that are shaped by the tragic situation of the oppressed. In this way, freedom in the American context can resound with a distinctive tonality that transcends normative interpretations of Scripture and are in no way circumscribed by the culturally limited nature of the Bible. Thus, cultural narratives in the Bible, like the story of the exodus, can become paradigmatic ways blacks participate in the realm of freedom. Freedom, of course, is then brought about through cultural participation in a transcendent reality, a view that is arguably resident in Barth's and Cone's theologies.[39] Unfortunately, the Western theological traditions have not always been serious proponents of the biblical traditions they inherited; and for that reason they fail as advocates who champion liberation.[40]

Because the black church is a scripturalist tradition, liberation remains a possibility. Moreover, this grand appreciation for Scripture led to a prohibition against "making the gospel into private moments of religious ecstasy or into the religious sanctification of the structures of society"—without literalism or fundamentalism.[41] Simultaneously and counterintuitively, the black tradition occasionally exercised the freedom *not* to use the biblical text. The admonition to love, for example, could certainly be extracted from the Bible; it could also be drawn from a black leader who was "a past tower of strength."[42] As Matthew Johnson intuits, this critical attitude towards Scripture is insulated from any modern movement of demythologization

38. Noel, *Black Religion*, 91.

39. See K. Barth, *Theology and Church*, 340–41. Barth writes, "When we hear God, we are not in a position to determine our relation to Church and culture as if we had not been claimed by both in a very definite way; as if we were not committed to and involved in both; as if a specific way of regarding both were not inevitable for us. We have called this way theological. Our *locus* is the Church; from there we understand, and we represent culture, not conversely. God we know speaks from a higher, freer place." Cone obviously approaches this issue from a very different place than Barth, but his position nonetheless includes the supposition that black history, black experience, and black culture play a role in biblical interpretation. See Cone: *Black Theology of Liberation*, 21–35; *God of the Oppressed*, 151–63, 182–83.

40. See Cone's discussion of the failure and his brief list of exceptions, including Gustavo Gutiérrez and Jürgen Moltmann, in Cone, *God of the Oppressed*, 163–64.

41. Cone, *Black Theology of Liberation*, 31.

42. See Washington, *Black Religion*, 4.

since it more or less emerged from "psychic and spiritual survival and the part that the myths, symbols, paradigmatic personages, and situations in the Bible have played in that effort."[43] Paradoxically, the crucible of the black Atlantic experience freed the biblical story to be critically (re)appropriated within the black community without notions of infallibility or parochial brands of literalism, which are ideologies that trend toward absolutization.

In Western traditions, historical criticism, historicist, and even ideological readings functioned to liberate the text from the dominance of tradition. For occasionally these traditions legitimize the status quo of the elite, and interrogating these positions requires that we avoid "obfuscating the issues of power and domination hidden in particular theological modes of discourse."[44] While it may seem naïve to assume that the historicity of the biblical text and black American experience correspond to one another, Cone rightly felt burdened with the methodological task of addressing these realities. He perceived that a methodology was needed to ensure our appreciation for historical events and the development of religious consciousness.[45]

Black Liberation Through Concrete Experience

According to Cone, our predecessors did not take the time to broach epistemological questions about *how* God was liberating them. There are no extended theological or philosophical treatises that address or test the truth of God's revelation as liberation from oppressed and marginalized sources.[46] God's revelation, on the contrary, occurs within the nature and history of the everyday world, and through the eyes and ears of faith as slaves perceived this world. So, through faith they apprehended the work of God. This position, according to Cone, is not an attempt to be consistent with the canons of logic put forth by oppressors, although it is not a rejection of logical consistency. He declared that "they [slaves] said what they said and did what they did not because of any 'logic' in the physical reality that encompassed them."[47] They

43. M. Johnson, *Tragic Vision*, 134.

44. See James Noel, especially his discussion called "Epistemologies Opaque: Conjuring, Conjecture, and the Problematic of Nat Turner's Biblical Hermeneutic," in Noel, *Black Religion*, 90–91.

45. Noel, *Black Religion*, 90–91.

46. Cone, *Spirituals and the Blues*, 65–66.

47. Cone, *Spirituals and the Blues*, 87. See also Cone and Hordern,"Dialogue on Black Theology," 1079.

lived and existed according to a different rhythm. On this point, Charles Long is illuminating and can be interpreted in concert with Cone.

> The religion of any people is more than a structure of thought; it is experience, expression, motivations, intentions, behaviors, styles, and rhythms. Its first and fundamental expression is not on the level of thought. It gives rise to thought, but a form of thought that embodies the precision and nuances of its source. This is especially true of Afro-American religion.[48]

According to Cone, white theologians, by contrast, constructed systems, but blacks drew intellectually on folktales, told stories, recited biblical stories about the exodus, and lived in a way that honored the insight that "it is not consciousness that determines life, but life that determines consciousness."[49]

From this standpoint, we can see why, hermeneutically, freedom is not reducible to a theoretical discussion in black theology. Cone prioritized praxis and addressed how the gospel relates to the concrete reality of the contemporary world. This concreteness is also evident in slave seculars and the blues and Monk's jazz. It even arises in narratives of reality that occasionally leave God out of the story.[50] In this line of thinking, there are no lengthy discussions of different types of freedom; there is no discussion of human being, and neither is there a genealogy of human freedom in America or Western development as it arises out of the black experience. Nevertheless, Cone does address freedom beyond the categories in "Barthian" understanding. His view of freedom, like Karl Barth's—who is not a "Barthian" any more than Luther was a Lutheran—is not reduced to a choice, that is, "possible alternatives." Freedom has a deeper ground in the struggle for liberation. In short, Cone mirrors what might be described as a turn on Barth's view of freedom, one grounded in the divine-human encounter. In his view, even "Barthians were correct on the personal aspect of freedom in the divine-human encounter, but they failed to place due emphasis on the role of liberation in an oppressive society."[51] Cone's discussion, however, focused primarily on the black liberation movement seen within the scope of the freedom movement, and as one can imagine, his concept of freedom is developed in relation to these events; and because of its distinctive emphases, it amounts to a freedom for *liberation.*

The concrete nature of black experience for this reason provides, for Cone, a fundamental critique of Western theology and persists as a primary

48. Long, *Significations*, 7.

49. Cited in Cone, *God of the Oppressed*, 47–48.

50. Cone, *Black Theology of Liberation*, 9–10; cf. Cone, *God of the Oppressed*, 24.

51. Cone, *Black Theology of Liberation*, 93.

impetus toward liberation. For example, when criticizing modern theology and arguing against the oversight of "Christian" thinkers, who appeal to their confidence in the human person, Cone declared that these thinkers missed the primary "evidence" that critiqued their viewpoint, i.e., "the period of black enslavement and Amerindian extermination, as well as European colonial conquest in Africa and Asia."[52] In this view, such atrocities should encourage liberal theologians to question their appeal to human goodness. And if one takes Barth's view of history seriously, such atrocities consummate in the liberation of blacks as an extraordinary witness or secular parable of the liberation of God, i.e., a "remarkable proof of the existence of God."[53]

Black Liberation Through the Method of Correlation?

Cone's situation was unique. Being troubled in his theological consciousness in the academy, he began asking questions that confronted the "particularity of the black religious experience," that is, the claims of faith on one hand and the reality of black suffering on the other. To address this dialectic, he adopted Paul Tillich's "method of correlation." He was clear in his appreciation for the biblical text and its contributions to black liberation. He was also prepared to modify the thought of Barth and Tillich—the best of his theological education—appropriating them *interpretatio in bonam partem* for his specific theological project.[54] Among other things, through Barth and Tillich, Cone grasped the important role sources and norms played in "shaping the character of theology."[55] Both theologians prioritized Scripture and the cultural situation, respectively. But Cone saw something more acute in Tillich, especially in terms of cultural liberation, precisely because he "does not share Barth's kerygmatic emphasis."[56] In Cone's view, Barth's *kerygmatic* emphasis was unable to communicate to the culture of the black

52. Cone, *Black Theology of Liberation*, 91. See also Cone, *Spirituals and the Blues*, 33–34, where Cone appeals to deliverance from slavery as the message of liberation in the spirituals.

53. K. Barth, *Gespräche*, 463.

54. This phrase refers to Karl Barth's method of teaching where he sought to interpret theologians by appropriating and often referring to their "best and therefore most useful parts." McKelway, "*Magister Dialecticae.*" James Cone, in a similar fashion, "did not bother to sort out their [Barth, Tillich, Bultmann, Bonhoeffer and others] differences or to analyze the problem of using them in the constructive development of black theology . . . I appropriated in order to say what I believed was the truth of the gospel as defined by the black experience." Cone, *My Soul Looks Back*, 82–83.

55. Cone, *Black Theology of Liberation*, 22.

56. Cone, *Black Theology of Liberation*, 59.

community, and although Barth confronted the powers of his day, Cone believed it was a mistake to read Barth and apply the arguments he used against Nazism to the black situation. Black people need examples that go beyond the rhythms of the European context.[57]

At this point, Cone is primarily concerned with the importance of the sociopolitical context for comprehending the liberative acts of God. He modeled the appropriate way to speak of God in a particular situation, rather than promoting ideological problems surrounding idolatrous equations between God and human culture. For Cone, moreover, to invoke or "apply Barth's words to the black-white context and interpret them as a warning against identifying God's revelation with black culture is to misunderstand Barth."[58] Another way to consider Cone's modulation here is to realize that God's relationship to the oppressed is not determined by the preciseness of a specific methodology. The historical backdrop or soundscape has its say in any situation. Cone thus attends to the power dynamics that occur within a particular situation, a fact that draws attention to the methods that oppressors use for approaching the problems of the oppressed. His concretizing turn raises several important questions, such as should a situation of oppression ever take a backseat to a theological model? Should normative procedures for theology be forestalled simply because we are speaking to the oppressed? Notwithstanding such questions, a perusal of Cone reveals that for him the answers to these questions are not in the sources per se, but resident within the occasion in which the sources are deployed.[59] Barth, for instance, seems to share a similar view, arguing that there are occasions when "you have to oppose your Christian brethren. A *decision* made at a certain moment may be more important than the most important Christian dogma!"[60] In light of the situation, theological sources may have to be considered in a different way. Cone's discussion thus raises intriguing questions about the word of God in relation to a particular theological system vis-à-vis the situation.

In taking a stance that favored the sociocultural context, Cone aligned himself more closely to Tillich than to Barth. He even appealed to Tillich's constructive form in systematics. Of course, he did not formally explore the risk that comes with using Tillich or attend the problems that accompany the Tillichian language of faith.[61] His concern was not to be true to Tillich

57. Cone, *Black Theology of Liberation*, 21–23, 27–31, 59, 113.

58. Cone, *Black Theology of Liberation*, 28.

59. Cone, *Black Theology of Liberation*, 35.

60. See Godsey, *Karl Barth's Table Talk*, 82. Emphasis in original.

61. Tillich, *Life and the Spirit*, 4. Tillich knows the danger of the loss of the Christian

but to the condition he sought to address. Still, his concerns at this juncture were more positively determined by Tillich's method than negatively determined by the specter of Barth's critique of ideology. Indeed, he depended on Tillich in terms of both the method of correlation and Tillich's concept of symbol discussed below. In this critical appropriation, Cone was more preoccupied with engaging the black situation theologically than with analyzing theological responses to it. Tillich, then, like Barth, became a useful ingredient for his project.

Cone's analysis of the human situation is far less ambiguous than Tillich's, however. Tillich used the method of correlation to analyze existential and philosophical questions. By contrast, Cone isolated the concrete experience of black suffering rather than pursing a "philosophically understood subject."[62] He addressed the *situation.* As a result, the situation emerged with much more clarity in Cone's theology, motivating him to bring the human situation to the Bible as a touchstone. According to the minister Carlyle Stewart, "Cone is more interested in establishing a legitimate theological basis for the conceptualization and eradication of oppression, while Tillich emphasized the ontological problem of humanity's estrangement from God."[63] Another way to conceptualize this difference is to imagine Tillich as being concerned with systematic theology and philosophical ennui, i.e., anthropological/philosophical discussions, while Cone is primarily concerned with theological/sociological problems created by the catastrophe of white racism.[64] Cone's concern with sociopolitical liberation then informs his perception and the extent to which he utilizes Western concepts in his theology.

As a matter of note, Tillich considered his theology to be a countermovement to Barth's, viewing Barth as starting "from above . . . and then proceed[ing] to man [humanity], and in his later period, even very deeply into man [humanity], when he speaks of the 'humanity of God.' Whereas, on the other hand, I start with man [humanity], not deriving the divine answer from man [humanity], but starting with the question which is present in

---

message. Cone, however, argued that the message is already lost because of white racism, and he attempted to employ "blackness" to recover and reorient the gospel message. See the discussion on heresy in Cone: *Black Theology of Liberation*, xiii; *God of the Oppressed*, 33–35.

62. The language of a "philosophically understood subject" is Karl Barth's language and critique of Paul Tillich in the "Introductory Report," in McKelway, *Systematic Theology of Paul Tillich*, 13.

63. See Stewart, "Method of Correlation," 31.

64. This language is ironically the language that Tillich used to criticize Karl Barth; however, it is fittingly descriptive of the difference between Cone and Tillich. See Tillich, *History of Christian Thought*, 536.

man [humanity] and to which the divine revelation comes as the answer."[65] To be sure, Tillich's apologetic style conflicts with Barth's kerygmatic focus and perhaps nudges Cone in a direction that advances both Barth and Tillich in relation to the social context. This extension is partly seen in Cone's relationship to Tillich's claim that he based his method on John Calvin's *Institutes*.[66] However, when this claim is scrutinized, it becomes discernible that Tillich deviated away from Calvin and into his own philosophical direction. As Calvin contended, "No man can arrive at the true knowledge of himself, without having first contemplated the divine character, and then descended to the consideration of his own."[67] It is a lesson that Cone learned well from Barth. This brings me back to Cone and his advancement of Barth and Tillich.

In his preliminary approach to the cultural situation, Cone established a christological position that corresponded to Barth's when he used Tillich's methodology to prioritize the black experience. His black theology project accented human suffering, asking, "How do we dare speak of God in a suffering world, a world in which blacks are humiliated because they are black?"[68] This strong position on suffering humanity functioned as the point of departure for Cone to address black liberation; it also provided an answer to the existential questions he had already posed in *Black Theology and Black Power*. Thus, when Cone asks how does Black Power relate to the gospel, the hermeneutical agenda is pursued in this aporia by juxtaposing the biblical account of revelation—which is fulfilled in the incarnation—with God's participation in the liberation of the oppressed.[69] Stewart is correct in his assessment when he writes that Cone's method of correlation is more reflective of a structure that centers on Scripture and experience than on God's response to existential questions, making it difficult to "logically refute God's liberation in a current context without negating the scriptural record."[70]

In my initial assessment I argued that Cone's approach made a breach between oppressors and God, but I would amend this criticism and frame Cone's theology as a call for oppressors to repent and be converted. Because blackness is the primary symbol for divine activity in America, oppressors must find freedom through their identification with the oppressed, i.e.,

65. Tillich, *History of Christian Thought*, 538.

66. Tillich, *Reason and Revelation*, 62–63.

67. Quoted in Tillich, *Reason and Revelation*, 63. See also a longer discussion in McKelway, *Systematic Theology of Paul Tillich*, 46–47. McKelway helped with this important distinction.

68. Cone, *Black Theology of Liberation*, 60.

69. Cone, *Black Theology of Liberation*, 60–61.

70. See Stewart, "Method of Correlation," 35.

through identification with blackness. In this way, "blackness, then, stands for all victims of oppression who realize that the survival of their humanity is bound up with the liberation from whiteness."[71]

> It is unthinkable that oppressors could identify with oppressed existence and thus say something relevant about God's liberation of the oppressed. In order to be Christian theology, white theology must cease being *white* theology and become black theology by denying whiteness as an acceptable form of human existence and affirming blackness as God's intention for humanity. White theologians will find this difficult, and it is to be expected that some will attempt to criticize black theology precisely on this point. Such criticism will not reveal a weakness in black theology but only the racist character of the critic.[72]

Cone is adamant that the Christian community must participate in the affirmation of blackness—the universal symbol of God's liberation in America—in order to engage in real Christian theology. To do so, however, requires that American Christians enter the rhythm of the black community that corresponds to the gospel. In this identification, which comes from embracing the cross and affirming black life in the resurrection, we find a witness to Du Bois's "tone too deep for words" and fellowship with the God of the oppressed. As Cone writes, God will "pick you up when you're fallin' and come to your rescue when you're in trouble." This support, found so resolutely in the rhythms of God's freedom, choreographs our "dance to the rhythm of freedom because Jesus is the Lord of all creation who gives the little ones liberating visions in wretched places."[73]

Black Liberation in the Rhythm of the Freedom of God

At first glance, one may presuppose that James Cone is primarily concerned with a narrow sociopolitical liberation only. But despite his concern for the situation as seen in his emphasis on addressing social problems through the "method of correlation," he was not focused on mere political or external liberation within the polis. A closer examination of his theology reveals a much more nuanced approach and a greater field of concern. When read in its best light, Cone's understanding of black worship allows for the

71. Cone, *Black Theology of Liberation*, 7–8.

72. Cone, *Black Theology of Liberation*, 9–10. Emphasis in original.

73. Cone, *God of the Oppressed*, 129. See also "The Revelation of Saint Orgne," in Du Bois, *Writings*, 1062.

identification of human beings as *having been created in freedom*. Black liberation, as a human political act, acknowledges the modality of this realm of freedom and the actualization of its possibilities within the sociopolitical context. The social reality alone does not grasp the heart of Cone's liberative ethics, however. For Cone, God is the ground of freedom. As Gayraud Wilmore asserted in *Black Theology: A Documentary History*, "our interpretation of history, its triumphs and tragedies, has come out of an encounter with the God of history."[74] More importantly, for Cone, God identifies with the oppressed. There is a rhythmical or dialectical relationship between black *liberation* and God's deeper freedom resonating throughout Cone's theology, one that culminates in human salvation, a salvation that "is not simply freedom in history; it is freedom to affirm the future which is *beyond* history."[75] This soteriological accent on freedom does not bifurcate human sin from the victim of sinfulness. What occurs in the life of God in Christ identifies with the victimized—individually and corporately. Such was the freedom heard by slaves who embraced new emancipatory rhythms for life.

> African slaves refused to accept Christianity as a given datum or as a deposit of fixed doctrines from white missionaries and preachers. Christianity as a rigidly defined system of beliefs about God, Jesus and the Holy Spirit was inconsistent with the African personality where rhythm, passion, and feeling defined the structures of one's being in the world.[76]

In his first book, *Black Theology and Black Power*, Cone addressed the relationship between freedom and liberation from the standpoint of the *imago Dei* where black liberation is grounded in the work of the Creator. In this respect freedom and liberation coexist dialectically for Cone. Any human laws, status quos, institutions, or ideologies that would stifle the human attempt to effectuate black dignity were resisted in light of God's liberative freedom. This liberative dimension makes an appeal to black theologians and the black church, encouraging them to participate within both civil disobedience and revolutionary policy formation(s) for the purpose of human maturation. Consequently, when defining black revolution in rhythm with the God of the oppressed, Cone paves the way for us to view participation in the Black Power movement as a duty that testifies to God. Delinquency from the revolutionary struggle is, inversely, a form of betrayal, of one's own humanity, the humanity of others, and, most importantly, of the sounding

74. Wilmore and Cone, *Black Theology*, 3.

75. Cone, "What Does It Mean," 23. Emphasis in original.

76. Cone, "Black Worship," 485.

melody of God because of the failure to respond creatively to the *imago Dei*.[77]

In his second text, *A Black Theology of Liberation*, Cone further contextualized the concept of liberation, lamenting medieval, Reformed, and modern theological obtuseness. He recognized that the image of God was obscured by personal and even anthropological approaches that fail to creatively address important problems in history, such as black enslavement, genocidal policies toward native Americans, and the enduring results of European colonization. Where such engagement is absent, an authentic actualization of freedom gives way to speciously abstract and pious conversation(s). Unsurprisingly, Cone reserved his sharpest criticism for neoorthodox thinkers. Turning to his criticism of Barth in particular, Cone criticized Barth, especially "Barthian" followers, for not sufficiently expounding the political element already resident in his use of the image of God.[78] This connection is important because it demonstrates at least three things. First, it reinforces Cone's distinction between Barth and adherents of his theology.[79] Here he regularly confessed in his literary reminiscences that he believed Barth to be "closer to him" than to others. Second, this section demonstrates that Cone viewed freedom, at least at this point in his development, as a concept that could perhaps be understood, not as an action, but as a realm of meaning. Third, Cone's incorporation of black cultural and theological resources clearly challenged the sources often used in white theologies.[80]

This liberative accent seems to be the case in several arguments where Cone declared that human freedom arises from divine freedom and human freedom liberates from oppression. He developed this section by appealing to prayer, testimony, sermon, and song as ways of encouraging blacks to "transcend the limitations of their immediate history and encounter the divine power, thereby creating a moment of ecstasy and joy wherein they recognize that the pain of oppression is not the last word about black life."[81] Cone's sustained efforts to privilege liberation in oppressive conditions contributed to the concreteness of his theology. He was not pursuing an

77. Cone, *Black Theology and Black Power*, 136–37.

78. Cone, *Black Theology of Liberation*, 89–93; cf. Cone, *God of the Oppressed*, 133.

79. Notice how Cone distinguished his earliest white interlocutors, Lehmann and Gollwitzer, from "narrow-minded Barthians." He took their analyses of theology much more seriously than others'. Cone's assessment implies an awareness of the need for a proper criterion for the task of theology. See James Cone, "Introduction: Black Theology and the Response of White Theologians," in Wilmore and Cone, *Black Theology*, 140.

80. See Cone, "Gospel and Liberation," 165.

81. Cone, *God of the Oppressed*, 132.

abstract concept of freedom; he was celebrating freedom as it unfolded in a particular context.[82]

Cone emphasized freedom in a lecture at the "Conference on Black Theology and Latin American Liberation Theology," in Geneva, Switzerland, in 1973. This lecture anticipated his development of freedom as the ground of liberation in his book *God of the Oppressed.* He asserted, as he reiterates later, that "human freedom is grounded in God's freedom to be with us in history, disclosing that our future is to be found in the historical struggle against human pain and suffering." Like Charles Long, Cone suggested that "human freedom is not a possibility that can be given or taken away by oppressors."[83] Freedom therefore has an objective quality, and in expressing this argument Cone demonstrated his proximity to Barth's project. Although he obviously relies on other sources outside of Barth, and on occasion underscored Barth's failure to advance the sociopolitical implications of the divine and human encounter;[84] Cone, at the same time, propounded his belief that Barth was closer to his work, imagining that if the Swiss theologian had had to endure the savage sixties, he too would have considered a different set of questions. When responding to Barth's challenge that American theologians develop a theology of freedom, Gayraud Wilmore enunciated a similar comparison between Barth and nascent black theology:

> Karl Barth, when he came to Chicago in 1963[,][85] did not know enough about Black people to appreciate how Martin Luther King, Jr. and Malcolm X laid the groundwork for a new American theology. If Barth had lived through that momentous decade he would have celebrated Black Theology as the answer to his question: "Will such a specific American theology one day arise?" . . . Black Theology did indeed arise as just such a "theology of freedom." A theology of liberation in response to critical events—events that had the unmistakable sign that God was saying and doing something unprecedented about oppressed minorities and freedom in White America.[86]

82. Cone, *God of the Oppressed*, 165, 190.

83. Cone, "Freedom, History, and Hope," 57.

84. This argument in Cone is a reiteration of his previous position where he argued that freedom is not a "rational decision about possible alternatives; it is a participation of the whole person in the liberation struggle." Cone, *Black Theology of Liberation*, 93.

85. Actually, Barth came in 1962.

86. Wilmore and Cone, *Black Theology*, 3–4.

Cone's proximity to Barth thus serves an important function. It throws into relief Barth's emphasis on the freedom of God in its juxtaposition to Cone's view of liberation. Reading Cone as a counterpoint to Barth's motif of objectivism builds on the same inner material content of his theology that established a rhythm in ethics. It also provides insight into how Cone himself pivots from the freedom of God to develop his independent subjective direction grounded in liberation. Cone began writing with an awareness of his proximity to Barth, being intent on affirming the difference—from the very beginning. As he states in his first book: "The black theology view of God must be sharply distinguished from white distortions of God. This does not mean that black theology rejects white theology entirely. . . . This cannot be done."[87] To the contrary, what Cone acknowledged is the degree of interplay between American black theology and white theology—an insight akin to a master musician who plays microtones on blues instruments.

In *God of the Oppressed*, we find Cone clarifying his theology and composing a line of thought designed to further capitalize on black history, culture, and experience to answer critics more thoroughly. He continued his critical appreciation for Barth's theology, however. For instance, one significant point in Cone's development occurred in his discussion of "Liberation as Freedom to Be in Relation to God." Cone emphasized the *imago Dei* to draw a distinction from Barth. He extended his view beyond Barth and others who relied primarily on Reformation thought. According to Cone, Barth limited the *image of God* to relationship, and although he revised the concept beyond the limitations of the Reformers, who defined it in terms of the human capacity to reason, Barth fell prey to an overemphasis on the "transcendent quality of God's presence." He surmised that such approaches interiorize the concept of freedom and fail to address "the political and social implications of the divine-human encounter." On account of this he extended the concept, making it constitutive for the political dimension of human encounter. In this way Cone can be interpreted as correcting Barth's sociopolitical limitations. This insight reveals where his intellectual rhythm is partly found. The image of God is not merely a personal relationship with God; it is that aspect of humanity that makes all people struggle against captivity. It is the constitutive ground of human rebellion and revolution among slaves.[88] For Cone, there is "no freedom independent of the fight for justice."[89]

As an aside, we are free to question Cone's description of Barth's viewpoint as stressing a "relational character" with too much emphasis on the

87. Cone, *Black Theology of Liberation*, 61.

88. Cone, *God of the Oppressed*, 133–34.

89. Cone, *God of the Oppressed*, 163.

transcendent quality of God's presence. Does this assessment understate the detailed and nuanced discussion Barth offered on the *imago Dei* in the context of covenant and creation?[90] Does Cone truly capture Barth's methodological choices as they relate to Barth's own theological context, form, and content? Is Cone's approach to Barth here an ironic dismissal of the importance of the situation *for Barth*? Does this mean that Barth—if he were experiencing a similar context—would not have responded akin to the way Cone did? Is it fair to describe Barth's theology as defective because it does not explicate its Christology in ways attendant to Cone's situation? To be sure, while the image of God for Barth is not only an analogy, expressed by the rudimentary relationship between man and woman, i.e., a form of togetherness, and a constitutive reality first of God and then of human beings,[91] and capable of being elucidated through a form of *analogia relationis*, which human beings only possess in grace, it is also *God's very image*. This standpoint permits Barth to see the image of God in respect to the fallenness in the world as a persistent reality that is modeled in the vocation of the community that provides hope and light in a fallen world.[92] Consequently, the *imago Dei* is not merely the ground of rebellion; it is the ground for reconciliatory acts that give way to concrete political consequences for human liberation in particular and human flourishing in general.

Still, in fairness to Cone, he is criticizing the degree to which Barth failed to provide practical ways of responding to social situations. In this case, black suffering would be foremost on Cone's mind. And yet what does that mean for Barth? It means that his theology is defective because it does not explicate its Christology in ways attendant to the polyphony of the human situation. Barth was familiar with the problem and expressed it in his *Ethics*. He argued that white privilege is "grounded in the superiority of one race and the subjection of many other races."[93] Moreover, in keeping with the German situation, he used the concept of the "image of God" so as to resist the advance of natural theology associated with the neo-Protestantism

90. See *CD* III/1:183–212. Cf. especially the episodic conversation throughout paragraph 41.2, and the brief conversation of "image of God" in an "English Speaking Colloquium" with Barth (Switzerland) in Godsey, *Karl Barth's Table Talk*, 57. Last, for a brief commentary on the *imago Dei* in Barth, see K. Johnson, *Essential Karl Barth*, 221–23.

91. See *CD* III/4:117; for the relation between man and woman, cf. *CD* III/1:185.

92. *CD* III/1:201.

93. I offer no excuse for Barth's participation in colonialism and the responsibility he shared for his relative silence on questions of slavery. For Barth's awareness of white privilege, see K. Barth, *Ethics*, 164–65.

and Roman Catholicism with which he struggled.[94] By rooting his view of the *imago Dei* in the grace of God, Barth solidified his stance against the idea of a *rectitude animae* (original righteousness) or *status integritatis* (state of innocence), which even now can be used to make a case for an ideal human being. His stance also prohibited the bad faith of a "constituent of humanity," an ideological way of valorizing a particular nation, race, tribe, or person.

The *anologia relationis* on the other hand does not equate to an *anologia entis* or some capacity to grasp the image of God. Rather, the free and gracious will of the Creator is fulfilled in humanity through divine actions and decisions, not through some "generational" or "natural" right as in an elitist view of Israel, idolatrous view of Aryanism, or as one may add today an "exceptional" view of America with all of its pomp and circumstance.[95] Most importantly, for Barth, the Old Testament (OT) concept of the image of God is correlated with the NT where Jesus himself is the image of God. Thus, the actualization of the image of God in Christ functions representatively for all human beings, regardless of gender, race, religion, etc. Jesus Christ is the substitute for every individual of humanity.

For Barth, "there could be no plainer reference to the *anologia relationis* and therefore the *imago Dei* in the most central, i.e., christological sense of the term."[96] In relation to the image of God, "the humanity of Jesus is the image of God." Here Barth anticipated any reading of a transcendent quality into his thought. If it is a form of transcendence, it is the transcendence of grace in that the eternal God has elected and received the humanity of Jesus in the eternal covenant.[97] The same reception of Jesus is reiterated in Jesus's reception of fellow humanity. As Barth writes, "The humanity of Jesus is not merely the reception and reflection of His divinity . . . or of God's controlling will; it is the repetition and reflection of God Himself, no more and no less. It is the image of God, the *imago Dei*." In terms of how he related God in Christ to humanity, Barth followed the church's tradition in Chalcedon, respecting the difference between God and humanity, but exercising care not to reverse the relationship. He argued, for example, "There is total sovereignty and grace on the part of God, but total dependence and need on that of man [humanity]."[98] Paradoxically, this movement from God to humanity shaped the melodic and rhythmic contours of Barth's theological ethics.

94. See K. Barth, *God in Action*, 20–22.

95. *CD* III/1:200.

96. *CD* III/2:221.

97. *CD* III/2:218. Cf. Lochman, "Theology of Christological Concentration," 213.

98. *CD* III/2:219.

Cone, by contrast, articulated liberative anthropological statements in the opposite direction, turning Barth, as I prefer to argue, *inside out.* He writes, "There is no revelation of God without a condition of oppression which develops into a situation of liberation."[99] For Cone, "God became human in Christ, so that we are free to speak about God in terms of humanity."[100] Humanity's capacity to speak of God in that event becomes the primary consideration in light of the incarnation. From this vantage point, unless we hear them together, Barth's theology becomes defective just at the point where Christ should be understood as a Liberator.[101] This distinction, rooted in their differing ways of accenting the cantus firmus, raises an important question for Barth's theology in terms of how Barth emphasizes the concrete liberation of humanity; moreover, this contrast raises a round of questions for Cone. How does he—in the wake of so-called "Barthian" constrictions—develop a theology that privileges the capacity of the human situation to speak of God and at the same time honor the sovereignty or grace of God?[102] How does Cone emphasize political liberation while prioritizing God as Liberator, without sacrificing the freedom of God with respect to human acts of liberation? To follow Cone's way of inverting Barth and others, I will delineate and interrogate some of Cone's most important theological concepts and resources before using Monk's notion of rhythm to make some concluding remarks about their relative differences at the end of this chapter.

Black Liberation, Tillichian Ontology, and Ontological Blackness

The order of his day served to highlight Cone's remarkable efforts to develop black theology in the milieu of the late sixties and early seventies. As described in chapter 3, world events required that theology be completely recast. The natural theology debate had become the *crux interpretum* among European and Anglo theologians, and the disputes surrounding this problem set a tone for cultural theology. Having already addressed the issue in his dissertation and books, Cone turned to Tillich, the theologian of culture, to circumvent the dangers of ideology that arose from strict identifications between God and cultural issues privileged in theological systems. It was a problem quite

99. Cone, *Black Theology of Liberation*, 45.

100. Cone, "Theology as the Expression," 123.

101. Cone, "Theology as the Expression," 122. See also Cone, *Speaking the Truth*, 6.

102. Cone's respect for Barth does not mean Barth's theology determined his full theological development; to the contrary, he remained aware of Barth's great contributions and, most importantly, the black tradition while accenting the identity of God vis-à-vis the identity of humanity; hence, my usage of the term theo*anthropology.*

common among dialecticians, including Barth, Bonhoeffer, Tillich, and others. Nevertheless, because of his *Sitz im Leben*, Cone engaged in the "risk of faith" to address the urgent needs of oppressed blacks. Regardless of "the problem of reductionism," to further develop his theology of black liberation, Cone turned to Tillich and adopted, *interpretatio in bonam partem*, two more ingredients in addition to Tillich's method of correlation. He adopted Tillichian ontology and what some have identified as "ontological blackness."

He retrieved insights from Tillich's ontology and theory of symbols, themes which are too often identified, reductively, as a problem called ontological blackness.[103] Notwithstanding the knotty problems of natural theology, Cone's early use of Tillich's philosophy of being was aimed at black affirmation in the "hostile structure of white society"—without reducing God to black existential anxiety.[104] This retrieval from Tillich was not a knee-jerk response to white racism nor was it merely black affirmation of a so-called "blackness that whiteness created."[105] Cone, by contrast, was responding to the danger of nonbeing. Having been converted to blackness through the Spirit, Cone embraced his own historicity and resourced black theology in order to further clarify his existential being. He is deliberate in his efforts, stating that this "is a word to the oppressor . . . not in hope that he will listen . . . but in the expectation *that my own existence will be clarified*."[106] This note of self-affirmation, therefore, was less about whether whites understood and more about the affirmation of the human mode of being. Even the task of unmasking the white ideological superstructures paled in comparison to the need for a black theology to express meaning for the black church constructively.[107] Thus, by drawing on Tillich, he resisted the threat of fate and death and affirmed blackness over efforts to frame black people as nonbeings.[108]

Although fate and death represent relative and absolute ways that human beings experience life, respectively, Cone framed new being as a way to actualize the courage to be, knowing that the anxiety associated with nonbeing can take hold of a person who is enmeshed in difficult human situations.[109] Cone championed new rhythms and advocated for a new beat

103. Cone and Hordern, "Dialogue on Black Theology," 1085; cf. Cone, *Black Theology of Liberation*, 7–8.

104. Cone, *Black Theology and Black Power*, 7.

105. V. Anderson, *Beyond Ontological Blackness*, 92. Cf. Hart, *Afro-Eccentricity*, 3–4.

106. Cone, *Black Theology and Black Power*, 3. Emphasis added. See also Cone, "Black Consciousness."

107. See Carter, *Race*, 157–60.

108. Tillich, *Courage to Be*, 42.

109. Tillich, *Courage to Be*, 45; cf. 26–27.

in the face of nonbeing. He "affirmed a freedom for *liberation*." Through Cone's black liberation theology, American blacks could affirm themselves in the face of death and nonbeing; and when read properly Cone's argument represents a step beyond the Black Power movement where we see this type of self-affirmation. Furthermore, because Cone found harmony in collectivist manifestations such as the Black Power movement, black people could affirm their own being and sense of belonging in the world.[110] The threat of white racism represented in this regard an elementary example of the kind of nonbeing that blacks must overcome through the courage to be.

The significant issue was the degree to which revelation permitted the possibility of "saying something about God that is not simply about ourselves."[111] Here we find Cone wrestling for the most part with the same question Barth confronted, that is, how does one speak properly of God, including the *what* and *how* of our sociopolitical situation? The term "natural theology," for example, came to be shorthand for an argument aimed at a principle reasserted in various doctrinal contexts. It describes—as interpreted in a Barthian context—problems such as the naturalizing of grace, appropriating of God, metaphysics of identity, etc.[112] Cone was sensitive, of course, to the issues, especially in terms of its connection to Nazi Germany, but he was never preoccupied with such matters in terms of a dogmatic idea of the transcendence of God or, to recall Kierkegaard's construction, in terms of an infinite qualitative difference between God and humanity. Cone was, frankly, dedicated to black liberation as "the new datum."[113] This means he had to attend to black being in the world; thus, his preoccupation with Tillichian ontology. In sum, his adoption of Tillich's thinking was not an attempt to be true to Tillich. It was rather a form of dogmatic improvisation signaling that Cone's aesthetic of "blackness" is not an argument for racial essentialism. His aesthetic is the result of historical circumstances and the interpretation of these experiences as resources for black theology.

To move beyond what some would call the cul-de-sac of black experience as an ideology, Cone retrieved several elements from Tillich's theology. First, as mentioned above, Cone employed the Tillichian method of correlation as a hermeneutical tool; second, he revised Tillich's "philosophy

110. Tillich, *Courage to Be*, 90–93. Cf. Cone, *Black Theology and Black Power*, 7.

111. Cone, *Black Theology of Liberation*, 123.

112. See Küng, *Justification*, xxv. Küng describes the problem called *analogia entis*.

113. See Cone and Hordern, "Dialogue on Black Theology," 1085. As Cone notes, "*Black liberation is the new datum*. Theology must now ask, What is the essence of the gospel in view of the oppressed of the land? What is good news for the oppressed and humiliated, the weak and downtrodden? I contend that it is the good news of liberation." Emphasis in original.

of being" to stress human participation in being over against the threat of nonbeing (under the auspices of courage);[114] and, third, he critically appropriated Tillich's concept of symbols to build on the two previous concepts. Again, Cone's usage of Tillich reveals his willingness to retrieve the best insights from various interlocutors.

While Cone's retrieval of Tillich's philosophy of being seemed straightforward enough, Tillich's philosophy of symbol has unintentionally led to a more difficult partnership. Tillichian theology harbors robust philosophical underpinnings. It opens the door to a radical particularity of blackness on one hand and extends in a universal direction on the other. The question of whether Cone's theological appropriation of Tillich's thought is compatible with the revelation of God must be negotiated in Cone's theological usage and not Tillich's.

Several scholars who attend to Cone's recombination of Tillich's theology interpret his usage too narrowly.[115] From Cone's perspective, blackness is not an exclusive term. It is an ontological symbol that utilizes blackness as the prism to observe a peculiar reality in America. Thus, by depicting blackness as an ontological symbol, Cone resolved two dilemmas. First, he was able to speak directly to the American reality, focusing on the problem of the color line, i.e., blackness as the center of a problem. This ennobles his theology, enhancing his ability to speak to the question of human dignity where the symbolic nature of blackness facilitated his interrogation of black suffering in America.

Second, it contributed a way for Cone to speak of blackness universally. Cone did not advocate a form of ontology that essentialized blackness. He elaborated this point routinely in dialogue with both critics and supporters. For example, he noted in a discussion with his former teacher, William Hordern, that "I do not insist that the concreteness of oppression is always and everywhere black; but I do think that it is a distortion of historical reality if one speaks of oppression in *America* that ignores black people." In this respect blackness sits at the heart of oppression in America because blackness as a symbol is born of the American *historical* experience.[116]

114. Cone, *Black Theology and Black Power*, 7, 54–55.

115. See V. Anderson, *Beyond Ontological Blackness*, 86–117; Eppehimer, "Victor Anderson's *Beyond Ontological Blackness*"; R. James, "Tillichian Analysis"; and Stewart, "Method of Correlation." See also my earlier misreading of Cone where I argued that "arguably, however, Cone's appropriation of Tillich's notion of symbol amounts to a form of essentialism. And although this usage amounts to Cone's own urgent existential need to appropriate what is immediately necessary to address black suffering it represents a profound problem area in Cone's thought." See Carr, "Barth and Cone in Dialogue," 282.

116. Cone and Hordern, "Dialogue on Black Theology," 1080. Emphasis in original.

Ontological blackness in Cone's theology represents a shorthand way of describing the literal and material particularity of black people who struggle in America. This symbolic identification of the black experience even accepts whites who participate in the affirmation of freedom for *liberation*, provided they lose their identity with the structures of oppression and become authentically converted to blackness.[117] On the grounds of their identification with the black struggle, whites participated in blackness and shared in a new form of freedom in America, a freedom for the "other." Ontological blackness has never been a catchall term designed to disregard delicate distinctions or nuances of historical problems in America. The symbol, in fact, "stands for the oppressed—anywhere and in every place." Cone with this in mind utilized blackness to preempt forms of hypocrisy and escapism, essentially guiding whites into the spiritual transcendence of whiteness. He knew that the more neutral language could be exploited, and he expressed this point to the editor of the *Frontier* journal as early as 1970:

> In the meantime he [James Cone] asks me to explain that his article was originally written in relation to the situation in the USA and that he is not "writing for the whole world." "Blackness is a symbol. Blackness stands for the oppressed—anywhere and any place. But you may ask, why choose blackness and not oppression? The reason is obvious. Most Americans think of themselves as oppressed and they would destroy the word's meaning by misusing it. Theological language is political language, and this means choosing words that are most appropriate for the situation."[118]

Ontological blackness does not only symbolize black particularity or the physiological struggles of black people in America. Cone employed the term as a universal symbol for all the oppressed. Although it is designed to draw attention to a peculiar social condition that exists for many today, it is an inclusive term. According to Cone, in other contexts theologies may be designated with terms such as "Black, African, Hispanic-American, Asian, Red, Latin American, Minjung, black feminist, and a host of other names that still sound strange to persons whose theological knowledge has been confined to European and white North American theologies."[119] Nevertheless, the term is not intended to valorize black religious aesthetics over other

117. Cone: "Christian Theology and Afro-American Revolution," 124; *Black Theology of Liberation*, 97.

118. Lawrence, "Editorial," 81.

119. See Cone, "Black Theology: Its Origin," 39.

perspectives. From the beginning of his ministry Cone knew that taking Jesus seriously meant that he must not forget the larger world.

What Cone rightly perceived is how the tendency to universalize oppression vacates the experiences of "others" of meaning. He therefore embraced a theological symbol meant to offset the American tendency toward abstraction, which spiritualizes the concrete dimension of faith and distracts from the immediate context. He identified a similar problem, for instance, when Christians minimize the impact of their economic status by saying the gospel is for everyone, the rich and the poor alike; and he identified those who minimize the problem of violence by speaking of nonviolence in a generic universal sense without recognizing the existing state of violence. This same tendency toward generalization or universalization occurs with the motto "Black Lives Matter." The response to the term, which is specifically aimed at addressing the problem of policing, is that "all lives matter." Again, this rejoinder inverts the intended meaning of the term and deflects from the matters at hand. Most importantly, the tendency to move away from particularity ignores the most important point of all, which is God's identification with the oppressed. God has elected the oppressed as God's own. Thus, Cone's position is that "this election signifies that the struggle of the oppressed for liberation is identical with God's intention for humanity."[120]

To see the strategic nature of Cone's theology, it is important to remember that Cone remains mindful of the problem of reductionism, and he had no interest in abstract notions of Christianity or blackness, but rather championed black liberation as the distinctive feature of his biblical theology. It is not only his point of departure, i.e., "*the biblical God as related to the black liberation struggle*," but it is also one of the two primary poles identified as Cone's "biblical-existential hermeneutic."[121] These two principles emerge and can be seen in the one italicized sentence quoted above, emphasizing the *biblical God* and *black liberation*. And because of his radical commitment to the situation, Cone considered any resistance to God as a liberating God to be a moot point, designed as an academic exercise. As a matter of fact, he even described the debates around "natural theology" as a distraction from the black situation in America, underlining those discussions with the following words: "*Karl Barth notwithstanding, the natural theology issue is dead*."[122]

120. See Cone's response to Lochman: Cone, "Violence," 167.

121. Cone, *Black Theology of Liberation*, 60. Emphasis added. See Stewart's discussion in *God, Being, and Liberation*, 25–30.

122. Cone, "Theology as the Expression," 123. Emphasis added. Cf. Cone, *Speaking the Truth*, 7.

When Cone is considered as functioning in the mode of Monk, the truth is that Cone used Tillich akin to the way he used Barth, distilling from Tillich what he considered to be best in an almost ad hoc manner, *in bonum partem*, adopting those ideas most relevant to black suffering in order to build his irregular theology. In Cone's usage of Tillich and Barth, he answered the question he proposed earlier: "What did Barth, Tillich, and Brunner have to do with young black girls and boys coming from the cotton fields of Arkansas, Tennessee, and Mississippi seeking to make a new future for themselves?"[123] I would suggest that the answer could be that, in a style reminiscent to a jazz artist, they provided the instruments on which Cone played the music of his black theology.[124]

Although the problem of ontological blackness remains as one of the more criticized areas in Cone's liberation theology, it would be a mistake to read his usage of ontology as a form of arbitrariness or as a loss of Christian identity to a form of cultural relevance. In sum, I have concluded that Cone is using the language of ontology strategically as a symbol to articulate the inclusion of others into blackness. Like Barth, this form of theological thinking moves from the particular to the general.[125] This suggests that the black struggle for justice is understood within the context of *Christ's* history. And although such justice includes all human beings, oppressors must come to terms with God's judgment as seen in God's identification with the oppressed. God's no to the oppressor is made known within God's yes to the oppressed in the same way that God's no to Pharaoh is made known within God's yes to Moses.[126] There is no bifurcation of Christ because the relationship between God and humanity is understood from God's movement in *history* for humanity.

123. Cone, *My Soul Looks Back*, 38.

124. With regard to this insight, which I made in the presence of Cone on more than one occasion, he corroborated this point in the posthumously released *Said I Wasn't Gonna Tell Nobody*, a book he was completing during our last conference together in 2017. He writes, "I was singing a new theological song, a blues song, messing with theology the way B. B. King messed with music. I used Barth's theology the way B. B. King used his guitar and Ray Charles used the piano. I had 'my mojo working' (Muddy Waters) as I danced the way I felt in my flesh and bones. I wasn't following Barth; he was simply an instrument I played and left behind whenever it got in my way." Cone, *Said I Wasn't*, 92.

125. *CD* II/2:8.

126. See *CD* II/2:225.

Black Liberation and the Black Christ

When further scrutinizing the relationship between James Cone and black liberation—as it relates to his transmutation of Barth—it is important to offer some qualifications. First, in his incipient black theology, Cone expressed a basic agreement with Barth in terms of the nature of revelation. His dependence raised the question of whether Cone's theological vision was overdetermined by Barth's radical emphasis on the transcendence of God. Cone, like Barth, prioritized Christ, but he turned toward a more immanent understanding of God in Christ, particularly in the way he stressed the "identification" of Christ with human suffering. Again, like B. B. King's tremolo, wavering with the spirit of blackness, he innovatively (re)framed the identification between God and humanity while simultaneously maintaining a christological priority in his thought, a shift that allowed him to unintentionally stay close to Barth.

Second, with the turn from more abstract methodological discussions to the black Christ, we shift to the most significant part of Cone's theological development. It is here that Cone differs from Barth and other progenitors of his thought, precisely in his emphasis on the human situation, accenting the world of human existence. Cone's theology, restated in Barth's provocative style, is not "Christ and human suffering" but "Christ and *human suffering*." Christ is prioritized, but suffering humanity is nevertheless the focus of his concern. Restated, Cone develops black theology by hermeneutically investing human experience, namely black suffering, with a logical priority *as it relates to Christ.* Therefore, Cone can argue, even against those with so-called Barthian sensibilities, that he does not begin with a truth derived ultimately from the human situation, but with the incarnation or "the proclamation that the divine has taken the human situation upon himself so as to redeem humanity."[127] When distilled we can simply say that James Cone has a "high Christology" and he has this in common with Barth.[128]

With this emphasis Cone's christological thrust is distinctively liberative. Christ is one with human suffering. Jesus Christ identifies with blacks and breaks the stranglehold of white oppressors. Predictably, in view of this

127. Cone's emphasis on the priority of black experience is resident in his criticism of Helmut Gollwitzer, who is one of the more important left-wing Barthian interpreters of Barth. See Cone, "Black Theology and Ideology," 76–77.

128. Cone's high Christology is evident in all three of his major texts on black theology. See Cone, *God of the Oppressed*, 245. Cone criticizes William Jones for overlooking his christological orientation. For more on Jones, see the first book in this trilogy, i.e., *Epistrophy*, ch. 2.

accent Cone offers an encouraging word to the black freedom struggle.[129] "Jesus is the black Christ!" And despite Barth's strictures against ideology, or any other theologian's protest, Cone takes the risk, believing that his "thesis about God's blackness was adequate then and is still appropriate today if we realize that blackness is a powerful symbol of oppression and liberation among the victims of the world."[130] The black situation—then and now—demands it. Blacks were hung and were dying in the streets. Racism must be interpreted in terms of the exigency of life or death, so for Cone the concrete situation trumped Western theological and philosophical methodologies, which are often used to overdetermine and dismiss black sources and black experiences.[131] Theologically, Cone knew the situation was less than paramount, but he opted to highlight issues that pertained to the black community while subordinating the methodological issues.[132] This may account for what can seem like an ad hoc approach to the various theologians he (re)combines, including Barth.

Third, as a close student of Barth, Cone cautiously proceeded while remaining deeply aware of the ideological nature of theology, and he recognized the need to explain why black theology could not be reduced to ideological talk about God. Black theology does not force "an alien contemporary black situation on the biblical sources."[133] To make this argument, Cone deepened his christological orientation through an appeal to biblical sources themselves. He attended to the biblical text to buttress his argument for Jesus's identification with the oppressed through both the "historic perception of coincidence between Israel's bondage" and an appeal to the biblical narrative.[134] However, his approach gives way to questions of whether Cone can claim to escape the danger of brazen identification while simultaneously presupposing a particular ontology for the oppressed. Who is allowed to determine the ontological nature of the oppressed and oppressor? Based on what kind of criteria does one proceed, the crucified Christ or the situation?[135] Furthermore, considering what is

129. See Cone, "Gospel and Liberation," 164.

130. Cone, "God Is Black," 104. For discussions of the black Christ, see Cone: *Black Theology of Liberation*, 121; *Black Theology and Black Power*, 68; *God of the Oppressed*, 122–26.

131. Cone, *Spirituals and the Blues*, 65.

132. Cone, *Black Theology of Liberation*, 113.

133. Cone, *Black Theology of Liberation*, 114.

134. It is no surprise that Wilmore spots the overall historic appeal in Cone. See Gayraud S. Wilmore's review of Cone's second book, *A Black Theology of Liberation*: Wilmore, Review.

135. A recent effort to create a *theologia crucis* by signifyin(g) on Luther, Barth,

traditionally called human fallenness and nonbeing in the world, is it presumptuous to assume black people are in a position to anthropologically analyze their own "existential fancies"?[136]

Black Liberation and Epistemological Conscientization

To propagate the blackness of Christ, Cone had to break away from limiting methodologies in the black empirical church. The black church contributed to difficulties in identifying Christ as black because of its long-term dependence on Western Christianity. Realizing this problem, Cone interrogated antebellum and postbellum meanings of church theology and described its theology as being uncritically indebted to both institutional and structural values of "whiteness." Here again, Cone, early in his theological development, demonstrated a critical dependence on his theological education and insight into black experience, culture, and history. Later, as he refined his insights into the early church, he recognized the church as being in the vanguard of God's liberating work in the world.

Following Barth, Cone identified the church as "God's provisional demonstration of his intention for all humanity."[137] Rather than valorizing the deleterious values of a "sick society which oppresses the poor," the black church must desire and participate in "Christ's continued work of liberation."[138] This means the church has to ground its orientation in a radical provisional reality in light of God's transforming presence in the world. An uncritical dependence on white theology could lead only to a kind of accommodation to cultural Christianity (*Kulturchristentum*) where God is identified with white ideological concerns that are at work within American Christianity, rather than taking seriously God's advocacy on the side of the poor or the experiences of the oppressed. Such a choice would reinforce the values of the oppressor, "being part of the evil which dominates that life."[139]

Bonhoeffer, and Moltmann through the conceptual framework of Cone's black liberation theology occurs in Brach S. Jennings's *Transfiguring a Theologia Crucis Through James Cone*. I became familiar with this text too late for a thoughtful inclusion into this project.

136. Cone, *Black Theology of Liberation*, 113.

137. In Cone, there is no original source cited for this particular quote but it is a repeated statement Barth used with reference to the church as "God's provisional representation of justification in Jesus Christ." *CD* 4/1:727, 739. Quoted in Cone, "Christianity and Black Power," 8.

138. Cone, "Christianity and Black Power," 8–9.

139. K. Barth, "Poverty," 245.

From the beginning of his theological development, Cone demonstrated skepticism about the church's accommodation to American social power. The antebellum church was born in protest, but it was soon clear to Cone that the church had accommodated, perhaps seeking solutions primarily in existing sociopolitical arrangements. Besides, Christianity, according to Cone, "was blatantly used to justify slavery, colonialism, and segregation for nearly five hundred years."[140] Certainly, no one should be surprised that many churches were concerned with their own political survival and institutional aggrandizement, etc. The break with such powers could occur with a turn to a more prophetic style of Christian faith. Cone acknowledged this concern in an unflinching manner:

> If the church is to remain faithful to its Lord, it must make a decisive break with the structure of this society by launching a vehement attack on the evils of racism in all forms. It must become *prophetic*, demanding a radical change in the interlocking structures of society.[141]

Breaking away from antiblack social worldviews (*Weltanschauungen*) and institutional structures would require a radical shift in Cone's epistemological orientation. Although he hesitantly acknowledged this, Cone experienced, ironically, just the sort of training necessary to overcome the Eurocentric paradigms he endured in the academy. The reason for this is Eurocentric theology had internal resources that were useful for breaking away from it, especially when read with Cone's blues-inflected sensibilities as the hermeneutical key. These are the sentiments that set Cone on fire.[142] Moreover, just as Barth understood himself as offering a radical break from liberal theology, Cone imagined himself finding freedom from his "liberal and neo-orthodox professors, to be liberated from defining theology using abstract theological jargon . . . unrelated to the life and death experience of black people."[143] In this case, Cone's biographical reflections are important because they reveal his theology as being initially born out of personal faith and praxis. As Theo Witvliet, the conscientious Dutch liberation theologian, points out, one must recognize that prior to any theological reflection there occurs a "commitment of faith."[144]

140. See Cone, "Looking Back, Going Forward," 253.

141. Cone, "Christianity and Black Power," 4. Emphasis in original.

142. Cone, *Said I Wasn't*, 93.

143. Cone, "Looking Back, Going Forward," 251–52.

144. See Witvliet, *Place in the Sun*, 25. Though he resisted attempts to frame his interests as theology, Charles Long perceived the necessary "faith commitments" that theology required. This faith, as Long would note, is "not faith that one's program will

As a result theologians should take Cone's question, i.e., "What could Karl Barth possibly mean for black students who had come from the cotton fields of Arkansas, Louisiana and Mississippi, seeking to change the structure of their lives in a society that had defined *black* as nonbeing?," as being aimed rhetorically to stress the alien nature of the theology inherited from Western Christianity.[145] In other words, all of Cone's experiences, both immediate and remote, are profoundly important forms of conscientization when referring to the epistemological break from "white theology": the civil rights movement, the Black Power movement, the assassination of Martin Luther King Jr., his marginalization at Garrett and Northwestern, and Cone's own desire "to create a Christian theology out of the black experience of slavery, segregation, and the struggle for a just society."[146]

Furthermore, the relative mood of the period of black theology, combined with the "progressive tendencies in European theology from the 1960s onwards," played a primary role in the development of black theology.[147] His overall personal experience embodies the rich combination of cultures that is true for any blacks living through the American experience. The words of Cornel West apply to James Cone: "We must call into question any notions of pure traditions or pristine heritages."[148] To be sure, Cone, at least initially, read black experience within the confluence of the negative experiences of evil associated with white racism. What is more remarkable, despite his own negative experiences and the sharp criticisms coming from black scholars, he continued his use of European sources even while developing black theology. In this I hear a radical form of freedom. Indeed, his attention to European and North American sources should be understood as an expression of both his theological freedom and, more importantly, his employment of the black tradition of signifyin(g). Cone's theology is a signifyin(g) form of theological music, and in it Cone displays a freedom for *liberation*.

When signifyin(g), just as I noted earlier, Cone, like Barth, approached theology and procured the most usable parts of various sources (*optimum*

---

succeed, or one's rights [will be] vindicated, etc., but Faith in the ultimate fact that God created the world and in so doing defined a purpose and meaning for all of its creatures." "Comments" (2006), in Long, *Codex*.

145. Cone, *God of the Oppressed*, 5. Emphasis in original. See also his later reflections on the same subject. Cone writes, "What did Barth, Tillich, and Brunner have to do with young black girls and boys coming from the cotton fields of Arkansas, Tennessee, and Mississippi seeking to make a new future for themselves?" Cone, *My Soul Looks Back*, 38.

146. Cone, "Looking Back, Going Forward," 250.

147. In agreement with Witvliet, the important role of European theology cannot be overlooked in the development of liberation theology.

148. West, *Prophetic Thought*, 4.

in bonam partem). In one sense his conversion to blackness set the agenda for his recombination of these theologies. This means that his conversion to blackness, then, shaped both how he attuned his hearing and how he (re)sounded the tonic or tonal center for the constructive use of black and white sources.[149] He argued that they were "like a smorgasbord of theologies from which I took what I wanted and left the rest, with Jesus Christ as defined by the Bible and the black experience as my central theological norm." Consequently, in order to break away from white concepts, Cone had to (re)read, (re)define, and refine his approach to the Scripture. Interestingly, Barth would play an important role for Cone, at least at the earliest point, because his central concern was the Bible and Jesus Christ, and following this "Barthian" melodic line and direction allowed Cone to focus intently on centering his thought.[150]

Just as Barth's theology required a development, Cone's theology became more conscientized over time—as he became more aware of the daily concern of oppressed people. This awareness is described by Cone as a development within the "world of men." So while Barth emphasized the vertical "from above," Cone embraced neither a movement "from above" (Barth), from below (Tillich, Pannenberg), nor from the future (Moltmann, Pannenberg).[151] In agreement with Theo Witvliet, the later Barth and Cone recognized revelation and revolution as God's acts *in* history.[152] Barth, of course, heard this in a form of the kingdom of God and its relation to socialism, distinguishing between *brazen* identifications and "identifications," read as analogies that actually "follow the movement of the gospel."[153] Cone, on the other hand, was concerned with the appearance of Black Power and what this phenomenon meant for black people in America. Barth and Cone, nonetheless, experienced a development in their respective theologies which led to Barth's refined christological concentration developed as the humanity of God and Cone's radical implementation of black sources heard

149. See Cone, *My Soul Looks Back*, 83. Note Cone's words, i.e., "when they suited my [his] purposes," they did "not determine his perspective," and at "no point did a European theologian, not even Barth, control what I said about the gospel and the black struggle for freedom."

150. Cone, *My Soul Looks Back*, 83.

151. See Cone, *God of the Oppressed*, 120.

152. See Witvliet, *Way of the Black Messiah*, 172.

153. See Gollwitzer, "Kingdom of God and Socialism," 81. Gollwitzer writes, "It made a difference whether we perceived an identity between God's kingdom and socialism, or whether we identify our socialism (as idea, movement, and finally achieved condition) with God's kingdom. In the first instance we follow the movement of the gospel, serving, believing, and obeying its promise. In the second we exploit . . . the utilization of God to serve our own respective interests." See also 80.

in *The Spirituals and the Blues*, *God of the Oppressed*, and other sources he used to respond to the criticisms of his black colleagues.[154]

Black Liberation and the Affirmation of Black Humanity

Regardless of questions attending Cone's Christology, his identification of Christ with blackness gives dignity to black self-understanding. He grounds his primary impetus for black affirmation in two sources, i.e., politically through the Black Power movement and, theologically, through the discipline of black theology. This affirmation of blackness is also tied to the liberation of the oppressed rather than acquiescence to oppression. As a result, Cone's theological development reveals hesitancy toward any theoretical view of freedom. This would be an abstraction. As Cone pointed out at the beginning of his development, "freedom is not a theoretical proposition to be debated in a philosophy or theology seminar."[155] Authentic liberation must be tied to the identity of black humanity, and for Cone this means acknowledging a much more pragmatic context. Black people must be free to participate in determining who they are. Cone's theology echoes a classical existentialist orientation since for Cone "man is [human beings are] in the process of defining himself [themselves]."[156]

Here the "process" of liberation in black theology occurs on several different levels, including liberation from white definitional self-understandings of black people. The racist character of white theo-politics not only prevented blacks from operating independently of white values; it prevented them from fully participating in their own communities, stifling their ability to make decisions for the black community.[157] Cone therefore affirmed blackness by isolating and unmasking how sin attacked black self-understandings. To be sure, white racism ignores God's liberating activity in Christ. Most egregiously, it actively resists the benefits of the incarnation where "God has taken upon himself human oppression and has, through his resurrection, transformed it into human liberation."[158]

154. Along with Cone's *Spirituals and the Blues*, *God of the Oppressed*, the article "Theology as the Expression," and the fourth chapter of *Cross and Lynching Tree* all represent Cone's more engaging turn to black religious sources. See Cone, *Speaking the Truth*, 1.

155. See Cone, "Freedom, History, and Hope," 61.

156. Cone, "Introduction to Black Theology," 72.

157. Cone, "Introduction to Black Theology," 59.

158. Cone, *Black Theology of Liberation*, 106. See also Cone, "Black Power, Black Theology," 211–12.

Black Liberation and the Rhythm of the Resurrection

Black conscientization and affirmation share a common theological ground. It is the ground of black liberation heard in the rhythm of the resurrection, making all things new. For Cone, "Christianity begins and ends with the man Jesus—his life, death, and resurrection."[159] This fact of faith informed and sustained Cone's adamant affirmation of blackness, which Cone used as a constructive turn to rhythms of faith designed to overcome Western forms of Christianity. These latter preestablished religious forms not only contradicted the genius of the gospel, but they were also hostile to black life. Even in the present situation, the first quarter of the twentieth-first century, nationalistic forms of evangelical Christianity identify Christ with political ideologies aimed at marginalizing and dehumanizing the material life of black communities, people of color in general, and LGBTQ+ communities.[160] In this kind of milieu, the resurrection frees oppressed humanity from such narrow identifications. The gospel therefore affirms black consciousness even as it overcomes the sin of nonbeing. Cone, as a result, argued for a knowledge that frees and liberates us "to be what we are and do what we must so that Black liberation will become a reality in this land."[161]

This emphasis on human liberation and the resurrection as the keynote means oppressed blacks will no longer listen to the cues of oppressors. Black people participate in a new reality as opposed to the "unreal reality" of whiteness, prophetically condemning white racist values and powers—even as their faith affirms blackness and courageously embraces new harmonics, new insights, and new sources arising from black life.[162] This new consciousness begins with a christological reading of Scripture that harmonizes blackness and Jesus Christ, the Liberator of black humanity. As Dwight Hopkins, a leading second-generation theologian, points out, "God's liberation . . . through Christ's cross and resurrection pinpoints the core of Cone's Christology."[163] Black liberation thus characterizes Jesus's identity. However, because of this emphatic trend in his thought, Cone is often perceived as offering a message alien to the Christian gospel. When he contended that blackness was his ultimate reality and rejected any "Ultimate Reality" that does not account for black experience, those listening through the lens of

159. Cone, *Black Theology and Black Power*, 34. Emphasis added.

160. Cone, "Dialectic of Theology and Life," 86–87.

161. Cone, "Black Power, Black Theology," 213. For Cone on nonbeing, see 210.

162. See Cone, *Black Theology of Liberation*, 20, 61. The language of "unreal reality" is adopted from Barth's definition and discussion of sin. See K. Barth, *Barth in Conversation*, 1:180.

163. Hopkins, *Introducing Black Theology of Liberation*, 57.

colonial logics heard only a contradiction. Indeed, for those who fail to hear black theological language, especially Cone's urgings, the response is often "you cannot have it both ways."[164] They hear black liberative faith and Christian faith as being mutually exclusive.

The failure is not in Cone's articulation of his position, however. It is a failure of hearing. There is a persistent inability to come to terms with black theological language whose "meaning is found in its style."[165] So, when elucidating his position, Cone came singing a new song in light of the resurrection, arguing that "like Scripture, the black experience is a source of the Truth, but not the Truth itself. Jesus Christ is the Truth and thus stands in judgment over all statements about truth." With this explanation, Cone turned the reader to his dialectic, balancing one statement with the other in order to underscore the fact that "no truth in Jesus Christ is independent of the oppressed of the land—their history and culture."[166] It is precisely at this point where Cone's new harmonics, sounding in the tensions between the "ultimate reality" of experience and the "Ultimate Reality," help us come to terms with what it means to be free for liberation and to live as signifiers of the resurrection. All along the melodic line of life (in experience and culture and history), when this divine dissonance is heard and set within the rhythmic scheme of the resurrection, black experience, culture, and history become alive and testify to radical political possibilities—even in a white world. The resurrection of life reveals so many unopened doors, affirming black identity in the face of nothingness and nonbeing.

This emphasis in Cone's thinking on the resurrection endured from the beginning to the end of his theological endeavors. In his first article, Cone contends—following Luther and the New Testament—that the resurrected One is "active even now in the midst of human misery . . . Jesus is where the oppressed are."[167] As he refined his turn toward blackness, the contemporaneity of Christ continually shaped his interpretation of Scripture, Christology, and praxis. Coupled with the engagement of black history and his emphasis on slave songs, sermons, sacred stories, and other black sources, whose rhythms reinforce black solidarity in black communities, it is not difficult to see how the historical Jesus as the Crucified and Risen

164. Cone, *Black Theology and Black Power*, 32–33. When discussing blackness as ultimate reality, Cone quotes Ron Karenga, the American activist and founder of Kwanzaa, who stated, "The fact that I am Black is my ultimate reality." He also addressed the charge that he was trying to have it both ways in "Dialectic of Theology and Life," 86.

165. Cone, *Said I Wasn't*, 89–90.

166. Cone, "Dialectic of Theology and Life," 86. For Cone's new song, see *Said I Wasn't*, 92.

167. Cone, "Christianity and Black Power," 8.

Lord participated "with us in the struggle of freedom."[168] While it is fair to question whether Cone's black theology has undergone an inspired one-sidedness, being evident in a kind of historicizing from the beginning of his theological work, we must not overlook his use of sources that are designed to recall and encourage faith in the faithfulness of God. As it relates to Scripture's witness to the Christ of faith and the historical Jesus, whom he reads dialectically, Cone's position on transcendence calls into question the tendency to read the later Cone over against the earlier much more Barthian Cone. Indeed, in my view it is best to hear the testimony of the earlier and later James Cone in their common witness to a freedom for *liberation* that resounds in the rhythm of the resurrection.

Black Liberation and the Transcendent God of the Oppressed

Although Cone built his Christology on the harmony between the biblical text and the liberative rhythms of black history, he maintained a profound appreciation for the otherness of God. Cone knew blacks could not live life meaningfully if we did not "see light beyond the darkness."[169] And if we follow the line of his overall theological corpus, we see his preoccupation with the theme of liberation in both the Old and New Testaments, separately and dialectically. Another way to state this is to note that, for Cone, God is not just the God *of liberation*. God is the *God* of liberation. God's revolutionary activity toward Israel exemplifies God's concern for humanity in general.[170] The biblical text reiterates God's concern for humanity. So, the exodus is more than a revolutionary event occurring in history. It is a priestly narrative that arises out of the Babylonian exile and identifies the Creator as the One who is not a metaphysically distant God, effecting questions of aseity, but rather the story of God's radically immanent concern for Jewish flesh and therefore black liberation.[171]

God's revelation remained primary for Cone; so much so, that he identified the call of Israel in the OT with the beginning of the church in the NT.[172] More importantly, Cone's dialectical appeal to Scripture allowed him to express liberation in a modality that prevented black theology from being sequestered by black experience. There were several critics who disagreed

168. Cone, *Spirituals and the Blues*, 57. For Jesus as "the Crucified and Risen Lord" in the struggle see Cone, *God of the Oppressed*, 111.

169. Cone, *Cross and Lynching Tree*, 154.

170. Cone, *Black Theology and Black Power*, 64.

171. Cone, *God of the Oppressed*, 57–59, 114–15.

172. Cone, *Black Theology and Black Power*, 64.

with Cone's dialectical appeal to the biblical message. J. Deotis Roberts, for instance, countered, believing Cone's precommitment to liberation and narrow Christocentrism misrepresented Scripture.[173] We are free to inquire whether Cone subordinated the transcendent richness of liberation in the Bible to a political principle of revelation, a question that I will address below.

Roberts's criticism of Cone's interpretation of liberation arose from his desire to pursue a view of Scripture that accommodates both the judgment and grace of God. In his view, the biblical story contains the bitter and the sweet, and for Cone "it is all sweet," meaning the dialectic in Scripture is in some sense exploited for Cone's own idea of liberation.[174] Nevertheless, a closer reading of Cone reveals that he prioritized and correlated the relationship between the social situation of the believer, Scripture, and traditions of the church that "moves beyond the subjectivity of our present." Moreover, he circumscribed the extent to which tradition is load bearing, positing that it does not "carry the same weight of authority as Scripture," although Jesus is mediated through Scripture.[175] This reading of Scripture and tradition, in juxtaposition, permits criticism of tradition on both sides while remaining open to the authority of Scripture. Spirituals, blues, sermons, secular and sacred texts are all free to amplify and illuminate the free-spirited task of theology and contribute to the discussion of Monk's relevance below.

Cone furthermore refined his methodology through an understanding of the transcendent Christ. As noted above, truth "is the divine happening that invades our contemporary situations." Although this is a subordinate theme for Cone, because of the primacy he gives to the situation, "Christ is the *otherness* in the black experience that makes possible the affirmation of black humanity in an inhumane situation."[176] This view situated Christ as representative of a type of transcendence. On one hand, his effort is an attempt to transcend Barth by using Scripture to paradoxically move the people of God into history by actively and reflectively engaging the biblical text from the standpoint of their situation, i.e., Scripture and tradition. On the other hand, he moved beyond Tillich concretely by subordinating philosophical questions in relation to the more concrete experiences of black people. This twofold approach tolerated less ambiguity regarding the human situation, particularly since Cone unambiguously identified God's ultimate concern for black people, i.e., God's concern to alleviate black

173. Roberts, "Critique," 60.

174. Roberts, "Critique," 60.

175. Cone, *God of the Oppressed*, 104.

176. Cone, *God of the Oppressed*, 105. Emphasis added.

suffering for the purpose of affirming black humanity, the *psychological* trait in blackness.[177] Culturally, he moved beyond Tillich since black theology represents the "theological circle" or the concrete synthesis Tillich was unable to achieve.[178]

Roberts, for instance, attacked Cone for methodologically using a Hegelian or neoorthodox dialectical methodology. He also chastised Cone, arguing that such an approach is not reminiscent of the black community. But despite Roberts's criticisms, it is unclear whether Cone is more reliant on Hegelian or a neoorthodox approach, depending on what one means by neoorthodox. It is clear, however, that he tried to mediate knowledge in a style similar to Paul Tillich since his method of correlation reflects an attempted self-transcendence aimed at coinciding with Tillich's argument that "the movement of life from self-identity to self-alteration and back to self-identity is the basic scheme of dialectics."[179] Cone's innovative use of dialectic in the method of correlation appears to reflect this movement for he explicitly argued that human identity undergoes some type of alteration:

> Through the reading of Scripture, the people hear other stories about Jesus that enable them to move beyond the privateness of their own story; through faith because of divine grace, they are taken from the present to the past and then thrust back into their contemporary history with divine power to transform the sociopolitical context. This event of transcendence enables the people to break the barriers of time and space as they walk and talk with Jesus in Palestine along with Peter, James, and John. They can hear his cry of pain and experience the suffering as he is nailed on the cross and pierced in the side.[180]

The experience with the biblical subject matter creates an *event of transcendence*. The people are *thrown back*, *encountered*, experiencing a passionate *transcendent leap* both into the first century and back into the contemporary situation.[181] Still, what is this moment of transcendence Cone describes? Is this the moment of encounter with Christ construed as the "*otherness* in the black experience that makes possible the affirmation of black humanity

177. The ultimate concern (being) for Tillich relates to both the ontological and scientific concept of experience. Through the juxtaposition of the two, Tillich gestures toward transcendence. Cone's clarity emerges because of his accent on black experience. It is the preliminary concern through which the ultimate concern actualizes itself. See Tillich, *Reason and Revelation*, 11–12. Cf. Cone, *Black Theology of Liberation*, 204.

178. Tillich, "Problem of Theological Method," 19.

179. Tillich, *Life and the Spirit*, 329.

180. Cone, *God of the Oppressed*, 102.

181. Cone, *God of the Oppressed*, 102–3, 109–10.

in an inhumane situation"? Is this perspective limited to Tillich's vision of transcendence? Is this rooted in Cone's earlier concept of transcendence associated with the secular, i.e., a transcendence from life itself?[182] Cone's audacious proposal leaves us to question whether we have ears to hear transcendence as it emerges from within the secular. Can we hear the light of this transcendent truth?

Central to understanding the meaning of transcendence and his christological point of departure is the idea of the so-called historical Jesus. The historical Jesus functions in several ways for Cone. First, the notion gives insight into the true humanity of Christ. There is no way to affirm Christ's identification with blackness if there is no way to know Christ was truly human. To overlook the humanity of Christ is to essentially marginalize Christ.

Second, the historical Jesus calls attention to the importance of Scripture as the basis for Christology.[183] This basic point enables Cone to move beyond what he determined to be *docetic* christological conceptions inherited from the nineteenth and early twentieth centuries—a problem area where Cone locates Barth, marking his reliance on Kierkegaard's notion of an "infinite qualitative difference" as one of the reasons Barth subordinates the historical Jesus and overemphasizes the eternal Word.[184] While we can certainly make a case for this interpretation of Barth, Cone's wrestling with the immanent side of Barth's notion of transcendence is more compelling. Does Kierkegaard's emphasis on a qualitative difference drive Barth's theology as much as Cone surmises? Is Barth's theology dualistic? Or, speaking more positively, did Barth's situation call for the same kind of inflection he suggested Jürgen Moltmann outgrow, i.e., the "inspired one-sidedness" of his nascent theology.[185]

Third, the humanity of the historical Jesus validates the identification of Jesus's racial identity. The particularity of Jesus reinforces the concrete nature of his humanity and actualizes the OT promises of God's deliverance of Israel. Hence the history of Jesus plays an important role in liberation. In fact, these various factors come together to emphasize how Jesus, interpreted through the pedagogical slogan "Jesus is who he was," functions in the struggle for freedom in Cone's theology. Among other things, with cursory reference to the problems of historicity, Cone sought to maintain transcendence or the

182. Cone, *God of the Oppressed*, 105. Emphasis added. See also 24–25. Cone associates this form of transcendence with the secular as in blues music.

183. Cone, *God of the Oppressed*, 107, 109.

184. Cone, *God of the Oppressed*, 107.

185. K. Barth, *Letters*, 176.

otherness of Christ by acknowledging that he does not believe in a separation between the historical Christ and the Christ of faith.[186] Here, in a departure from Pannenberg, who was also a critic of docetic interpretations of Christ, Cone argued for a dialectical relationship between the Jesus "from below" and the Jesus "from above."[187] In this way, he presupposed Christ as being dialectically present with blacks in the struggle for liberation and freedom. Transcendence occurs through faith and experience of the past of Jesus "in the historicity of his life and death on the cross."[188]

The problem with defending the historical Jesus, however, is that even when one makes room for the Christ of faith, as Cone attempts to do, the identification of the historical Jesus misses the key burden of the incarnation and human bondage for which only a redeeming deliverance will suffice. Is every so-called historical manifestation of liberation revelatory? Furthermore, how does one avoid the way divine revolutions, happenings, or events eventually end up serving institutional interests? In such cases how does one identify revelation? At any rate, Cone's brilliant work on the historical Jesus presses me to reconsider the way Western logic limits our ability to speak of God in relation to humanity. In an earlier discussion of this subject, I presumed that Cone's approach led to speaking of the poverty of Christ and the world's poverty in a univocal way.[189] Such a conclusion would make an equation between the freedom of God in relation to the poverty of oppressors.

However, if we read Cone as "stretching the form" and emphasizing a dissonant note, rather than as a simple equation (univocity), then we are not forced to conclude that when arguing that "the Kingdom belongs to the poor *alone*" we are excluding all others.[190] Thus, this signifyin(g) on Barth could involve deepening his christological concentration by embracing Jesus the suffering Jew and God's identification with his humanity as a way of proclaiming God's identification with the finitude of all people, especially blacks—in addition to the identification with the poor and with blackness interpreted as an *ontological symbol*. Both options are possible when thinking in the mode of Monk.

186. See Cone, *God of the Oppressed*, 109. A distinction should be honored at this point. Cone tends to think of historical Jesus as Jesus in his true humanity. Nevertheless, the term and his dependence on Pannenberg raise the apologetic question of a closer relationship between Cone and a Jesus who is somehow verified historically.

187. Cone, *God of the Oppressed*, 111.

188. Cone, *God of the Oppressed*, 114.

189. See Carr, "Barth and Cone in Dialogue," 300.

190. Cone, *God of the Oppressed*, 72. Emphasis in original.

Rhythm-a-ning with Barth and Cone on Freedom and Liberation

Despite Cone's development and criticism of Barth's theology, there is a generative fruitfulness we receive if we advance the theologies of Karl Barth *and* James Cone, particularly when playing in the tension of their respective differences. This effort requires that we cultivate an appreciation for the same antithetical modes of thought in the modern world that we see in the Hebrew Bible, in Jewish tradition, and in dialectical thinkers like Barth and Cone who draw on the legacy of what I am calling harmonious thinking. In this way, even their differences are not binaries where we view one choice over against another; nor are differences meant to be resolved into easy solutions. On the contrary, the approximations, the ambiguities, the silences that naturally occur within all human experiences in the external ground of creation provide space for the alternating rhythms of freedom and liberation.

In much the same way Monk's style of making music allows us to hear space, a kind of rhythmic virtuosity is possible where ethics is grounded in a dimension of depth. The alternating rhythms of God's freedom and acts of human liberation in the mystery of Christ, which urges us to live *into*, *with*, and *beyond* the ambiguities of life, transcend Western modes of life and thought, particularly when they seek to resolve differences into neat theological categories and solutions that rub away the brilliant corners of our lives too quickly. To put it simply, American Christianity culminates, ethically speaking, far too often into modern forms of casuistry or moralistic codes that become substitutes for the deeper life of faith we desire in our inner being. Such rules undermine the spirit of playful freedom God has gifted to believers. And while it is important to avoid reducing revelation to human experience, to the moods of a particular moment, to personal passions or to caprice, we must not sacrifice the joyful rhythms of human life at the altar of an abstract realm of divine freedom. I am convinced that it is in this context that Cone speaks of freedom as not being a gift but a risk, a risk we must all be willing to take.[191]

This continuum between God's freedom and human liberation explains in some respects why I occasionally stumble when assessing Barth, feeling a twinge of discomfort. For although I respect Barth's commitment to theology as a dogmatic discipline and the wisdom that leads him to avoid natural theologies, strict identifications, and the drawing of parallels—especially given his situation in the shadow of two world wars, Vietnam, and

191. "Black Theology and the Black Church," in Cone, *Risks of Faith*, 48. In this article Cone used freedom interchangeably with liberation, presupposing human participation in freedom.

other conflicts—I still struggle with the degree of his emphasis on God's freedom and its meaning for human liberation, although I know the conceptual structures he relied upon came from many years of being steeped in Scripture. I can only imagine the extent of his suspicion of the modern liberal mind that all too often substitutes facts for faith on the one hand, and those who in reaction to such thinking—even when facts are used in their proper environment—resort to "alternative facts," on the other hand, in order to justify their ideological ways of living.

To fully appreciate Barth's nuance, it is helpful to hear how Cone's counterpoint is actualized in relation to human experience, distinguishing between the humanity of Christ and the Christ of the *kerygma*. By analyzing the relationship between the scriptural view of the historical Jesus and black experience, Cone attuned himself to history in a way that complemented revelation. Moreover, by attending to a particular historical context, he interpreted revelation from the standpoint of history. Although this is risky, interpreters should note that Cone did not ask what is the relevance of the black community to Christ. He asked, "What is *his* relevance to the black community today?"[192] With that noted, it is still fair to ask if Cone's question presupposes a general definition of humanity rooted in ontology, symbolically speaking. This suggests we must attend to the way Cone constructively developed his theology through praxis. As he notes, "Praxis (i.e., a reflective political action that includes cultural identity) comes *before* theology in any formal sense."[193] Symbolically speaking, then, Cone creates room for the constructive development of new theological language.

In questioning Christ's relevance to the black community, Cone actualized the "soteriological value of Jesus' person," going beyond Pannenberg's understanding of the historical Jesus and extending Jesus's relevance *into* and in identification with the condition of the oppressed.[194] Jesus's identity and relevance are thus determined by what Jesus did. Cone thus demonstrated a theological dexterity that is rarely exercised by the historical Jesus scholars.

192. Cone, *Black Theology of Liberation*, 119. Emphasis added.

193. Cone, "Black Theology: Its Origin," 38. Emphasis added. This observation is offered even though Cone utilizes blackness strategically. As Trevor Eppehimer notes, "Cone's 'blackness' was never developed in the interest of articulating a comprehensive theological anthropology." He was primarily concerned with concrete blackness to provoke interest in black liberation. Following Tillich, this furnishes the heroic energy to overcome white oppression. Eppehimer, "Victor Anderson's *Beyond Ontological Blackness*," 104.

194. Pannenberg, as Cone implied here, would limit the historical Jesus to Jesus the carpenter or to the way the narrative depicts Jesus. See Cone, *Black Theology of Liberation*, 119. Cone later takes up this argument and contextualizes liberation with respect to Christ. See Cone, *God of the Oppressed*, 106–10.

In this shift Cone prioritizes and actualizes Christology so that it speaks to the history of blackness. The historical Jesus—in his identification with the liberation of the oppressed—aligns himself with the oppressed. Cone writes, "He was for the poor and against the rich, for the weak and against the strong."[195] This priority for the oppressed is deliberately one-sided in Cone. He bends the notes as it were toward a preferential option for the oppressed. So, theologically speaking, the sociopolitical situation in America outweighs the danger of ideology. If Jesus is the Crucified and Risen Lord then the identification itself happens in Christ, and in doing so God's identity provides the melody for the situation. If this is the case, I would suggest that the mystery of God's presence is evidenced in the struggle to be black. In the words of James Cone, "*We must become black with God!*"[196]

The potential problem here is not that Cone understands the historical and *kerygmatic* Christ in an undialectical way; rather, it is in how he launches his Christology from the standpoint of historical Jesus who is heard in a flat identification with black liberation. The humanity of Christ, following Cone, gives the impression of being pressed into service in an abstract and insular way. This way of reading Cone proffers the question of whether history can be deployed on par with Christ and perpetuates a narrowly exclusivist vision of Jesus whose openness to the multidimensional nature of humanity is interpreted from an exclusivist form of blackness. Thus feminist, womanist, queer, crip, and other forms of reality are marginalized in relation to "blackness." Most importantly, Christ is equated unwittingly with a black political revolution rather than with God's revolution expressed fundamentally in its eschatological dimensions. Of course, Cone does not frame black theology in this narrow way. God in Cone's theological music does not just become black. Blackness proexists for others in rhythm with God: "Teaching theology," according to Cone, "is about giving voice to people and helping people find their voice. It's not about my voice. My voice should elicit theirs. It's a process for the purpose of bringing their voices out."[197]

Cone's emphases partly explain why Barth and Cone, when rhythm-a-ning together, become so invaluable to a theology of freedom and liberation. For Barth offers a complementary position since he argued that "this revelation of God, is the work of the eternal Son, it legitimately confronts the whole world of creatures, excellent beyond compare."[198] Barth's notion

195. Cone, *Black Theology of Liberation*, 120. See also Cone, *Black Theology and Black Power*, 36.

196. Cone, *Black Theology of Liberation*, 65. Emphasis in original.

197. See the interview in Comstock, *Whosoever Church*, 213.

198. K. Barth, *Dogmatics in Outline*, 84.

of the humanity of God as a contrapuntal rhythm-a-ning with Cone helps liberate theology *for* history. As Paul Ricoeur acknowledged in dependence on Gadamer, "historical knowledge cannot free itself from the historical condition."[199] And since Christ's works are too often interpreted by historico-critical scholars abstractly rather than historically (interpreted as the event of God), the significance of Christ's movement is forfeited. To the contrary, Christ's movement or revelation "is above all powers; not of the revelation of a divine Above or Below, but the *revelation of God Himself [as Godself]*."[200] Marquardt recalls this emphasis in Barth, noting his recognition of Christ's history as *Urgeschichte* (primal history), which is "not supernatural, but revolutionary history."[201] Thus, rather than a vision of the historical Christ that presupposes one can come to a knowledge of God in Christ through the science of history (*historie*), Barth, by contrast, utilized history or story (*Geschichte*) in order to distinguish the history of Christ from other histories. In this way God's history (*Geschichte*) liberates one from the trap of historicism, rationalism, totalism, or any other narrow epistemological orientation.

This christological formulation anticipates J. Kameron Carter's contention that Cone shifted to being theologically "beyond-Barthian" at this point.[202] While Carter's interpretation also precludes scholasticized visions of Barth, like those depicted in American Barthian thought, Cone also argued against reading Barth scholastically and distinguished himself from European and North American Barthians who "used him [i.e., Barth] to justify doing nothing about the struggle for justice."[203] It is not necessary, then, to imagine Cone as being "beyond-Barthian," especially if we take seriously the left-wing portrayal of Barth where we see a more radical christological understanding of the two natures of Christ. The question at issue is how to advance Barth and Cone together in a way that is theologically ambidextrous, akin to two independent rhythmic lines, as opposed to using one theologian to stand in judgment on (or beyond) another.

199. Ricoeur, *Hermeneutics*, 76.

200. K. Barth, *Dogmatics in Outline*, 84. Emphasis in original.

201. Hunsinger, *Karl Barth and Radical Politics*, 54.

202. Carter, *Race*, 166–67.

203. Cone, *My Soul Looks Back*, 45. Cone, in fact, saw Barth as against the "Barthians" and their failure to actualize what I identify as a "freedom *for* liberation" (in Barth), modulating toward the oppressed. One example is Cone's commendation for theologians of hope whom he described as being "[un]like Barth who ignored Marx." See Cone, *Black Theology of Liberation*, 93. On Barth and Marx, see Cone, *God of the Oppressed*, 116. For an extended discussion of "the Marxist elements in Barth," see Marquardt, *Theologie und Sozialismus*, 313–32.

This kind of rhythm-a-ning is why it is so important to hear Barth's innovation(s) as being born out of his efforts to navigate the strait between the Scylla of Lutheran thought and the Charybdis of Reformed teaching. This *locus theologicus* provided him with unique insights; and of course, such insights can cause oversights, since Lutherans sought to radically transcend any form of one-sidedness by going beyond the pattern of Chalcedon (accenting the identification of God's deity and the humanity of Christ in the *Communicatio Idiomatum*) in order to highlight the ubiquity of Christ in the world.[204] The Calvinists, on the other hand, appealed to the otherness of God (accenting the distinction between God and Humanity in the *Calvinistic Ad Extra*) in order to protect the sovereignty of God. Karl Barth attempted to transcend these emphases on both sides by developing a theology "from above to below" (*von oben nach unten*) and has endured criticism for his emphasis on a *freedom* for liberation that supposedly sacrifices human liberation at the altar of some kind of Christomonism.[205]

Cone, in my view, resounds with a healthy counterpoint to this problem, notably in his efforts to articulate a theology "from below to above" (*von unten nach oben*). Of course, Cone has endured criticism for what he identifies as the blindness of those who refuse to see power in powerlessness, namely in the "power of the oppressed against their oppressors," failing to hear the light in the "immanent presence of a transcendent revelation, confirming for blacks that they were more than what whites said about them."[206] Cone therefore had to avoid the Scylla of heretical white American churches steeped in racism on one hand, and the Charybdis of ideological danger(s) that shaped quietist, christomonist churches on the other. Strangely, rather than hearing Cone's freedom for *liberation* that testifies to God's judgment on the oppressor, Cone is perceived as sacrificing the freedom of God at the altar of an ideological form of liberation.

At this point, what should be coming clear is I am suggesting that Barth's and Cone's theologies coexist in a peculiar familial kinship, a form (*Form*) that finds its conformity (*Konformität*) in the turning, the rhythm, or the impulse of God.[207] And like counterpoints that share the same

204. For a brief discussion of this problem and Barth's solution, see Carr, "Barth and Cone in Dialogue," 304–6.

205. This partly explains why the political interpretations of Timothy Gorringe and others have such a profound importance, especially in the articulation of political responsibility as seen in Barth's stance against National Socialism, which finds a troubling corollary in the Christian nationalism at work in American settings today. See Gorringe, *Against Hegemony*, 154–63.

206. Cone, *Said I Wasn't*, 10; cf. Cone, *Cross and Lynching Tree*, xviii. For Barth's emphasis on above and below, see *CD* IV/4:22; *KD* IV/4:24.

207. *CD* II/2:511–12; *KD* II/2:567.

melody, these rhythms revolve around the gravitating power of the mystery of Christ, the divine melody, whose musicality is recognized if we hear the light of its truth. To be sure, the mystery of this coherence is not found in the conceptual balance of a theological system or a carefully thought-out syllogism or well-balanced dialectic. It is found in "the light of life," in the spirit of free play around the *melodic foundation*, articulated in a way that transcends even our vacillations and contradiction(s). It is here in our embrace of the cantus firmus where, as Bonhoeffer notes, "the counterpoints can be developed to their limits,"[208] giving way to a polyphony that includes the history of Israel and the church even as it "goes out into all lands, to the whole world and all the nations."[209] In the alternation of this rhythm we find a new beginning in the mode of Monk.

Listening Guide

Thelonious Monk, "'Round Midnight," 1951,
https://www.youtube.com/watch?v=Dj_XxuEQTnY

Louis Armstrong, "Nobody Knows the Trouble I've Seen," 1962,
https://www.youtube.com/watch?v=SVKKRzemX_w

Nina Simone, "Strange Fruit," 2022,
https://www.youtube.com/watch?v=Bn6DKuEleUg

Billie Holiday & Her Orchestra, "Strange Fruit," 2022,
https://www.youtube.com/watch?v=649wWWkW_10

Thelonious Monk, "Abide With Me," 1958,
https://www.youtube.com/watch?v=RHctGCUS2fE

Thelonious Monk, "This Is My Story, This is My Song," 1967,
https://www.youtube.com/watch?v=FIQ6fj1BJX0

208. Bonhoeffer, *Letters and Papers*, 303.

209. *CD* 4/3.1:61.

EPISTROPHY (Reprise)

Back to the Beginning

It is midnight of an autumn day . . . All is death. There is no sound; and yet somehow somewhere beneath lies some Tone too deep for sound—a silent chord of infinite Harmony.—W. E. B. Du Bois[1]

We were at times remarkably buoyant, singing hymns, and making joyous exclamations almost as triumphant in their tone as if we had reached a land of freedom and safety.—Frederick Douglass[2]

Lift every voice and sing / Till earth and heaven ring / Ring with the harmonies of Liberty—James Weldon Johnson[3]

There are no wrong notes; some are just more right than others.—Frequent saying of Thelonious Monk

There is a jazz artist in us all.

1. "The Revelation of Saint Orgne," in Du Bois, *Writings*, 1062.
2. Douglass, *Life and Times*, 109.
3. Johnson, "Lift Every Voice," st. 1.

HEAD

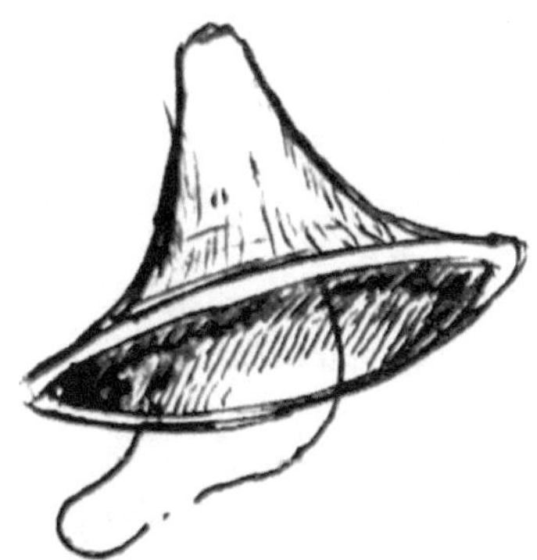

(Re)orientation as "Epistrophy"

In the early years of a Thelonious Monk performance, the tune "Epistrophy" was played more than once during a jazz set. Monk performed "Epistrophy" with regularity, sometimes five or six times with astonishing improvisations and without formulaic replication.[1] The song was even used as "a sophisticated way of announcing intermission,"[2] an interlude for adoring fans to unwind and hang loose. This reiteration of a melody without

1. Gourse, *Straight, No Chaser*, 172.
2. Fitterling, *Thelonious Monk*, 198.

reduplicating it makes "Epistrophy" the ideal song for thinking of the turning about (epistrophe) as a new beginning that I hope to make in relation to Barth and Cone.

Invoking "Epistrophy" in this final chapter, then, means I intend to demonstrate how Monk's musicality contributes to more than just the overall form and architectural structure; and more than the inner material content of this aesthetics of freedom. Monk's musicality opens the way to a range of symbolic representations and informs the creative consciousness. Indeed, when we take seriously the mystery of the cantus firmus, especially when heard in its most radical biblical sense, we encounter the revealed secret (*mysterion*) that gives insight into a world of meanings. I hear in Monk's music a theology of playful freedom whose aesthetic mode and symbolic force suggest a way to freely begin again at the beginning (where the end is insinuated in the beginning).[3] Put another way, the (re)orientation I am suggesting is the epistrophe that prompts us to (re)imagine matter and (re) consider the Sacred and sacred spaces. Thus, the illustrative power of Monk's music models a way for us to reimagine our world and advance Barth's and Cone's theological contributions to the social imaginary.

In the same manner, "Epistrophy" represented a historical turn toward modern music, which is also emblematic here of another potential turning point for modern theology, a threshold experience for new questions in theology about critical turning points for (de)*constructive* conversations.[4] It may come as a surprise, in fact, that Monk originally wanted to create a new turning point for jazz. Even as a youth he knew something had to be done about the relationship between jazz and America, feeling that music had lost its way.[5] With Monk's aesthetics as an artistic analogue, then, we can ask what does it mean, for instance, to bring two theologians whose theologies *turn* on more kerygmatic and analogical viewpoints (Barth) and on a *(re)turn* to black religio-cultural sources (Cone)? How can we today (re)interpret these two in what I believe is a burgeoning age of the imagination? How can we, Barth suggests, "*say the same thing* in other words," and not "say the same thing *in other words*?"[6] In essence, how can we say the

3. In invoking the language of a "theology of playful freedom," I find myself in profound solidarity with Raymond Kemp Anderson, who coined this term. Anderson, an independent-thinking theologian, was one of Karl Barth's last doctoral students. See my foreword to his important book called *New Testament Micro-Ethics*: Carr, "The Living God and Playful Encounter," ix–xi.

4. Hentoff, *Jazz Life*, 194. Note that even the (de)*constructive* emphasis turns on the constructive.

5. Van der Bliek, *Thelonious Monk Reader*, 117.

6 *CD* I/1:345. Emphasis in original. Cf. K. Barth, *Barth in Conversation*, 3:229. In his advice to a young Indian theologian (named Jevis), Barth sums up what this

same thing differently and still proclaim the gospel of freedom without losing the vitality between the object of revelation and the aesthetic surplus of our histories?

In my view, one way of saying the same thing differently is to hear Monk's compositional stylistics as a sign or witness to the kingdom of God, viz, as a form of testifying to God's musicality, the subject matter of faith (*die Sache*), and a way to transcend the limitations that accompany much of our conceptual modes of discourse about creation. This means we should stretch to hear Monk's attention to the melody, his bold rhythms, and his harmonics as representative of more than mere musical relationships. For if we hear in Monk's music a harmonics analogous to the harmony of redemption, then we can imagine his music as representing this *more than*, and hear beyond the counterpoint that exists between Barth and Cone.

When imagining Monk as an icon, we are able to articulate a vision of faith outside the walls of the church (*extra muros ecclesia*). Of course, our listening should be done while maintaining respect for the proper sequence, order, or priority between God and all things other than God; between the eternal and temporal, redemption and creation, and Christian faith and praxis. Monk's stylistics spring open to the abundance of phenomena in creation, metaphorically suggesting as a paradigm the various ways our world can be interpreted, i.e., its brilliant corners, its rhythmic displacements, its dissonant harmonies, its alignments, conjunctives and disjunctives that all characterize the diversity and versatility between God and history, even demanding that we embrace a more enchanted view of the world.

This irreversible and irreducible relationship between God and "the other" (and otherkind and God) provides a foretaste of the kingdom of God and the earth, meaning the grace of God as it resides in every domain, including the temporal, the profane, the secular, post-secular, and the suffering of life where the silent harmonies of infinite mercy often speaks its peace. Such domains are not less important because of what we endure, but more important because materiality must be imagined in light of God's own identification with the world.[7] For this reason we began first with the sacred

approach means for an indigenous theology. Cf. Carr, *Epistrophy*, 122–23, 130, 134.

7. Here I appeal to the Christian church, a forerunner of this "kingdom," and the academy or other religious and nonreligious institutions in America. I confess that I refer to "America" with a thickness beyond its normal usage. I have in mind a kind of creolization as a microcosm, which is a form of diversity typically identified regionally within places like New Orleans or the multiculturalism in a city like Los Angeles or New York, i.e., regions in the nation that include ancestral, aboriginal, and even modern connotations of what it means to live in the United States. These ways of being are often marginalized in traditional American self-understandings. Cf. Long, "New Orleans as American City."

harmonies existing between Barth and Cone and my interpretation of their turning points, which produced the emphatic trends I employ in order to (re)imagine the relationship between God (in Barth) and humanity (in Cone).

As noted in the preface, I return to "Epistrophy" in this final chapter to "vamp and fade"; setting forth an opportunity to hear the harmony existing in the seemingly dichotomous relationship between these two principal notes in our theological music. In counterpoint, Barth and Cone represent the yin and yang of freedom and liberation. Like the meeting between Martin and Malcolm in Cone's thinking, a rapprochement between Barth and Cone has a range of symbolic meanings for black theology and theology in general.[8] If we attend to the existential depths of faith in the alternating action between freedom and liberation, if we listen to the silences, junctures, and ambiguities, betwixt and between the loci of our lives, then we can come to terms with the false sense of security we place in our adamant claims to truth and authority. I think then we have a chance to truly understand what Monk's harmonic language represents for theology. Therefore, I appeal to the deeper harmony created by the God who finds human beings in a world of darkness and makes the oppressed's condition God's condition.

Attending to this harmony means acknowledging new modes of expression that accompany black religion in ever new contexts. So rather than simply "improvising on the *melody*" as is most common to Barth's style of theology or "*improvising* on the melody" as accented in Cone's God talk, I employ another pedagogical slogan to witness to this deeper harmony: "I improvise on the melody *at the rendezvous.*" Thus, the harmonious thinking I am advancing here is inclusive of a variety of voicings that revolve around the cantus firmus, the divine center, that gives meaning to the institutions, creeds, the apostolate, and "other" religious and nonreligious witnesses that materialize episodically at a distance from the divine center. To be sure, it invites us to affirm and attend to our radical differences from the standpoint of the resounding unity heard in the Du Boisean "Tone too deep for sound," a mysterious unity that extends beyond the relationship between Barth and Cone, whose theologies are nevertheless fundamental resources for the imaginative theological reflection I offer in this book.[9]

This harmonious interplay also moves in a direction from a christological concentration to what I identify as a pneumatological expansion. I use Monk's music *and* his experience, understood as a secular parable, to attend to what Max Weber called the *religiös unmusikalisch*, the religiously

8. Cone, *Martin & Malcolm & America*, 3. Cf. Cone's conversation in Kirylo and Cone, "Paulo Freire, Black Theology," 208–9.

9. "The Revelation of Saint Orgne," in Du Bois, *Writings*, 1062.

unmusical soul of modern humanity.[10] Weber's apt phrase brilliantly captures how Western culture attunes to the divine. The West's so-called "coming of age" has led to disenchantment with the divine. It is no secret in the modern "West" that many disciplines have excluded the religious life, drawing instead on methodologies that give pride of place to the legacy of nonreligious modernity.[11] The specter of secularism haunts American society; but the description of a religiously unmusical soul, while apt for many who privilege European traditions, fails when broadly applied to black Americans. To be frank, it is rather naïve to presume that black religious experience is somehow coterminous with the white imaginary. Blacks in America resist the ways white nationalism, colonialism, and even American religion have framed this culture. As a matter of fact, when such discussions are broached theologically in the Western world order, there is seldom an acknowledgment of the uniqueness of black soul, black rhythms, black religion, or black cultural consciousness functioning as a critical component of the American theopolitical economy.

To address why terms such as *religiös unmusikalisch* are uncritically and presumptuously applied universally to oppressed persons, particularly as an object of the postmodern/Christian world, I employ below the metaphor of Minton's Playhouse as a way of highlighting how black nonreligious and religious identities congregated and developed organizing frameworks for their free play. Thinking in the mode of Monk takes seriously the harmony between the internal consciousness of the "black soul of reborn humanity" and sites, such as Minton's, that provide the external space (or ground) for radical human experience in America. To suggest otherwise, especially akin to those who misread Weber's insight, applying nonreligious ways of being too broadly, is to conceal from America both the tragic dimensions of its experiences and the possibilities that arise from the dissonances and tensions emerging from the interplay between Europeans in North America (who "quickly developed a sense of being 'white people' distinct and apart from blacks whom they enslaved"[12]) and those "others" who represent counterpoints to their ways of being. To state the matter more succinctly, neither Weber nor Vahanian, who builds on Weber's insight, can be referring to "the souls of black folk" when speaking of the unmusical soul. As C. Eric Lincoln, Lawrence Mamiya, Charles Long, Jon Michael Spencer, and many others testify, religious consciousness is constitutive of the black experience,

10. See Gabriel Vahanian, who employs Weber's term in *Wait Without Idols*, 43.

11. Here I am indebted to Charles H. Long. See "Mircea Eliade and the Imagination of Matter," in Long, *Ellipsis*, 117; and Cox, *Feast of Fools*, 167–68.

12. Noel, *Black Religion*, 5.

which is evident in the correspondence between African heritage *and* their conversion to Christianity.[13] God, of course, is reducible to neither.

This criticism does not mean, of course, that black experience and Western paradigms of progress are mutually exclusive from one another. There is no radical disharmony, but there is discord, non-Procrustean, without conscripting human life in the world and forcing upon these "others" the preestablished harmonies determined by powers, institutions, and ideologies in the world come of age. The blues tradition with its dissonances and laments reveals, by contrast, the creative imagination that resists Western overdetermination, being fired within the crucible of oppression in American society. As Amiri Baraka occasionally riffs more colorfully, blues and jazz traditions reveal the truth that "jazz artists mastered European instruments."[14]

It therefore strains credulity to suggest that the musical souls of black folk that function as the channel by which "believers may devote themselves to greater service to God and humanity" is somehow lost in the disenchantment born of modern skepticism.[15] This supposition on the other hand validates my summons to white Americans to become cocreators with blacks as fellow witnesses to the new creation, rather than framing black folk into specious arguments based on fabricated orientations. Faith witnesses not only to a radical harmony between God and humanity, but also to formative contacts and exchanges that occur between humankind and otherkind in the modern world.

This aspiration justifies why Barth, when read contrapuntally with Cone, is a useful theological resource, since his attention to the harmony of redemption highlights the ground tone on which the improvised community of blacks *and others* witness to Christ's reconciliation. This (re)orientation, based on the reconciling work of Christ and the liberating work of the Spirit, is the epistrophe; the turning about of the soul and the recognition of saving knowledge (the new orientation) whereby we assent to a more profound relationship to humanity and God. It represents, moreover, the way beyond disagreements that hinder our multidialogical and multidimensional solidarity with one another.

Barth's assessment of Schleiermacher is instructive at this point. Regarding his disagreements with Schleiermacher, Barth attested to redemptive solidarity, stating that in the eschaton, "there will be agreement in the disagreement, and no more disagreement in agreement."[16] Such harmony

13. See Lincoln and Mamiya, "Religious Dimension."

14. Baraka, *Blues People*, 70–80.

15. Riedel, *Soul Music*, 47.

16. Godsey, *Karl Barth's Table Talk*, 14.

finds its melodic foundation in the christological center of the church. This center renounces melioristic optimism about the future while advocating for a radical realism about our present reality. Barth (and Cone) rejected such optimism but also accepted dialectically the truth that there is a certain harmony, even in our disagreements. As Barth opined, "It's a great deal that we [the churches] are now talking to one another. And even when we talk alongside one another, there's a certain harmony."[17] This judgment represents an acknowledgment of a peculiar source for our union beyond the soundings of any narrow form of unison. Harmony is thus found in our radical difference and in the polyphony of our being together. This togetherness *in difference* is where the symphony of humankind and even "otherkind"—the otherness in everything—share in a harmonic universe of melodies and countermelodies.

Thinking in this mode will hopefully offer new seeds for contemplation and ways to a new beginning, a new turn, *at the rendezvous*, a beginning that has its locus not in a tune or book or an idea or a color; and not even in a dialectical movement based on reimagined forms of theology, but rather in the eschatological transformation that has already occurred objectively in Christ, the living center of faith, who gifts us with our harmonic language for living in the world. This new mode of being has its ultimate ground in what Du Bois identified as a "Tone too deep for sound—a silent chord of infinite Harmony."[18]

Theological thinking occurs therefore in God's harmonics, in a thoroughgoing eschatological orientation in creation. The call to discourse in this manner is a summons to think in terms of God's free, spiritual movement for the concrete ground of redemption; to think of God's eventful activity in history as demonstrated in the polyphony of voices in religious and nonreligious nations, tribes, and traditions; or put more simply, to think in relation to the action of the God who marshals us into a symphony of harmonized melodies. Indeed, I pray that the tonality of this final critical turning point (*Epistrophy*) resounds in ears bent toward the eschatological tones of the new beginning (*'Round Midnight*) and gifts us all with insight into the mystery of what it means to live in creation (*Misterioso*).

> Like violins, music begins
> It starts to swell, then I can tell
> That pretty soon we going to be in tune
> Our hearts will be in perfect harmony
> —Marvin Gaye, "Symphony"

17. K. Barth, *Final Testimonies*, 28.
18. "The Revelation of Saint Orgne," in Du Bois, *Writings*, 1062.

III

Noon of Night

Improvising on the Melody *at the Rendezvous*

"Watchman, what is left of the night? Watchman, what is left of the night?"
The watchman replies, "Morning is coming, but also the night." (Isa 21:11–12)

To live meaningfully, we must see light beyond the darkness.—James H. Cone[1]

There are also lights in the darkness, clarities in the confusion, constants in the oscillating dialectic of our existence, orders in disorder, certainties in the great sea of doubt.—Karl Barth[2]

Hear the light!—Thelonious Monk[3]

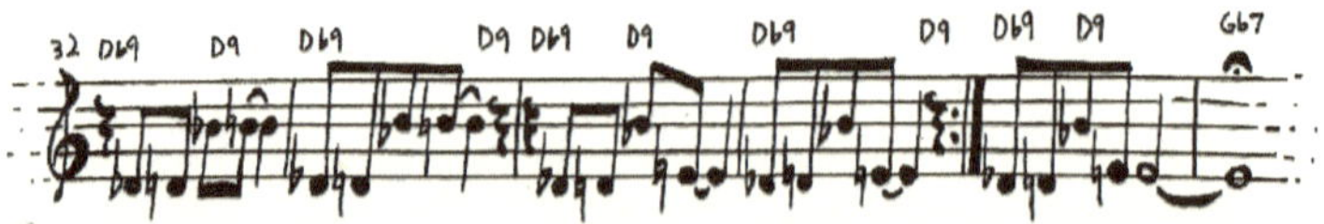

1. Cone, *Cross and Lynching Tree*, 154.

2. *CD* IV/3.1:476.

3. Van der Bliek, *Thelonious Monk Reader*, 56. I have identified no direct quote of Monk saying "hear the light." However, it is reported that Monk wanted his records to help "young, modern musicians hear the light."

As noted in the head above, the song "Epistrophy" represents a new tone for theology in this final chapter. It is an affective tone where the "harmonization" between Cone and Barth is employed to advance new modes of discourse arising from their theological contact and exchange. The convergence between these two theologians corresponds to the interchange between *God* and *humanity*, bridging the impasse that separates theological categories from human experiences. In this respect, Barth and Cone are contrapuntal. When alternating between their accents on the freedom of God (Barth) and the liberation of humanity (Cone), they signal a way to realistically expand and engage in a more complex conversation in modern society (with its postmodern claims of enlightenment and its pragmatic performances of theological praxis). Therefore, in this chapter, I address the essential location or *locus theologicus* for thinking about the rendezvous between Barth and Cone, that is, the American academy. I have chosen this location because the academy represents both a site of contestation and a site of fecundity, being a location with generative possibilities that allows us to think in a constructive direction while keeping in mind the stratagems of a white aesthetic regime.

Although the rationality of academic life often fails black people because of the profound mendacity in American life in general, academia may paradoxically be the setting where a radically inclusive revolutionary Spirit can arise, at least episodically, a Spirit that ameliorates some of our most inveterate problems.[4] Simply put, the academic complex is a setting where there can be a restoration of the problems of the status quo on the one hand, or a revolutionary redemptive Spirit can arise and give way to new modes of thinking, on the other. In this burgeoning age of imagination, it is important to remember that success will come when we acknowledge, as stated best by Malcolm X, that "there just has to be a new system of reason and logic devised by us who are at the bottom, if we want to get some results in this struggle."[5]

Since I ultimately seek a *modus vivendi* between Barth and Cone to champion new theological directions, I privilege Cone's black theology in this chapter. Black theology is more pertinent as a theological approach, even though it remains on the margins of the modern academy, which is turning more deliberately to religious thought. This accent allows me to underscore black religious experience as a paradigm for other victims of history and

4. See Cone's recounting of King's "kitchen table experience," in Cone, *Martin & Malcolm & America*, 124; cf. also his confrontation with the contradictions of seminary education in the face of black students, in Cone, *God of the Oppressed*, 5.

5. Cited in Cone, "Black Theology: Its Origin," 40.

their relationship to the divine center of theology. Moreover, while Barth and Cone are committed to the melody that underlies the differences between them, Cone's accent on experience more directly anticipates the pneumatological direction I believe is necessary for theological advancement. The pneumatological vision of the black church—already resident within Cone's theology—opens to a constructive theological development that honors the aesthetic rhythms of black freedom in America. This aesthetic mode of religious apprehension promotes (re)enactments of faith that qualify the authority of traditional institutional frameworks, creeds, sacraments, and positivistic doctrinal promulgations of historic Christianity.

Furthermore, a liberating freedom in the global context arises from Cone's more qualified vision, and it provokes criticism of secular institutional powers, church authorities, ideological traditions, curricular interests, and aesthetic persuasions that accompany the historic expressions of faith. This constructively supports black resistance against ideological ideations, notably the secular cultural institutions that reinforce and extend the status quo. One example of such an ideology would be American notions of freedom that trade on what Jaroslav Pelikan, following Paul Tillich, called the Protestant principle.[6] These freedoms often rely on older arguments, on questions of authority, and bootstrap mentalities that now depend on the spirit of capitalism, which is rooted in what Willie Jennings has identified as the exclusionary logic of the colonial plantation. Such modes of thought supplement the power valences that reside in the dominant categories of theology—categories we often fail to interrogate and realities we ignore to our peril.

In addition to emphasizing a break from existing historical and hermeneutical frameworks, principles, conventions, and categories, this project champions a turning about (epistrophe) toward a kind of "dark wisdom" that exists on the underside of dominant exclusive realities, being located even in the secular creative sphere that has been captured by Christ, whose redeeming power catalyzes the performative dimensions of faith that are grounded in the pneumatic counterpoint and lived in constant confession and repentance. This faith thrives where churches remain open to the reconciliation (or harmony) with God and to radical communion with improvised religious *and* nonreligious communities.

In this turn toward what I will call *improvised communities*, black churches may find a willing audience within the larger context of the black religious experience. Too many black Americans—because of their tenuous relationship with traditional churches and church structures—have become unchurched and disaffected, but as James Cone would intimate, not

6. Pelikan, *Obedient Rebels.*

irreligious.[7] These unchurched but non-irreligious people ought not be wedded intellectually to an essentialism that minimizes the great diversity among black people, i.e., the different voices and eventful activities arising within black life. Nor should they be tied to a provincial view of the black community—understood in primarily spatial terms such as the churchly sphere or some other religious locale. Black life should not be restricted to either secular meanings or sectarian religious understandings; its complexity and richness are irreducible to a monotonous unison that drowns out difference.

The imaginative reorientation I am suggesting resounds in harmony with the divine and opens to the world's variegated voices and countervoices that have been set free within the social imaginary—above us, below us, around us. It opens to radical acts of love in creation. This is not the harmony criticized by womanist and feminist theologians who are rightfully suspicious of a "harmonizing" that leads certain groups to feel whole in Christ but fail to engage the "dreadful, bloody, brutal reality that we describe with the cross, the ancient symbol of torture" or a harmony that ignores black women who arguably "were sometimes substituted for black men who happened to escape white mob violence."[8] On the contrary, the bounteous God abides at the center of our advocacy for the world and spurs us on to harmonious acts of peace, justice, loyalty, love, and freedom, acts that affirm the radical humanity in women's lives in creation even as it affirms the particularity of all others.

This turn to the God of freedom imparts us with a mode of being that manifests itself in a joyful dance in rhythm with God—a liberated form of playfulness in human life where the creativity and giftedness of the *humanum* is dramatized, not merely in God's presence, but in human solidarity within the orbit of God's redeeming power.[9] This community begins with the Spirit of Christ who creates community, who creates the harmony of life in the free witness to the divine, and who *has been*, *is*, and *will be* the rhythmic source of our redemption. Although churches have not always been so, they are called to be the forerunners of a peculiar form of community and should testify to (re)conceived rhythms and notions of space and time in light of the *giftedness* of God—the God who gifts us with life in

7. James Cone offered this sentiment in his discussion of the blues as secular spirituals: *Spirituals and the Blues*, 97–100. Cf. Noel, *Black Religion*, 79.

8. Soelle, *On Earth as in Heaven*, 95. Cf. Cone, *Cross and Lynching Tree*, 120–51 (esp. 121). Cone here powerfully appeals to Delores Williams to question the "surrogate roles black women have been forced to assume by white men and women as well as black men." Cf. Carr, *Epistrophy*, ch. 3.

9. Barth discusses the *humanum* and the concrete possibility of Christ in *CD* IV/2:48–49.

the redeeming power of Christ through which we dance within the orbit of redemption in ways that reflect noncompetitive harmonies and shape what we *know* and *do.* Because of the general negligence of churches, we should always be prepared to hear the Spirit's witness *extra muros ecclesia* (outside the walls of the church), a truth that brings me to Minton's Playhouse as a parabolic expression of God's creation.

Minton's Playhouse and God's Playground: Hearing the Light 'Round Midnight

At the beginning it is important to remember that bebop as a genre of music occurred in a world where the artists who created it were treated as second-class citizens. Their sociopolitical context privileged the de jure rules of Jim Crow. Thelonious Monk, Charlie Parker, Dizzy Gillespie, Mary Lou Williams, and many others composed and performed in a strange land where on certain occasions, according to Gerald Horne, they came into sharp conflict with the metaphorical midnight in the American political order. Horne recalls, for instance, that "when they played in Los Angeles in the early 1940s, they were treated like lepers, and even worse. . . . Their music was either laughed at or violently attacked and one radio station officially banned it."[10] Monk and his friends did not make music by changing their world, however. They made music by affirming their aesthetic imaginations and pivoting into their own testimony, into a world of life-affirming witness, despite all the pain. Even as America remained hostile and unchanged, captured by the dark ideology and mood of the distinctive American zeitgeist in the first half of the twentieth century, jazz artists engaged in history-making endeavors that sustained their humanity.

In essence they embraced life, redeemed the time, and sought to actualize their humanity during the midnight hour. And because the matrix out of which jazz developed was already deeply shaped by what Cornel West identifies as strong institutional channels that supported the black musical tradition, it was possible for black agency to be celebrated and sustained.[11] In much the same way that books helped Richard Wright, the author, to imagine a sense of freedom in the southern darkness, the aesthetic creations of jazz artists and their performances at Minton's Playhouse and other so-called hot spots benefited from the spatiotemporal dynamics that allowed Monk and others to affirm their humanity in a hostile world—a strange,

10. Horne, *Jazz and Justice*, 95.

11. West, *Cornel West Reader*, 306.

alienated world that often made no sense.[12] Minton's thus became the "incubator of bop" or modern jazz. But it was more than this. It was the birthplace of a revolutionary mood and spirit in humanity, being lively and filled with "living, dancing, and drinking . . . as if everyone was talking at the same time." Neil Leonard describes the community there as "one big, happy family on 118th Street."[13]

The affirmative nature of this community therefore plays a powerful role in the developing of the music since the *epistrophe*, the turn that accompanies an encounter with otherness, is linked to the dynamics of their proximity in a peculiar place of authenticity, simplicity, and impassioned commonality. Hence, the community itself was something akin to a living congregation with its unique priestcraft, serving both the creation and development of their music and testifying to their common humanity. As Ingrid Monson points out, jazz artists were not only the cultural heroes in locations like Minton's and Five Spot, but the racial hierarchy in a world full of noise, hatred, conflict, and disdain was "symbolically inverted, with black excellence setting the aesthetic standards by which non-African American musicians were evaluated rather than vice versa."[14] Thus places like Minton's already had secreted within them—for those who can hear the parable—the same pattern we observe in the gospel community. It was a world whose model testified analogically to the belief that the first shall become last and the last become first.

The representational meaning of places like Minton's is thus relevant theologically. Since the church represents the firstfruits of a spatiotemporal gathering where people, in a mode akin to jazz musicians, gather in solidarity to humanize, edify, and create frameworks that make for human flourishing, jazz artists in such locations represent a parable of the momentary liberation from social death that is experienced in the institutional legacy of the Atlantic world whose slave ethics still reverberate in many of the policies, systems, and social structures within the US. With black music being "the first major cultural point of contact between whites and blacks," the spirituals, blues, and jazz not only had a major impact on America's democratic values, but also profoundly shaped the religious and nonreligious contours of the nation, appealing to the antiestablishment youth and the rise of rock, rhythm and blues, and hip-hop.[15] The question is how do we use

12. See Wright's quote as an important epigraph in Cone, *Cross and Lynching Tree*, xiii.

13. Quoted in Leonard, *Jazz*, 78–79.

14. See Monson, *Freedom Sounds*, 170–71; Born et al., *Improvisation and Social Aesthetics*, 79.

15. West, *Democracy Matters*, 92–93.

these paradigms to unmask chthonic powers and confront the havoc left by the white aesthetic regime?

Experiences akin to those that occurred at Minton's also reveal why we must maintain James Cone's emphasis on the "secular" in the black religious experience. In Cone's estimation the religious experience is "secular only to the extent that it is earthy and seldom uses 'God' or 'Christianity' as the chief symbols of its hopes and dreams." These experiences conceal within themselves the special charismata of the black church's meaning in the world. In this case, then, secular does not mean anti-religious or even nonreligious. The sacredness of the secular is tethered to its creation, being "created out of the same historical community as the church experience and thus represents the people's attempt to shape life and live it according to their dreams and aspirations."[16] Cone's audacity to wrestle with the history of black experience as a symbolic expression of the gospel is born out of this orientation. While Barth likewise conceded that "God may also speak from outside the Church as we now know it or as it really is," and that the "cosmos now *becomes* a parable" in light of the governing agency of God, he did not audaciously construct his theology in this direction, except for scattered appeals to Mozart and other words, lights, and truths.[17] Barth's theology of culture was underdeveloped to some extent, an oversight that should be taken seriously.

When assessed in view of the life-affirming activities of these early boppers, Cone's emphasis reminds us of the reasons why such humanizing activities are significant and worthy of the attention of theologians. To be sure, although much of this improvising or free play began in seminal jam sessions at Minton's Playhouse and not the church house, these locations, whose architecture was aesthetically and pragmatically reminiscent of storefront churches, became the genesis of a revolutionary spirit that transcended bourgeois culture, commodity fetishism, and even conventional jazz rituals. The quasi-ritualistic style of dress, language, and attempts at individuation were clearly testimonials to their radical sense of humanity in a world that demonized and marginalized black creative productions, even as it capitalized on their inspired genius to promote a form of progress that trivialized their humanity. But despite the so-called darkness of their world, Monk and other creatives, in Monk's words, "heard the light" in the darkness and lived into what Martin Luther King Jr. called "the sunlight of opportunity," into the grace of creation—God's playground.

16. Cone, *God of the Oppressed*, 22. Cf. Cone, "Dialectic of Theology and Life," 80.

17. K. Barth, *Heidelberg Catechism*, 61–62. Emphasis in original. Cf. *CD* I.1:81; IV/3.1.

Minton's Playhouse as a Witness to God's Playground

The need to "hear the light"[18] leads us to think with Jürgen Moltmann, who noted that "the conflict between the rising sun and the departing shadows of the night is already being fought out."[19] This conflict sits at the heart of reality, and we cannot resolve it by evading or simply (re)imagining the darkness in the secular world as being somehow separate from the light. The light shines in darkness! Thus, our critique and creativity are symbolized in secular spaces, and at the heart of human creativity resides the sacred in the depths of the secular, albeit in its broken witness.[20] This reality for Monk and his fellow musicians can be heard in the unconventional symbolism of Minton's Playhouse, a space where musicians thrived in what seemed like an alternative reality, enjoying the opposite side of the hardness of the life they endured in America.

This symbolic view of creation does not presuppose two worlds. It takes for granted the new creation that sits at the heart of the old and witnesses to a noncompetitive harmony between the Creator God (the giver of every good and perfect gift) and the versatility and inexhaustibility of the various witnesses in creation. Barth argued that the "freedom of the saints is grounded and enclosed . . . in the dignity and power of the gift made, or rather of the Giver of this gift, in the freedom of the royal man Jesus to whom they are summoned to look."[21] So, in recalling Monk's accent, analogically, on the melody as the centering reality for thinking of the relationship between our part and the whole, I imaginatively think in a mode *from* and *to* God to embrace the aesthetica, the great versatility of witnesses in the world, and to inspire us to celebrate past traditions without measuring them by one-dimensional methodological metrics or the modern scientific protocols of the contemporary academy. Of course I do not intend to crudely dismiss modern ways of knowing. Thinking in Monk mode revels in no break with the past. It, rather, celebrates the past and its variations, i.e., new tones, new harmonic structures, new rhythms, even as it (re)purposes the resources of our predecessors, venerating the past and voicing new chords. Just like Monk recomposed or reassembled the "stuff" of the past.

My hermeneutical dependence on the way Monk approached composing, particularly his way of recombining the past and the present, draws on the fuller meaning of "improvisation" that is deployed throughout this project. Much like the improvised constructions of a French bricoleur I use

18 Van der Bliek, *Thelonious Monk Reader*, 56.

19. Moltmann, *Source of Life*, 72.

20. Paul Tillich argued for a similar point: *Theology of Culture*, 9.

21. *CD* IV/2:531. See Jas 1:17.

the term "improvisation" to describe my efforts to fabricate a theology out of the brilliance of Barth's and Cone's insights and then, secondarily, I refer to the spontaneous variations required to improvise theologically while engaging existing melodies and rhythms in the world. Being equivalent to a form of bricolage, this form of improvisation often remains unexamined in view of the more prevalent understandings of improvisation, that is, improvisation as extemporizing in music making.

This former, painstaking aspect of composition in jazz is rarely appreciated and seldom discussed. Many listeners are unaware of the part of Monk's jazz where he draws on the vitality and versatility of jazz traditions that preceded and informed his efforts at composing. This aspect of his jazz is present in "'Round Midnight" where he constantly returns and reworks the song, improving on what some call the "wrong mistakes" he made.[22] This background reveals Monk's recognizable contributions to the genre; and as noted by Robin Kelley, it calls attention to Monk's inventive style, proving that he did not just sit at the piano and play in a rough-hewn and willy-nilly fashion. His music was practiced and his developmental logic was honed thoughtfully even when improvising spontaneously.[23]

Monk's procedure of thoughtfully honing one's craft applies to what I am calling "theology in the mode of Monk." Intending to advance a more creative theological effort, at least aesthetically, I acknowledge the various ways theology can be crafted and the way a theological world can be created, if theologians remain open to the various and sundry turns and (re)turns that are often trivialized because of the complex demands of a peculiar historical locatedness or *locus theologicus*. Otherwise, the existing conceptions of theological discourse will reify and become a hindrance to our theological creativity. Andrew Greeley, the Catholic sociologist and popular novelist, recognized this failure as a problem in the modern theological imagination.[24] So what is needed today is the creative space to (re)envision theology so as not to repeat the mistakes of the past. Barth notably came to a similar conclusion after wrestling with Schleiermacher for many years.

Writing in a postscript for his book *The Theology of Schleiermacher*, Barth deliberated with the theologian he considered to be the "church father of the nineteenth (and also the twentieth?!) century."[25] He articulated

22. I am dependent on Kelley, whose definitive work on Monk has no parallel. Listen to Monk "in progress": "'Round Midnight (In Progress)," https://www.youtube.com/watch?v=ZYT5HNgPbBY&t=203s.

23. See Kelley, "Secret Life," 9; cf. Szwed, *Jazz 101*, 171–73.

24. Greeley, *God in Popular Culture*, 9–12.

25. K. Barth, *Theology of Schleiermacher*, 261.

unforeseeable turning points as he continued to glean from Schleiermacher's sermons, letters, and other writings that eventually came into his possession. He discovered new information he had not considered about his predecessor. Eventually, his experiences and encounters with new writings deepened his understanding of Schleiermacher's efforts to craft theology in general. Barth even concluded that Schleiermacher's Copernican revolution was more the result of "an older development rather than the initiation of a new one."[26] Thus his reading of this "father of modern liberal theology" revealed that his precursor's theology remained worthy of consideration, and his personal critique and direction reflected his own idiosyncratic intellectual and creative choices. Such experiences disclose an important truth about theology, viz, that the Spirit of God often uses human beings whose insights bear implicit ambiguities, contradictions, and personal predilections that remain extant even when one responds in an extemporaneous manner to peculiar historical circumstances during critical moments in history.

The sources Barth used to construct his "regular theology," for instance, included his exposure to grand theological visions that he integrated from the thought of theologians such as Augustine, Luther, Calvin, and—more contemporaneously—Friedrich Schleiermacher and Herman Bavinck. His coterie of theological voices also included somewhat overlooked "irregular" thinkers such as Hermann Kutter, Leonard Ragaz, Franz Overbeck, and particularly the stylized sermonic contributions of the Blumhardts, father and son. As we have seen throughout his development, these and many other contemporaries resourced and provided momentum to Barth's recasting of modern theology.

The same is true, *mutatis mutandis*, for James Cone. As mentioned in the first two volumes of *Theology in the Mode of Monk*, Cone was profoundly influenced by the work of several predecessors, including Karl Barth, Paul Tillich, Reinhold Niebuhr, and other theological luminaries of his day.[27] But, more importantly, Cone incorporated the insights of Martin Luther King Jr., Malcolm X, James Baldwin, and contemporaries such as Charles Long, Gayraud Wilmore, William Jones, and black womanist theologians, such as Delores Williams and Katie Cannon, and many others who supported and challenged him as he encountered and endured the crucible of American oppression. He was further buoyed in his thought by what he called "other black expressions," including folktales, black artists, and the aesthetics of the spirituals, blues, and so-called "secular spiritual" contributions. Cone curated his theological resources and responded in a distinctive cultural

26. K. Barth, *Göttingen Dogmatics*, 9.

27. In conversation, James Cone once mentioned to me his deep appreciation for Thomas Merton.

milieu, even as he contributed to the discipline in a way that reflected his experiences, interests, stylistics, and tastes.

Such reframing of things is not necessarily a revolution in the classical sense, but it is revolutionary in its turning to something new. As noted in *Epistrophy* (ch. 1), bop was born of a revolutionary spirit in much the same way the theologies of Karl Barth and James Cone materialized during the cultural zeitgeist of their day. Events coalesced and opened doors to new ways of making theological music. These developments reveal what makes Thelonious Monk's music such a fitting parable to imagine Barth's and Cone's theological development. Monk's improvising on the melody was an exercise designed to make sense out of a world where the break from the past, the emphasis on small improvising quintets, and the focus on inventive themeless chord changes rather than melodies required that a sense of order be brought to the music—if one planned to make a real contribution to the genre.[28] I think the sense of order Monk brought to bebop is one of the reasons Monk is described as a bebopper who never played bebop. Indeed, he transcended bop in the way he created a world in the midst of a so-called revolutionary moment. Stanley Crouch is one of many who described Monk as conducting what I refer to as a "revolution within a revolution."[29] In so doing, Monk attests, analogically, to a revolution beyond all revolutions, that is, an existing truth beyond human revolutions.

Theology Without Aesthetics?

Still, even revolutions are threatened by the way various "principalities and powers" function within the ordered world. Such competing structures or powers possess the potential to constrain humanity, particularly where there is no aesthetic sense or where aesthetic symmetry is predetermined by some other regime of thought.[30] For this reason, the will to freedom or self-affirmation as demonstrated in jazz is important for theologians. Theomusicology as developed by Jon Spencer, for example, follows this line, viewing

28. See M. Williams, "What Kind of Composer," 435.

29. Crouch locates the language of revolution in the movement. He states that Monk "brought about a movement within a movement," a point that I interpret as a revolution within the revolutionary movement of bebop. See Crouch, *Considering Genius*, 88. See also where he quotes Regis Debray, who states that Monk was conducting a "revolution within the revolution" (86). I should note that my language of revolution comes from the left-wing Barthian tradition.

30. For insight into the way a predetermined racial aesthetic can shape our ways of seeing the world, see W. Jennings, "Aesthetic Struggle."

"music as a transparency through which to peer upon deeper ideas."[31] The same is true of the encounter between artists. For where jazz aesthetics and ethics correspond, the surplus from aesthetics often overcomes the impasse between aesthetics and ethics.

Because aesthetics in the main are presupposed in African American classical music, the need to establish an aesthetic ground was not a primary issue in the world of jazz. The question of a black aesthetic in theology, however, was an issue fraught with problems and possibilities. But what is the black aesthetic? Who or what determines blackness? As a matter of fact, in the jazz world, aesthetic styles tended to be "more malleable, mobile and pluralistic than social structures despite their roots in particular cultural communities and geographical locations."[32] There are as many ways to be a jazz musician as there are ways to play a melody.[33] In the world of theology, however, aesthetics encounter a different kind of resistance, since modern academic settings and churches exist within fundamental, almost unacknowledged aesthetic orders; and the attendant discipline of our concern, i.e., theology, routinely appropriates modes of thought and categories that are governed by sociocultural contexts and designed to secure certain fixed hierarchical structures within the world.

This domesticating agenda may partly explain why Barth and Cone were so sharply criticized for their theological innovations and revisions of Christian faith. Because doctrinal frameworks are often designed to protect existing structures of power from uncomfortable truths that are subversive to their history, they often have to be turned upside down from the bottom up, rather than addressed from the top down.[34] These powers also must be (de)constructed, meaning they must be recast from our own constructive mode of thinking.

This tension between human agency and the influence of the market morality that reigns in the corporate sector makes its appearance precisely at the point of aesthetics. The sociocultural problem of black affirmation means that composers of modern jazz provide an important analogue for articulating the assertion of freedom in the midst of various forms of institutionalization. Modern institutions are primarily concerned with production and profit or "products over promise."[35] Still, in terms of aesthetics,

31. Spencer, *Theological Music*, 146.

32. Monson, *Freedom Sounds*, 74.

33. See Gordon, *Her Majesty's Other Children*, 220.

34. Cf. Gutiérrez, *Power of the Poor*, 21.

35. Gerald Horne provides an insightful discussion of how Jim Crow and economic decisions to tax dance halls impacted black music: *Jazz and Justice*, 97–98.

I am less interested in black aesthetics as a terminological concept (or in terms of the malleable and mobile nature of aesthetics) and more interested in the forces that tend to overdetermine, flatten, and frame black aesthetic sensibilities that, when turning to music, have the potential to provide important insights and inspiration for thinking theologically and living improvisationally. James Baldwin, for instance, in his essay called "The Uses of the Blues," paved the way toward using the blues as a metaphor for life. He was hoping that Americans would take advantage of the possibility of learning from the spirituals, the blues, and jazz to gain insight and inspiration from their great contributions to the nation.

Although he did not identify it, Baldwin explored what Charles Long identified as "negative revelations," that is, experiences that insinuate themselves in the West, even as it seeks to refine itself and create a new era by ignoring such experiences.[36] The truth is the modern world fails to account for such experiences. Baldwin contends that Americans "came from Europe, we came from Africa, we came from all over the world. We brought whatever was in us from China or from France. We *all* brought it with us. We were not transformed when we crossed the ocean. Something else happened. . . . We no longer had any way of finding out, of knowing who we were."[37] Thus, in Baldwin's view, America's failure to come to terms with the blue note of American experience—coupled with racism and extreme materialism—cheated us all out of a deeper sense of humanity. Even now our tendency to avoid the chaos, the ambiguity, and the reality of the tragic plagues our churches, which have become sites designed to escape death rather than avenues to encounter and confront it.[38] But it is not merely forms of death we end up escaping. We fail to engage the mundane, the ordinary, ignoring the profane realities in the world and overlooking the "lights in the darkness, clarities in confusion, constants in the oscillating dialectic of our existence, orders in disorder, certainties in the great sea of doubt, genuine speaking and hearing even in the labyrinth of human speech."[39]

This insight suggests that current tensions with institutional powers, even with their capacity to conscript human life and fashion it in their image, are latent with possibilities, harboring the potential to teach us to confront life-affirming realities in the midst of death again. And similar to Baldwin, Cone believed the spirituals did not seek escape from various

36. Long, "Passage and Prayer," 15–16; cf. Baldwin, *Cross of Redemption*, 61.

37. Baldwin, *Cross of Redemption*, 61. Emphasis in original. See West, who highlights Baldwin on the importance of black thought and culture: *Democracy Matters*, 84–85.

38. Cone, *Cross and Lynching Tree*, 63–65.

39. *CD* IV/3.1:476.

sufferings in the world, for "slaves faced the reality of the world 'ladened wid trouble, an' burden'd wid grief,' but they believed that they could go to Jesus in secret and get relief."[40] In going to Jesus, slaves expected to achieve a radical community. Barth, on the contrary, described the church's resistance as a form of tension-filled "revolt against disorder," while others described Barth's position as going "against the stream," with the implication being that the eschatological impulse in the life of the church always places the church in a peculiar tension with traditions, institutions, ideologies, methodologies, categories, etc.

Simultaneously, for Barth, the eschatological impulse relativizes any theology, especially those that claim to have no aesthetics, since pneumatology embraces the subjectivity and the historically effective consciousness of those who are theologizing, including both affective aesthetic and rational discursive categories, which are often falsely separated. Said differently, the Spirit of God embraces the entire person, soul and body, sacred and secular, temporal and eternal. The Spirit of Christ is indeed the locus where such differences are distinguished, affirmed, and harmonized. Perhaps for this reason Barth "believed that the problem of art or the arts must be dealt with in connection with the eschatological apocalypse," and he, moreover, outlined this in his earliest version of ethics.[41]

We are free to ask, of course, if theology—or any cultural form of expression—is ever truly without aesthetics. For even when the aesthetic dimension is suppressed, ignored, avoided, or seemingly eclipsed by an outside agency, there remains the question of whether a cultural aesthetic is still present or not. This problem is revealed in the anecdotal experience of Donald Byrd, the bebop jazz trumpeter and educator, who wrestled with this question in his article called "Music Without Aesthetics." Using a straightforward realism, Byrd drew attention to the way crucial factors beyond music influenced the *what* and *how* of his composing.[42] He maintained that "non-musical forces and institutions"—existing outside his music—overdetermined black music and impacted its creative impulse, shaping how the music was developed and deployed. Byrd scrutinized the conspicuous influence of record companies and other corporate entities on his music. Like Alain Locke and Harlem Renaissance scholars, Byrd identified the "white-dominated commercial industry as the problematic variable."[43]

40. Cone, *Spirituals and the Blues*, 57.

41. K. Barth, *Letters*, 100.

42. Byrd, "Music Without Aesthetics," 2.

43. Spencer, *Theological Music*, 146.

What he sensed was not merely a kind of white paternalism, channeled through an institutional apparatus; Byrd intuited the ideological interests of record companies and their attendant emphases on economics. These powers operated in an economically oriented, custodial relationship to black creative products, and such commercial enterprises exerted power and influence that is still more characterized by "its capacity as a corporate entity or a business enterprise."[44] Byrd properly identified this influence as a "non-aesthetic environment," and in such environments black aesthetics become auxiliary, relegated to an inferior status, or ignored altogether. Thus, if we hear the light in Byrd's notion of "music without aesthetics," we gain insight into a problem that is not limited to the music industry nor is it representative of only a negative relationship.[45]

As a musician Byrd was sensitive to the impact of record companies on his creative contributions and this reveals the discontinuity between his worldview and the commercial agenda executed by the custodians of record companies. These custodians in his view represented a locus of *power* that was "soulless and *unmusical*."[46] The problem was not just that these forces diminished black creativity; it cut deeper. They were ultimately "disharmonious to the social fabric of black music." This situation provoked a central controlling question for Byrd, a query we shall examine below in a theological context: "The question is [writes Byrd] can black people afford to become involved in using white standards of measuring greatness and thereby contributing to those forces which stifle creativity and give false direction to our music?"[47]

In essence, Byrd's concerns beg the question of whether black identity and black music can be channeled to spring from black giftedness rather than being co-opted by institutional powers that racialize, commercialize, and unscrupulously editorialize black life. While the power to shape the aesthetic range of our choices is not limited solely to the banal processes often tied to production itself—whether we are speaking of music or other black creative contributions—the question as to how we liberate ourselves from such powers to (re)channel the heroic energy to strike a blow against materialism remains extant. The cultural critic bell hooks correctly identifies this problem, proposing that in America we are subject to an "ideological framework that breeds domination and a culture of repression."[48] For this reason

44. Byrd, "Music Without Aesthetics," 2.

45. See W. Jennings, *Christian Imagination*, 279–82.

46. Byrd, "Music Without Aesthetics," 3. Emphasis in original.

47. Byrd, "Music Without Aesthetics," 5.

48. hooks, *Outlaw Culture*, 146–47.

we must repudiate both racism and an ethic of materialism, for not only do whites benefit from the structured nature of a one-dimensional society that is rooted in productive forces that commercialize and commodify human life, but many blacks and people of color participate in the established rhythms of this market morality. This explains to some extent the effeteness that accompanies a politics of respectability in academic settings.[49]

Thelonious Monk Created a World[50]

In relation to Barth's and Cone's accomplishments, a way to illuminate this "playground" is to recall the description Gabriel Solis used to describe Monk's composing. Solis describes Monk as "creating a world."[51] So when composing, Monk displayed a kind of self-referentiality in his musical thinking that revealed the distinctive nature of his music, that is, his radical subjectivity. For example, Solis appeals to Monk's early version of the song "Blue Monk" where, during his playing of an extended solo, Monk referenced songs from earlier compositions. He did this frequently, and he also forecasted songs not yet recorded.[52] Monk's world of self-referentiality sounded a break with the old world by redeeming past traditions and introducing new possibilities—including black sacred music and stride piano. In doing so Monk forged a new sonic future.

He not only created a world in terms of playful self-referentiality in the music; but he also coined imaginative titles when choosing names for his songs: "Epistrophy," "Misterioso," "Pannonica," "Crepes with Nellie," and "Rhythm-a-ning," to name a few. All these tunes reveal Monk's sense of agency expressed in an act of self-definition. This act of naming requires that we understand and appreciate his creative musical sensibilities as we enter his world, and his life to some extent. One must come to terms with not only his intent but also the ambiguity residing in his choices.

Theologically, this act of naming recalls, symbolically, human participation in the act of creation, although the biblical text and later interpretations need a good bit of demythologization. In the Genesis account, for

49. This background or soundscape led James Cone to express a profound concern about second-generation black theologians who seemed more concerned with careerism than with a commitment to the cross. See Cone, *For My People*, 24–28.

50. In this section I am reminded of my debt to the indispensable research of Gabriel Solis, whose oral history composed of interviews with Monk's contemporaries provided remarkable insights into Monk's world. See Solis: *Monk's Music*, 56–59; "Hearing Monk."

51. Solis, *Monk's Music*, 56–60.

52. Solis, *Monk's Music*, 57.

instance, through the *act of naming* one encounters a narrative about power, agency, and the question of free participation in the creative order, an important act especially in a world where hierarchical claims are often made in light of a privileged caste. Hence, this creative act of naming, especially for the oppressed, redounds to the question of self-definition, self-agency, and self-affirmation as is evident in the long history of blacks in America who existed as numberless souls who still wrestle with divergent views revolving around names such as Negro, Black, or African American. These names are transposed or easily lost in our more generic terms such as "people of color" or mixed race. Indeed, throughout this text I have emphasized primarily the term "black theology" in order to echo the aesthetics of color symbolism deployed by James Cone in his immediate sociopolitical setting, rather than choosing for instance the term "African American theology."[53] I have also chosen "black theology" rather than Charles Long's term "theologies opaque," which can subtly center whiteness even as it exposes it.

In addition to producing a specific nomenclature for his music, Monk created new ways of playing the piano. His flat-fingered approach, which was/is sometimes judged as poor technique, besides being somewhat scandalous to technocrats, provided a way to resist the tendency to play fuller chords and, perhaps, a way of dealing with the problem of having small hands. Thus, his breaking with conventions was not in essence about the conventions themselves. On the contrary, new techniques allowed him to crush sounds, produce fresh harmonic tonalities, and disorient rhythmic clichés, even as he engaged in the harmonic explorations that were necessary to pursue the *sound* he heard in his mind and the possibilities he imagined.[54] Gunther Schuller succinctly summarized Monk's keyboard style with reference to the sound he pursued:

> Monk was able to fashion a uniquely personal keyboard style and technique with a touch on the piano that by any conventional standards would be considered hopelessly clumsy and wrong. It took a long time for listeners and critics . . . to comprehend that what seemed just ponderous or inept or weird was actually

53. See Ware, *African American Theology*. Gayraud Wilmore used the term "Black Theology" to distinguish and signify the academic expression of Black Theology. In addition to using the term "black theology," I have purposely used lower case for "black" in most instances in agreement with Cone's past works. The pertinent question is when did style guides and other traditions decide to capitalize the term? Who decided for this change? To what degree was it debated among black folk?

54. John Szwed describes Monk's song "Well, You Needn't" as a new rhythmic modality that problematizes or disorients a swing cliché. See Szwed, *Jazz 101*, 172.

consummate music of real substance, of striking ideas—a whole new sound world.[55]

Yes. Monk created a world. He creatively extended the harmonic boundaries and broke with the aesthetics in the world of bop at the time. His so-called strange voicings, dissonant chords, and tonalities, including desiccated notes, all pressed hearers to appreciate new harmonic schemes and provided a way to (re)imagine the world of music. It is not surprising therefore when Gil Mellé, upon hearing "Epistrophy," described Monk as "a man who doesn't think like any musician in all of musical history, let alone jazz." This new world of music was echoed in the burgeoning style of life expressed by many blacks who broke with European models, producing what Amiri Baraka called a "rough, raw sound the black man [black people] forced out of these European instruments . . . a sound he [they] had cultivated in this country for two hundred years."[56] This sound is a metaphor for black life and, theologically speaking, a voicing (a secondary analogue, *analogatum*, of the primary analogy, the *analogans* of God) in concert with the creative voice of God.[57]

Following Monk, whose music can be imagined through this metaphor of Minton's Playhouse as part of Monk's world, we encounter a symbolism that provides a way to (re)imagine Cone as a theologian who expressed his voice distinctly, exacting a toll on readers but rewarding the studied patience of those who strive to understand his theology, especially since he grants insight into black lives in the strange world of American whiteness. With Barth, on the other hand, one encounters God in the strange new world of the Bible. In either case, theologians do not create history and so transform the message of the Bible; but, rather, the message of the Bible is about a God of history (*Geschichte*) who transforms history. So, in the ultimate sense, theologians witness to a strange God in a strange new world, a world that has been materially transformed by God (Isa 28:21b).

This world of witness discloses to the reader the peculiar "theological personality" of the theologian who frames the conversational dance between God and the world. The theological personality is recognized in the harmonious interplay between creation history and experience, in various aptitudes and limitations, and in notable stylistic choices and other

55. Schuller, *Life in Pursuit*, 600. Leslie Gourse notes how "Monk's technique was ideal for his music, that he had devised his technique to achieve his sound." Gourse, *Straight, No Chaser*, 153.

56. Baraka, *Blues People*, 79.

57. For the relationship between the *analogans* and the *analogatum* in Barth, see *CD* II/1:238.

intangibles, which are too numerous to catalogue. This explains why—in the second section of this book—Barth and Cone, despite their differences, are affirmed without undermining their common witness, which is ultimately based on the divine harmony, the melodic foundation of their common ground.

Fundamentally, what epitomizes Monk's way of creating a world is not merely his self-referentiality, his way of naming, or his new techniques. His creating of a world is evidenced in his audacious freedom as is expressed in the thoroughgoing vitality of his aesthetic, that is, his musical language. His adventurous musicality offers profound insights into the meaning of free space for the development of new ideas. There is room for surprise, silence, dissonance, melodic fragments, rhythmic displacements, and, yes, even playful self-referentiality. His creative freedoms suggest that the intramusical references in Monk are, to put it simply, part of the world Monk created and part of his ethics of playfulness. Minton's simply became the laboratory for the generative nature of freedom and Monk's explorations in "free play." His music inspires the same freedom in my approach to Barth and Cone, who, because of the kind of harmonious thinking I am suggesting, are brought together in a common theological keynote, witnessing and testifying to the same reality, but uniquely so.

I also believe this order of aesthetics can contribute to a theology of the Holy Spirit that honors the centrality of Christ, the divine melody, and the spiritual calling into a radical advocacy that prioritizes the subjectivity of our creative endeavors over against prevailing powers that—in their one-dimensional nature—diminish the richness of human life and the originality of our productions in the world. Monk's audacious stylistics, then, if we have ears to hear, can move us from rationalistic and discursive categories toward elementary insights into a deeper freedom and stimulate our theological imaginations to ponder the diversity of God's kingdom and its gifts and the promised eschatological scene as a place where all things resound. It is a world-open theology where the blue notes of our experience—bent notes, even the so-called bizarre, the dissonant, and the unpredictable can all be heard as representing, analogically, the versatility of God's rhythms and cadences in God's polyphonic creation. An affirmation of difference anticipates and necessitates, as we shall see below, an "ethic of playful versatility" in existing differences that correspond to the inclusive nature of the kingdom of God—differences that honor and support our very real aesthetic experiences.[58]

58. I adopted the term "an ethic of playful versatility" from Riggins Earl Jr. See Earl, *Dark Symbols, Obscure Signs*, 149–58. See my extended footnote in the section called "Spiritual Seculars and Their Playful Versatility" below.

Improvising on the Melody *at the Rendezvous*: The AIC as the *Locus Theologicus* of a Theology of Freedom

When aesthetic problems, akin to those endured by Byrd and other musicians, are extrapolated into an academic context, we move beyond questions of mere academicist forms of expression. The problems related to invisibility, cultural appropriation, and the misapplication of power resonate within institutional structures/corporate powers and black aesthetic practices. These difficulties materialize in the realm of religious experience. At the core of black religion, however, is black culture functioning in a mode of being that includes folk practices that are still rendered as "other" within academic contexts. Consequently, it is helpful at this point to ponder these problems—notwithstanding Karl Barth's emphasis on the church and James Cone's emphasis on the black community, respectively. In fact, because Barth and Cone accomplished their most important theological work within the halls of academia, the modern academic context represents the *locus theologicus*, a meeting place, where a rendezvous occurs between Barth's and Cone's theologies. The academy, furthermore, comprises a site where the traditional and the modern find reciprocity. It is a generative site where various perspectives collide, converge, and correspond with the potential to manifest a world of possibilities and problems.

Whether we are speaking of private or public universities, divinity schools, or seminaries, these establishments, including governing agencies, publishing houses, granting institutions, archival settings, and various powers (particularly within Christian higher education), represent collective structures, social systems, curricular interests, and protocols that coalesce into a constellation of powers. Along with surrogate institutions they form what I will identify as the academic industrial complex (AIC), an informal silent partner to the two primary industrial complexes often discussed in American sociopolitical thought, i.e., the military industrial complex (MIC) and the prison industrial complex (PIC).[59]

While it is common knowledge that President Dwight Eisenhower in his farewell address on January 17, 1961, is the first to describe the burgeoning military industrial complex as such, and as a potential threat to democratic governance, it often comes as a surprise for many to learn that Eisenhower removed the term "military-industrial-*academic* complex" from his initial remarks.[60] And while this latter phrase sounds the alarm concern-

59. For the MIC, see Schiller and Phillips, *Super State*, 29–34; Davis, *Abolition Democracy*, 39.

60. Giroux, *University in Chains*, 14–15. Emphasis added. Cf. Lee, "Academic Industrial Complex"; Del Gandio, "Neoliberalism."

ing military power, corporate structures, and their potential for influencing the curricular interests of the nation's leading research universities, this relationship is not limited to research universities. It is also connected to seminaries, divinity schools, and evangelical communities that are similarly sustained by the rhythms of corporate interests. As an industrial complex, the AIC echoes and embodies many of the same corroding corporate influences that occur in the relationship between the military and prison life in the nation, influences that warrant its inclusion into conversations with the former two powers, but simultaneously reveal idiosyncrasies that make it a distinct power.

Being aware of the many interdependencies of the AIC to subsidiary institutional powers and agencies and their responsibilities to the public, I offer no sustained focus on these relationships, such as the "school to prison pipeline" or the rising costs of higher education or the consequences associated with educational policy and other important points of interest that represent areas of focus within the AIC. On the contrary, I have a more modest agenda in mind in this brief section. I simply aim to sequester and unmask the AIC and "its institutional spirit" as a peculiar power without viewing its alliances with the agendas of the prison or military industrial complexes as the primary reason for its sociopolitical identity. I am also less interested in the AIC as represented by institutions within the larger constellation, such as Graduate Theological Union or Union Theological Seminary or Pepperdine University for instance. These organizations express what Rosemary Ruether, the feminist theologian, identified as "rules of life, structures for enforcing these rules, educational systems that socialize people into its identity, and rituals that celebrate its vision of itself."[61] At any rate, the AIC is simply identified here as a social system in its own right and as a "principality and power"—to use biblical language—being subject to industrialization, commodification, and ideological manipulation.[62]

Interrogating the AIC, nevertheless, is essential since the preservation of black religion, black theology, and their "collateral contemporaneity," to use a term from William James, reside in this context and include power valences that have not always been amenable to black life or black expressions of faith. The location in the academy is thus part and parcel of "the *real* order of the world."[63] It rewards us therefore not just to consider these institutions but to ponder the possibilities that surround them.

61. Ruether, *Christianity and Social Systems*, 2.

62. In conversation with Barth, William Stringfellow alluded to this important discussion during Barth's visit to America in 1962. See K. Barth, *Barth in Conversation*, 1:188–90.

63. W. James, *Will to Believe*, 119. Emphasis added. James Cone recognized the

Round and Round: The Harmony of "True Words" in the World of God[64]

One way to engage this "real order of the world" is to enlist our creative imaginations to accent the multidimensionality of life in harmony with God. Thelonious Monk helps with this since the aesthetic he employs can function as a comprehensive symbol or artistic analogue to signal how all of creation participates in the divine mystery. Even the variations—whether we reference the key, various notes, timbres, harmonies, and rhythms—become meaningful representatives that witness to the melody, and although I intend to expand this paradigm in *Signifying Monk*, where I seek to (re)imagine matter, the trajectory I am seeking can already be heard in Monk's voicings here, which symbolize the polyphony of human voices that embellish the cantus firmus. Of course there are other harmonies, melodies, and rhythms in the world, but the melody of God is sui generis in its potential to reconcile all of creation. In this respect even such classificatory language is inadequate since, as Thomas Aquinas rightly notes, God is of no genus whatsoever.[65] Still, God's aseity should not be heard as a metaphysically distancing concept, but rather as a way of speaking counterintuitively of the external world in union with the freedom of God.

In the external ground of the covenant the whole periphery of creatorial life is alive to God. God in the form of a "*free, pneumatic counterpoint*" simultaneously embraces the whole creation, yes, every created thing, the oceans, the rivers, the trees. The mystery of the divine center inhabits and (inter)rupts the possibilities on the periphery, calling us into a joyful correspondence between the melody of God and the external ground of

---

hostility and alienation between black religion and the black church early in his career, a fact that stemmed from the rise of black consciousness and black nationalism. Cone, *Risks of Faith*, 129. Charles H. Long also tied the marginalization of his work on black religion to the "race issue." "Comments," in Long, *Codex*.

64. This language of "round and round, outside in, and right side up" is a reversal of the methodological order in *Epistrophy* (ch. 4) and the structural order in *'Round Midnight* (chs. 1–2). I note the following in the former volume: "When pursuing a conversation between Barth and Cone, the historical sequence from my point of view is as follows: Barth turned Schleiermacher *upside down*, Cone turned Barth *inside out*, and an aesthetic approach to the relationship between these two theologians will support a hermeneutical methodology that proceeds on the periphery of their common center, that is, *round and round*." In this volume, I engage in a turning about to operationalize Barth and Cone in my hermeneutical strategy and address a new situation in the modern academy, maintaining through harmonious thinking what I consider to be a family kinship that starts on the periphery and moves to the center: *round and round*, *outside in*, and *right side up*.

65. Aquinas, *Summa Theologica*, 1.3.5.

creation.[66] Barth, drawing on this metaphor would say, "Each note of a melody contains the entire melody."[67] The parts witness to the whole, and the whole is contained in the parts. This mystery is not an enigma. It rather reveals and gives meaning to all of creation, especially the particularity in creation, a fact that leads me to the theology of James Cone.

Cone exercised his imagination in a way that coincides with the framework I am suggesting. He freely employed black voices, which we can identify as "true words," to use Barth's turn of phrase, in witness to God. In doing so, he charted a new way by deliberately signifyin(g) upon and expanding the horizon of the Christian community. The world of probabilities and contingencies are envisioned in concert with God. I would even contend that Cone's black aesthetics, like the aesthetic mode Monk employs, models an imaginative theological turn toward "true words," toward the polyphony of voices.[68] And although Cone was initially criticized for not actualizing new pathways, but rather charged with blackenizing white theology, he used black voices and "secular spirituals" to transcend the biblical witness and the limited narratives about black religion in the black church. Corresponding to Barth's notion of "secular parables," black voices are sources that speak "outside the walls of the church" (*extra muros ecclesia*) and outside the standard narrative of black church religion and theology.[69] These words arise from the surplus of black history and culture. In fact, it can be argued that these words "stem more from the cultural environment of the Church in its journey through history than from disagreement as to the material substance of the faith."[70]

To be conversant with such words, theologians should attune themselves to history and culture, particularly the concrete world as interpreted

66. This thoughtful construction, a *free, pneumatic counterpoint*, is derived from one of Karl Barth's last graduate students, Raymond Kemp Anderson, who was interested in a theology of playful freedom. R. Anderson, *American Scholar Recalls*, 416. Emphasis in original. See also my foreword to his *New Testament Micro-Ethics*, ix–xi.

67. See K. Barth, *Faith of the Church*, 57.

68. Cone's emphases on the church's lively engagement in the world occur in the opening salvos of black theology. See Cone: "Christianity and Black Power," 4; Cone, *Black Theology and Black Power*, 84. In the latter book, he stresses this point: "Theology . . . if it is to serve the need of the Church must become 'worldly theology.'" For the term "signifying," see Cone, *Said I Wasn't*, 102. Although Cone rarely used the term "signifying," it was his practice, a practice I underscore in *Epistrophy*, ch. 1.

69. *CD* 4/3.1:110–11. Cf. Hart, *Beyond the Standard Narrative of Black Religion*. See also V. Anderson, "Flesh-Stuff," 27–33.

70. Torrance, *Theology in Reconciliation*, 10. I am not suggesting that Torrance would interpret Cone as such, but that his recognition of the importance of cultural backgrounds for formulating our viewpoints corresponds to what the black tradition brings to the historic faith.

by various sources comprised of anthropology, ethnography, both continental and analytic philosophy, critical race theory, and history. They should freely cultivate insight from these frameworks and many others to constructively employ true words to confront powers like the AIC. The goal is to humanize our institutions and audaciously enlist their service on behalf of humanity. In this way, institutional powers are liberated unto their proper role in the social imaginary. This brings me to an important point about the harmony of redemption. I do not emphasize our need to recognize possibilities, ambiguities, or approximations in the interstices between freedom and liberation to press for a radical relativity, but rather for precisely the opposite reason, that is, to acknowledge God's lordship over all of our relativities in time and space for the purpose of sanctifying the times and spaces we occupy.

Theologians should therefore attune to the witness of more than liberation theologies, existing across denominational lines, including black, womanist, Minjung, Indigenous theologies, and others too numerous to name. We should hear the testimonies of world religions, including historical, cultural, and institutional modes of being that represent *an-other* to those traditions that are typically indulged in the "West." They should, moreover, hear and embrace secular traditions where our common witness against idolatry exists.[71] Thus, rather than constraining our multivalent modes of being in a faltering one-dimensional way, religious and secular institutions must be redeemed and inspired to treat human beings as ends in themselves rather than as means to an end for institutional agendas.

This kind of harmonious thinking leads me again to Thelonious. Monk's voicings broke with traditional musical discourse to embrace the interstices, the ignored possibilities with each melody and the irrupting and erupting possibilities within music in general. These possibilities, which are not limited to the periphery, are an extension of the melody, and they are relative to *its* ordering. If I might reiterate this point with the geometric figure of a circle as a metaphor, the area around the center of a circle represents space laden with possibilities. So, these incidentals or contingences exist even on the inside, "in between the notes," as it were, if the reader will bear with me as I shift back to a musical metaphor. To think therefore of Monk's understanding of the cantus firmus as the dimension of depth at the center of our musical movement means we must recognize the music

71. An exemplary model of common witness occurred between the Trappist monk Thomas Merton and the critical theorist Eric Fromm, who argued that believers and nonbelievers have a common fight against idolatry, including institutions, production, orders and all man-made things: "Whether or not one believes in God is a question secondary to whether or not one denies idols." Fromm, *Revolution of Hope*, 136.

around the music, the possibilities of "true words," of the voices *round and round*. This means acknowledging how Monk's extraordinary witness, when imagined in a way that is analogous to God's word, testifies to God's grace, which harmonizes these possibilities (or "true words") as they revolve around the mystery of the divine melody. Again, I am reminded of Nica, the Jazz Baroness, whose inspired words accurately summed up Monk's music—and my theological concern—when she said that what "shook me up about Thelonious was how he could hear the music around the music," and how he "explored all those possibilities that one never dreamed of."[72] This insight speaks to the symbolic force of what Monk was doing musically. The reader who is in tune with what I am suggesting will recognize an allusion to the "christological concentration" that corresponds with the thinking of Karl Barth, James Cone, and others who began in this special place—*in the mystery of the divine melody*.

When interpreted in the proper way, the cantus firmus, which can be signified analogously as the center of the spiritual ground of God's covenant with us, opens up to a dynamic and versatile, kaleidoscopic view of creation, which is the external ground of our playful joy. It opens to the relativity of our creations, the triumphs, breakthroughs, failures, trials, sorrows, and vanities; it opens to a world where even the cynical wisdom of Qoheleth relays its truths—where every word and work "is brought into judgment" (Eccl 12:14).

Barth suggested that "we must not miss the *cantus firmus* of the positive continuum above the dialect of the prophets." Moreover, he extended this argument, as I noted earlier, writing that "it [the *cantus firmus*] goes out into all lands, to the whole world and all the nations, but it is also perceived continually in Israel itself."[73] Barth expresses here a view of the prophetic that transcends the dialectic of the prophets themselves, setting forth a doctrinal affirmation, through Christ, that extends to all creation. This vision for Barth begins with Israel, and with Israel Barth frames his "*theo*-anthropology," that is, his critique of any "theology" that fails to properly account for the relationship between God and human beings. As it happens, theoanthropology, according to Barth, underscores "God *and* the human being! . . . God *for* the human being, God *with* the human being, God *before* the human being, God *above* the human being, and *behind* the human being."[74] God is *round and round*, indeed.

72. Rothschild, *Baroness*, 223.

73. *CD* 4/3.1:61.

74. K. Barth, *Barth in Conversation*, 3:103. Emphasis in original. See also K. Barth, *Evangelical Theology*, 12.

While Christian institutions should spearhead a form of radical openness and humanizing agency in the erupting possibilities around the melody, many Christian institutions tolerate provincialism, advocating for ideological or parochial forms of sectarianism that nurture Christian egotism. This attitude leads some Christian colleges and divinity schools to unwittingly frame themselves as adversaries against non-Christian secular society. For instance, when Christian theologians employ language like "secular progressivism"—which in our partisan political environs is ambiguous and coded terminology—conservative ideological predilections conceal the religious dimensions of their respective evangelical institutions.[75] Moreover, the relationship of the divine to the world at large is lost to a mode of "sacred protest" that fails to encounter the problems in the material world more comprehensively.[76] Thus the imagination of matter is eclipsed.

Considering how black people are often recruited as a commodity to sustain certain academic climates—as opposed to being authentic participants who contribute to substantial changes within these institutions—it is no wonder that many blacks (who make up religious and nonreligious faculty, staff, and students) have resigned themselves to approaching the AIC from the vantage of the subversive intellectual. Following Harney and Moten, this means that we "sneak into the university and steal what one can. To abuse its hospitality, to spite its mission, to join its refugee colony . . . to be in but not of" the university—this is the path of the subversive intellectual in the modern university."[77] Another approach, however, may be to inquire about other ways of reframing the relationship, ways to (inter)rupt these spaces for the good of a radical form of humanity.

If we take seriously, for instance, the meaning of black religion, that is, the *charismata* of blackness as a "true word" or part of the harmonious structure of faith and attend to its meaning in black communities, then there is no reason we cannot establish improvised communities that recognize common bonds and participate in communal networks within the modern academy. Despite the AIC's tendency to ignore the religious dimension in black life, the black religious experience persists as a symbol of *otherness* to some degree. These *others* represent a radical subjectivity that is grounded in a form of community which is modeled on the same kind of cooperative independence and affirmation of life that is symbolized in places like the Five Spot, Minton's Playhouse, Open Door, Clark Monroe's Uptown

75. Highfield, "Opinion."

76. With these comments I have in mind my own tradition, Churches of Christ, which has marginalized aesthetic questions and forms of embodiment for the purpose of doctrinal uniformity.

77. Harney and Moten, *Undercommons*, 26.

House, Birdland, and many other types of improvised communities within the United States. During the bebop period, human solidarity (and sanity) took precedence over careerism, individualism, and so-called progressive secularism aimed at marginalizing the genius of black folk traditions and black religious understanding(s).[78]

Transcending institutional powers means we must first identify and unmask them, especially as they create problems for black aesthetics and aesthetes in general, including musicians, painters, poets, folklorists, thespians, and even those more remote artistic types who engage in sports and other endeavors, bringing a certain kind of stylistics that challenge and (de)*construct* the structures of the institutions themselves. Artists are often the purveyors of new ways of seeing the world, and one finds *an-other* attitude that comes to terms with the beauty of life in novel ways, confronting the status quo and its stratagems and forms of commodification. But acknowledging such orientations requires more resourcefulness than any single academic can marshal in any one book (or even a discipline for that matter). This work of unmasking is made more difficult because political and economic integration has established reconciliation on terms that lack the centered existence we all need.

What is needed is a harmonic scheme that is inclusive enough to embrace the radical pluralism in American society. This uniquely American problem is epitomized in the words of Charles Long, who criticized institutions that celebrate productions of knowledge that marginalize the kind of freedom arising from cultures of the oppressed.[79] Monk's jazz serves therefore as a symbol, an aesthetic mode that assists us in (re)imagining free relationships between faith and history, that is, between the harmony of redemption and the rhythms of production, suggesting a freedom that draws on the "free, continuous, creative energy as produced in song."[80] As is his custom, Monk said it most succinctly, noting simply that "jazz is freedom." Moreover, if James Cone is correct, the "functional character applied to the slave seculars, ballads, spirituals, as well as the blues" can be applied to jazz as well. Therefore, if we are to embrace the jazzology of life through such paradigms we must attend to the locations where those harmonious gatherings occur and appraise the ways the AIC functions as a site where black voices can again intersect in a harmony of true words in a creative new world.

78. Cone, *Spirituals and the Blues*, 57.

79. Long, *Significations*, 210.

80. Rudi Blesh, the jazz critic, as quoted in Cone, *Spirituals and the Blues*, 98.

Outside In: The Harmony of Redemption and the Academic Industrial Complex

Coming to terms with the harmony of "true words" in a context marked by institutional crises means we should recognize three significant implications tied to the relationship between faith and history. First, we should acknowledge the harmony between God and human history as seen in Christ. As noted in the bridge of *'Round Midnight* (vol. 2), this harmony is set forth by the two melodies of the Father and the Son (and their perfect collaboration), where Christ represents God and humanity. And through the Spirit of Christ, we participate in the plenitude of the Son's redemption, being incorporated into Christ.[81] Second, these harmonies or true words, to use a term from Jan Lochman, are directionally "ex-centric."[82] This means, whether on the periphery or some other space within the area of the circle, that redemptive harmonies find their orientation in the center, i.e., in the mystery of Christ, the center of the covenant. Stated differently, these harmonies represent a lively movement of the work of Christ without losing their integrity and authenticity *in being what they are in their own mode of being.* As noted in the prelude, Monk's jazz remains jazz—even as it functions as theology—without violating its integrity as jazz. This would also be true of other genres of music, literature, philosophy, and aesthetic forms, including institutions that are far too numerous to list here. This *stuff*: words, lights, truths, and harmonies may witness to the Word in their own way; without, of course, displacing the harmony of redemption in any way.

This brings us to the third implication of the relationship between the harmony of redemption and the powers that be. We must attend to the way power functions in institutions like the AIC. Minding such power means we must unmask their claims and counteract their power of signification by relativizing ersatz claims to dominion. As maintained above, one way to decenter power of this kind is through an appeal to the christological

81. In a way similar to Monk, who was "so far inside the [musical] tradition that he seemed to demand that the listener have a thorough enough knowledge of the African American legacy to appreciate how he was playing around with it, off it, and through it," I am somewhat drawing on Trinitarian language to articulate the way in which we participate within the musicality of the divine, the inner material content of divine life. See Crouch, *Considering Genius*, 88. For the perfect collaboration between the Son and Spirit, see Durrwell, *Holy Spirit of God*, 92.

82. The notion of thinking in an "ex-centric" direction toward reconciliation with Christ as the center is grounded in Barth's view of the covenant as the internal ground of creation. The language of "ex-centric" is adopted from Jan Lochman: "Reconciliation and Creation," 171–72. Lochman also occasionally uses the term *ec-centric* to mean the same thing. See Lochman, *Lord's Prayer*, ix; cf. Lochman, *Encountering Marx*, 43–46.

concentration where Christ's harmony outstrips the so-called priority of the powers. In this way, the reality of Christ—read inclusively and not in a negative exclusive sense—gives shape to the corporeal reality of black Americans. This form is the "cantus firmus of the polyphonic life of Jesus." This is the center that (re)orients us in our relationship to powers in the world,[83] grounding us in grace so we can signify on the signifiers and turn institutions, at least their claims to power, upside down in a sense.

This kind of paradigm shift is evident in the New Testament. An instance of it is recorded in the apostolic testimony where early witnesses are described as "turning the world upside down" (Acts 17:5). Surely, if the inversion of such orders is not recognized, no redistribution of power will occur. Rather, black self-affirmation, which is in accordance with the will of Jesus Christ, will be overdetermined by whiteness and other ideologies.[84] Ergo, in hopes of advancing Barth and Cone what follows here is an attempt to briefly address the AIC in relation to these "true words," "lights," "parables," or as I prefer to say, "harmonies," that hopefully complement other burgeoning discussions of institutional powers and the way they participate in systemic structures of racism.[85]

If we track along with Barth and Cone, a turn to the academy is important because the black experience has a locus in academic settings where, prioritizing Cone, it means walking through a door he has sprung open, at least in terms of theological and religious studies in the academy.[86] The academy therefore contains a paradoxical significance for black theologians, particularly those who engage communities of color where young African Americans often travel the established routes of social mobility, a trajectory that typically includes also the military industrial complex and, more tragically, the prison industrial complex.

83. Although I discovered the notion of cantus firmus in Monk, my emphasis corresponds with Jan Lochman, Chung, and others in the left-wing Barthian tradition. See Lochman, *Reconciliation and Liberation*, 66; Lochman, *Living Roots of Reformation*, 29; Macchia and Chung, *Theology Between East and West*, 9–10. Compare Jürgen Moltmann's important foreword to this latter book (4).

84. Cone, "Toward a Black Theology," 114.

85. In terms of important discussions of the problem with the AIC, I have in mind the important work of Henry Giroux, Rosemary Ruether, and the more recent contributions of Willie Jennings in *After Whiteness.*

86. It is common knowledge among Cone and black theologians that his endeavors were designed to clear the way to deeper engagement in the field rather than make a hermetic turn designed to seal off and provincialize black theology in the academy. This is not to suggest Cone was the only one who participated in opening the doors to the academy or in developing black theology as a discipline.

Far too often, however, the university complex is separated from the critical discourse aimed at these other centers of power, as if its so-called traditional commitments to the ideals of academic freedom and civic intellectual engagement advance it as a corporately endorsed power that truly supports human potentiality and excludes racist ideology. On the contrary, the American educational system not only mirrors the values of the warfare state, it naturalizes it through bonds of common interest with other powers. Consequently, it perpetuates conflict.[87] Being an establishment that commodifies human resources, it marginalizes the radical otherness (that speaks to the real depth of harmony at the center of reality) that springs from black folk religion, and it undermines the contributions black religion makes to common ways of being.

The university often functions this way because as a system it maintains the sources that serve the status quo, limiting risk and safeguarding the economic and ideological agendas of those who are most powerful. And although the alliances that make up the AIC are not necessarily coordinated or conspiratorial, theological agendas are commercially and ideologically driven to the point of being profoundly shaped by the racial imaginary, including neoliberal concerns and outright attempts to ideologize the gospel of Christ for corporate capitalism and other institutional purposes.[88] In conjunction, some academic institutions regularly conceal their ambitions, baptizing their ideological impulses by extending Christian language to camouflage idealized conceptions of purpose or service or leadership. They demonstrate no real-world concern for the new world of faith, i.e., for the transformation of human life in witness to God in the common life of the world. These institutions, rather, engage in feigned attempts to honor the "problem space" occupied by blackness and black bodies in the academic domain.[89]

The AIC, to be sure, may not exert its most significant influence in the transactions occurring in the material world or the realm of economics, but rather in the realm of ideas, beliefs, and the aesthetic orderings that shape the ambiance of the academy.[90] Ordinarily, such problems are associated with

87. Fulbright, "War and Its Effects," 173–74. Compare also Nelson Maldonado-Torres's book, *Against War*, 1–19. He offers an insightful discussion of the naturalization of war as a death ethic that is shot through coloniality/Western modernity.

88. W. Jennings, *Christian Imagination*, 279–82. Jennings's brilliant project explores the origins of race in the Christian imaginary.

89. See Walker, "Serious Human Discourse," 99–100. Walker pinpoints the problem space that blackness represents in the academy and in broader society.

90. I am also mindful of Karl Barth, who suggested that a new light might shine on theology in terms of its academic ambiance. K. Barth, *Evangelical Theology*, 16.

conservative institutions, because of the rise of the "new right" and the role of neoliberalism, but it should be noted that this is also a perduring problem within institutions that incline toward a certain political piety on the left, including those who identify with so-called revolutionary agendas.[91] The failed record of black inclusion in many elite religious institutions attests to this truth; and the channeling of black students toward particular disciplines reveals the legacy of white supremacy in its academic ambiance.

Of course, the aesthetic values propagated by such provincial intellectual resources and categories of thought are not limited to problems based on color symbolism or long-standing malignant attitudes about the physical characteristics of blacks. To the contrary, as Delores Williams points out, aesthetics is "coded into American language and literature."[92] I would add that such aesthetics are coded into the more subtle metrics of whiteness used to "standardize" religious and theological protocols in university curriculums, in publishing houses, and in the editorial boardrooms of scientific publications. The truth is that many institutions—and I have purposely resisted naming any—have not taken the intractable problem of racism as seriously as they ought, naïvely ignoring the charismata given to the church and the American society in black religion and black theology. What is the meaning of the message of the gospel when it is born out of the medium of the black experience whose witness still indicts so many of our institutions, especially divinity schools, seminaries, and institutions of higher learning that aid and abet the exclusionary logics of the white aesthetic regime?[93]

In truth, many of these seminaries and universities have resigned themselves to treating the problem of racism, as Fanon noted, more like a "mental quirk" or "psychological flaw" rather than a normalized way of being that "has achieved a perfect harmony of economic relations and ideology."[94] Racism, which clearly transmogrified into classism and sexism in America, has given way to the preestablished harmonies of white supremacy in postindustrial capitalist America. This development has weakened the vitality of the churches' prophetic voices in relation to institutional powers, and perhaps most importantly, it has dulled our ability to hear the harmony

91. See Darren Dochuk's award-winning *From Bible Belt to Sun Belt*. Barth levels a critique that sees conservative evangelical institutions on the right and liberal institutions on the left as two sides of the same coin.

92. D. Williams, *Sisters in the Wilderness*, 91. Williams is quoting Winthrop Jordan, *White over Black*, but the emphasis on theological aesthetics in her text should not be missed.

93. A profound treatment of the white aesthetic regime—in symbolic and discursive terms—is developed in W. Jennings, *After Whiteness*.

94. Fanon, *Toward the African Revolution*, 38, 40.

of redemption in the midst of the powers. Consequently, the metaphorical knock at midnight, so eloquently spoken of by Martin Luther King Jr., remains unheard. The door has been left unattended because churches and other religious institutions—with no ears to hear the aural aesthetics associated with the higher frequencies of God (Barth) or the lower frequencies coming from the cries of the oppressed (Cone)—simply refuse to answer.[95]

Right Side Up: Harmonies of Redemption and the Academic Industrial Complex

Complicating the dilemma with the AIC are problems that extend beyond the impact of commercialization and corporatization. Consider, for instance, the theological content of what one researches and teaches. When Barth visited America in 1962, he criticized the ambiance of the academy in relation to the task of doing theology. His visit was an evocative and memorable moment, because his caveat threw into relief a number of questions about the academy as a site for theological engagement. While it may be too speculative to flirt with what Barth ultimately had in mind, his profound hermeneutical suspicion, his radical engagement in the class struggles in Safenwil, and his abiding concern with the priority of confessional theology as a counterrevolutionary force to social movements in Switzerland—including his stance against the "lordless powers" epitomized by Nazi Germany—all point more or less to an educated guess about what his stance would be against the academy as a resident power, as a principality, or as a living site of the "original disorder." This problem is what Barth would identify as the human alienation from God that "darkens and burdens human life and fellowship," a resident fact of all radically autonomous institutional and corporate structures.[96]

Barth, paradoxically, argued that the way beyond the disorder is to imagine the world in its true reality, i.e., right side up, in correspondence with the gospel of Christ. In other words, (re)imagining the world as already having been dedemonized in a sense; and then to engage the chaos through the preservation and renewal of human life. In this way, the harmony of redemption, guided by the renewal of the Spirit, will give structure and organize these established harmonies, provoking them to engage in the work of human justice, human peace, and human liberation in solidarity with others and in concert with Christ's lordship. What is remarkable about Barth's paradoxical turn is his suggestion that the rational and scientific approaches

95. See Carr, "More Certain Sound."

96. K. Barth, *Christian Life*, 213.

are inadequate to address the problem. He was more impressed with the so-called "magical thinking" as seen in the New Testament and churches in Africa and Asia, although he demythologized these views to some extent. Barth's argument calls to mind his early evaluation of historical criticism, a methodology whose value Barth viewed as "a means of attaining freedom in relation to [church] tradition,"[97] rather than constituting a new form of liberal theology. On the other hand, it is somewhat difficult to imagine the mythical (magical) worldview of the younger churches in Asia and Africa as playing an important hermeneutical role in liberating the gospel from narrow, rationalistic, and scientific theologies without constituting a return to old forms of orthodoxy.

Barth's approach actually complements Charles Long's argument that theologies are modes of discourse about power. As noted in the bridge (*'Round Midnight*), Long concluded that theological discourse functions hegemonically, being not only discourses "about power, the power of God but equally about the power of the specific form of discourse about power." Such discourses are in this respect ultimately "about the hegemony of power—the distribution and economy of this power in heaven and on earth—whether in the ecclesiastical locus of a Pope or, more generally since the modern period, the center of this power in the modern Western world."[98] With this insight, Long brings the theological enterprise itself into a critical light, unmasking the hidden power working within theological categories and the tendency for such categories to circumscribe the beauty of harmonies (voices) that witness to the Word in their own way.

Moreover, since the adjudication of these discourses have their locus in divinity schools, seminaries, and universities, the agenda of the AIC ends up shaping a "public pedagogy that teaches all members of society how to think, act, believe and live."[99] And when these discourses are framed by arguments that ignore social stratification "by targeting student-consumers, channeling students into corporate careers and reinforcing rather than reducing social stratification," we see why these modes of power must be unmasked.[100] To be sure, the corporatized system of higher education, which has proliferated during the twentieth century, reflects this social stratification and echoes the same violences Barth confronted at the beginning of his pastorate in Safenwil.

97. See K. Barth and Thurneysen, *Revolutionary Theology*, 36; cf. K. Barth, *Christian Life*, 218–19.

98. Long, *Significations*, 209.

99. Del Gandio, "Neoliberalism," para. 12.

100. Del Gandio, "Neoliberalism," para. 8.

The industrial capitalist system, as revealed in Christian higher education, yields a form of social injustice. This system is not simply hostile to humanity; it endangers the ecology and often exploits the gospel of Christ by camouflaging and concealing its motives in Christian garb, masking neoliberal agendas, treating students as commodities for the purpose of brand building, and conflating the relationship between the revelation of God and ideological pursuits—even occasionally promoting political or religious leaders who represent partisan ambitions and pragmatic choices designed to preserve the status quo, rather than providing choices that humanize and mete out justice. Because it reinforces such agendas, the AIC represents what Felicia Lee describes as the "hallmark of a new era in the relationship between corporate culture and higher education." This relationship has given way to a burgeoning literature that sounds the alarm about the risk posed by increasing commercialization and its impact on the mission and standards of divinity schools, seminaries, and universities.[101]

This parochialism was evidenced in the aesthetics of white seminaries and universities when black theology first broke intellectual ground as a discipline, and because of its polemical message and its eventual location within primarily elite, bureaucratized settings, including institutions such as Union Theological Seminary, for example, black theology was initially perceived as having nothing to do with the black church since many of these religious institutions, according to Cone, had no long-standing relationship to the black Christian community. Cone himself felt as if he was being taken away from his people.[102] In one respect, we can argue that Cone was experiencing what Cornel West calls the dilemma of the black intellectual, but I believe this dilemma is much more than an intellectual problem.[103]

The problem was not simply that bureaucratic academic institutions rendered blacks opaque, but the lure of seminaries, divinity schools, and universities and the drive for academic respectability (for black theology as a discipline in the academy and black theologians as participants in the guild) led black theology to a second stage characterized by black professors who lacked, in Cone's estimation, the prophetic orientation and audacity of the clerics who represented the NCBC (National Committee for Black Churchmen) and other more prophetic organizations that preceded what he described as ambivalent institutions like the SSBR (Society for the Study of Black Religion)—which itself was partially established to prophetically confront the white academy and affirm black intellectual life.

101. Lee, "Academic Industrial Complex," para. 2.

102. Cone, "Looking Back, Going Forward," 250.

103. West, *Cornel West Reader*, 305; Cone, *For My People*, 99–121.

Nevertheless, because the black prophetic voice accommodated itself to the academy, a corresponding failure of the affirmation of black aesthetic life has surfaced, a fact that reinforces the white aesthetic regime. This means that the problem of entering the academy was of signal importance for black theologians since it concerns the introduction of blacks into modern academic spaces that create what Cone identified as not merely an academic problem, but a question about the task of theology and our subsequent commitment to community. Cone wanted to know if black theologians were prepared to "define our lives by the *cross* of Jesus." And more pointedly, he challenged black theologians, asking, "What are we prepared to die for?"[104] In his view, therefore, the prophetic voice of the church suffered a loss even as it gained respectability in the new world of academia.

Thus, from the very beginning of his turn to black theology, although Cone maintained a more critical attitude of the way racism was sponsored in academic institutions, his personal experiences in America and the absence of black theology as a discipline required that he work at the threshold where black theology was neither an academic affair, requiring that one put real "skin in the game," nor to be found in Karl Barth, Paul Tillich, Wolfhart Pannenberg, or any other white theologian or institution for that matter. Instead, parachurch organizations like the National Committee for Black Churchmen (NCBC), Society for the Study of Black Religion (SSBR), and other emerging theological base communities echoed the harmonies of redemption and created the milieu where Cone found space to articulate the freedom of his unique theological individuation.

His theological sensibilities resisted the constraints of white supremacy, not because he had necessarily found hope, but I would argue that because hope—as expressed through his ancestral tradition and blues legacies—had found him.[105] The lived sense of black music that transcends narrow rational and discursive categories were part of his social context at Macedonia AME. As Cone noted, black life is a spiritual, capturing the rhythms, hopes, and freedoms passed down through generations. Therefore, for Cone, "whatever form black music takes, it is always an expression of black life in America and what the people must do to survive with a measure of dignity in a society which seems bent on destroying their right to be human beings."[106] Accordingly, if a theological aesthetics is to persist as a hopeful and disruptive way of proceeding along this line, it must follow the prophetic accent as

104. Cone, *For My People*, 219. Emphasis in original.

105. Angela Sims, for instance, captures the power of memory, i.e., the momentum it gives to Christian experience through its words and silences, in Sims, *Lynched*.

106. Cone, *Spirituals and the Blues*, 130. For "*Black history is a spiritual!*," see 31. Emphasis in original.

represented by the chorus of voices that stand against dehumanization and in harmony with redemption, especially in the perduring midnight hour in America.

Moreover, because of hopeful liberative rhythms, the academy possesses potential to be more than a cipher and a mere site of contestation where the slow creep of ideologization, institutionalization, and commoditization deleteriously mark all intellectual endeavors. The academy can become, paradoxically, a site of fecundity—a hopeful generative space where the harmonics of black creativity can potentially arise as witness to something "other"—syncopating, (inter)rupting the status quo, and affirming new possibilities for human life and dignity. This is the proper vision of the world, the "right-side-up" vision. This is the orientation Barth imagined, and the theological possibility Cone's theology represents as a grand contribution to American academic life. Indeed, even a cursory view of his more developed contributions reveals the theological advances of womanist theologians, such as Katie Cannon, Delores Williams, M. Shawn Copeland, Emilie Townes, Angela Sims, Cheryl Kirk-Duggan, JoAnne Terrell, and many others previously mentioned in earlier chapters in this project. Black theology's influence abroad through Cone's colleagues, such as Gayraud Wilmore, J. Deotis Roberts, and second-generation theologians like Dwight Hopkins, Kelly Brown Douglas, Will Coleman, and Willie Jennings have extended the significance of the discipline. Even the theological enterprises of white allies who attempt to legitimize and disciplinize black theology within seminaries and universities throughout the United States riff off the cultural harmonics of redemption Cone and others initiated in the academy.[107]

These resounding countermelodies must be heard in their own unique registers. More than this, the harmonies radiating from the kingdom of God, i.e., the mystery of the divine melody, include the richness of not only womanist theologies, as strong and needed voicings, but indigenous religions and theologies, African theologies, Minjung and Asian theologies, Latin American liberation theologies, queer theologies, feminist theologies, crip theologies, and even radical visions like secular theologies that are living

107. Here is a good place to acknowledge again that I do not intend to mythologize Cone as the sole voice in the movement, but only an important one. We should be wary of any kind of intellectual elitism or cisgender normativity that privileges male voices over others, rich over poor, singular over communal, and so on. I also agree with Angela Davis and her argument for "women's blues" as an indispensable indicator of a "gendered consciousness that transformed collective memories of slavery as it worked with a new social construction of love and sexuality." Davis, *Blues Legacies*, 47. With that said, I agree with Riggins Earl that Cone's proximity to the Black Power movement made him "the normative interpretive voice in the academy" for black liberation theologies. Earl, *Dark Symbols, Obscure Signs*, xi.

alternatives to traditional perspectives. These harmonies represent melodic counterpoints rather than strict contradictions. They are best read *optimam in bonum partem* (in terms of their best gifts); and they should be joyfully heard as part of the multidialogical witness of God's harmony of redemption. These various perspectives testify to the gravitational pull of the cantus firmus, which through them has "turned the world upside down" (Acts 17:6). Another way to state this more constructively is to note that these countermelodies should be heard *ex-centrically*, outside in, as they contour and give shape to what the academy *can become* when it is redeemed and experienced in the musicality of the right-side-up kingdom of God.

We must, finally, assess how these voices can be interpreted in relation to the AIC without falling into the naïve trap of reproducing theology as a hermetic discipline that reinforces isolationism or separation. We should also avoid a church that is insulated and concerned with its own self-maintenance over against the summons to multivalent attestations. It seems to me, in fact, that black theology in its initial development by Cone was already traveling along a line that allowed for a positive contribution or inversion of this dilemma. In his first article, for example, Cone acknowledged the need to "challenge the power-structure with the power of the *Gospel*, knowing that nothing less than *immediate* and total emancipation of all people is consistent with the message and style of Jesus Christ."[108] Read in one way, as Victor Anderson indicates, Cone was faced with a choice between disentangling theology by "acknowledging its indebtedness" to Western theological sources or insisting for "the radical disjunction of black theology from European sources," and he chose the latter.

In another way, however, when read more charitably, Cone's use of Barth, Tillich, Niebuhr, existential philosophy, and many other European sources reveals a more nuanced move on his behalf. His signification on Barth (as a representative locus) and the loci of theology in general means that in turning of Barth inside out—an emphasis that opens the way to questions about the churches' relationship to the AIC and other principalities and powers—Cone opened the door to thinking constructively about sources right side up. To be sure, the primary sources for black theology became, according to Cone, "found in the spirituals, blues and sayings of our people." His goal was designed to effect change and utilize the prophetic power within churches to help them "move closer to the calling to be God's instrument of liberation to the world."[109] The question is whether this is possible in the context of the modern AIC. Will the established harmonies and rhythms of

108. Cone, "Christianity and Black Power," 4. Emphasis in original.

109. Cone, *For My People*, 117–18. Cf. Cone, *Black Theology and Black Power*, 24.

the academic complex—along with its allied satellite institutions, projecting what Henry Giroux has called their "crude emphasis on quantity"—make space for new rhythms of black creative freedom that constructively address black oppression and the flailing life of black churches? Will institutions that reside in the established patterns of American consumer society, being so overdetermined and bound by rhythms of industry, break away from the commodification that raids the spiritual life of the church?

In my view, the way beyond the limitations of aesthetic and sociopolitical problems that plague the AIC is found in a renewed theological vision. This view of the world is not limited to an inversion of the power of the AIC, turning it upside down and acknowledging the harmony created by God in the midst of the darkness, a position in the order of Barth's understanding of the relationship between God and humanity. While I support the view that the cantus firmus objectively secures victory over the powers, I also think we should disrupt the AIC by functioning in a way or mode of affirmation that resists the powers. Using aesthetic approaches akin to Cone's theological undertakings, we must protest against the banal hostility of such industries—without functioning in a one-dimensional oppositional mode—and constructively fill the void the powers created, leading us into deeper aesthetic engagement, enhancing creativity and the human imagination through various forms of literature, art, and music. I am suggesting we turn toward history making as modeled in *The Spirituals and the Blues*, *The Cross and the Lynching Tree*, and Cone's more constructive endeavors, such as his editing of the significant book series called the Bishop Henry McNeal Turner Studies. In these productions of knowledge, we are introduced to Cone at his very best, affirming programmatically black religious life in history. This is the constructive mode we must follow as we revel in the "right-side-up" harmony of redemption.

Noon of Night: The Spirit's Witness in the Polyphony of Creation[110]

Having taken seriously the symbolic meaning of midnight throughout this project, I further address the midnight hour in this final section. At

110. Although my introduction to the notion of "polyphony" initially came from Thelonious Monk's way of playing variations on a tune, which some argue should be heterophony, Dietrich Bonhoeffer's phrase "polyphony of life" is useful. Bonhoeffer anticipates the way I deploy Monk's music as a metaphor in this book. See Bonhoeffer, *Letters and Papers*, 302–6. Monk's explicit emphasis on the cantus firmus can be found in Van der Bliek, *Thelonious Monk Reader*, 269–70, and of course in other discussions of melody.

this juncture, however, I make an appeal using the poetic phrase "noon of night," hoping to convey the meaning of midnight in the American moral and sociopolitical order *and* to furnish a way to engage the midnight hour with a constructive aesthetic agenda that is grounded in the Spirit's witness. We must confront our times, highlighting the paradoxical situation of the light shining in midst of sociopolitical darkness. Perhaps Jan Lochman, the Czech theologian, captured this sentiment best when contending that the church and the modern world greet each other with contradictory greetings. The church says to the world, "Good morning," and the world says to the church, "Good night."[111] Still, if theology is to have a kind of humanizing influence in this encounter, it must address the dichotomy with a faithful correlation between morning and night, noon and midnight, darkness and light. "Noon of night," then, is my way of speaking to this faithful encounter.

As a turn of phrase, "noon of night" poetically captures how I would like to constructively imagine what Monk and other jazz artists (who honed their gifts in the world of the nightlife and thrived as subalterns and were allowed to breathe without a metaphorical knee on their necks) contribute symbolically to our thinking about the current midnight hour. The poetry in the term treats midnight with the same reverence as midday, and in doing so it liberates us to think beyond simplistic binary frameworks often found in the dichotomies between the holy and profane, eternity and time, grace and judgment, sacred and secular, or objectivity (Barth) and subjectivity (Cone)—even liberating us to expand theology as a grammar and reconcile what Cornel West calls "the two *organic* intellectual traditions in Afro-American life: *the black Christian tradition of preaching and the black musical tradition of performance*."[112]

Standing constructions, conventions, and traditional binaries, particularly those that perpetuate difference as division, rather than affirming the difference, must be (re)imagined as we rethink what it means to confront postindustrial capitalist America. We must respect the contradictions and sometimes open hostility that accompany the multidimensional nature of what it means to be human. This accent on radical forms of humanization suggests that we find a way to imagine noon and midnight simultaneously and honor the juxtapositions that attend such thinking. For this reason, I used the Chinese proverb "At midnight noon is born" to accent or affirm the difference between Barth and Cone in their respective contexts, signaling a way to imagine a healthy form of totality.[113]

111. Lochman, "Church and Humanization," 133.

112. West, *Cornel West Reader*, 306. Emphasis in original.

113. As a reminder, this proverb is a caveat that "life sooner or later goes over into

Imagining Barth and Cone within the movement of the whole indicates why black music is so important. To invoke Aaron Copland, "music provides the broadest possible vista for the imagination."[114] Hence, when we find individuals or even traditions within the movement of the whole, we find the whole in each position.[115] Musicians, in fact, often breath this air of creativity almost naturally and contribute to a form of thinking that can lead us toward dynamic productions of knowledge that move according to different rhythms—that fire the free play of the imagination. For this reason Monk's musical aesthetic offers a symbolic touchstone for new modes of thinking.

In Monk's heyday bebop artists worked, for the most part, according to a different circadian rhythm, one that transcended the dichotomy between midnight and noon. Their daily rhythms were nurtured by the evening hours and the mystery of the night that expands artistic creativity and freedom beyond the binaries we employ to categorize human life and thought. Many artists, generally speaking, are even more attuned to the nonhuman components of creation, revealing what Andrew Greeley, the Catholic priest and popular writer, called "otherness in everything"; otherness in the mountains, oceans, lakes, and rivers, even otherness in the darkness—akin to the way the darkness became Howard Thurman's friend and comforted him in the nighttime.[116] During the flowering of bop, Monk and others treated the midnight like a metaphorical noon and attended to its meanings. Midnight was embraced. His popular tune "'Round Midnight" signifies the paradox that also resides in the term "noon of night." Even the connotations that occasionally plague the term "midnight hour" with its ominous tones were abandoned by Monk and his friends, including those soulful whites, such as the aptly named "Jazz Baroness," Nica Koenigswarter, who retired from the clubs and regathered at various places like the home of Mary Lou Williams and the Baroness's "Cathouse" where they literally created music well into the morning hours. These were improvised communities, that is, secular parables, and they created new modes of expression that expanded the darkness round midnight into morning, making it luminous, honing their crafts in the dark and playfully creating new rhythms, riffs, and chords as they shared musical wisdom with one another—that dark wisdom

its opposite." We see things one-sidedly and thus we must not sacrifice the whole by exceeding ourselves in a part of ourselves. For this description, see Van der Post, *Dark Eye in Africa*, 119–20.

114. Copland, *Music and Imagination*, 7.

115. This is a paraphrase of Barth's metaphor of the whole and parts. K. Barth, *Faith of the Church*, 57.

116. On this point, see Greeley, *Religion*, 72.

that Davíd Carrasco, the historian of religions, calls the "dark cornucopia," celebrating the light of community in the dark.[117]

Perhaps this explains why the social and political witness of slaves—who thrived to "make a way out of no way," who worshiped in brush arbor meetings, who created the invisible institution, and who often lived closer to the creation—became a preserving reality for Christian faith and the (inter)rupting possibilities thereof. As Thurman noted, "[By] some amazing but vastly creative spiritual insight the slave undertook the redemption for a religion that the master had profaned in his midst."[118] It is also no wonder that early black witnesses to the gospel began with self-affirmation rather than some preamble that addressed black suffering.

Even today as black Americans persevere in the richness of their experiences, theology must be true to the collective identities of these uprooted people who developed a constructive relationship to the "talking book." Still, black people must remain hermeneutically suspicious of modern techniques that claim mastery in the world, especially those that degrade the surplus, the richness and density, and the depth of complexity emerging from black religious life. We must embrace methodologies that spiritually nurture the creative imagination. To be sure, if we hear the light, such modes of thought, when adopted, can reframe our relationship to the natural world, and nurture a style and form of theology that transcends Christian nationalism and civil religions, which are nourished by categories of whiteness and stifled by dogmatic denominational concerns.[119] I will not belabor this point, or as they say in jazz, "stretch out," but perhaps a way forward can be found in how we attend to the darkness.

The Spirit in the Dark: A Melodielehre as a Theology for Nature

During some of the darkest moments in American history, music mattered. More importantly, music elevated black lives spiritually by ritualizing black existence and testifying to "a dimension of promise and new reality that could not be contained in human theologies and philosophies."[120] Music still harbors this potential today. Although a lack of allegiance to heritages,

117. Carrasco uses this language in personal conversations.

118. Thurman, *Deep River*, 36.

119. This framing is a critical response to Charles Long, who draws on C. Eric Lincoln to suggest a way to expand the data and methods for doing black theology. "African American Religion in the United States of America: An Interpretive Essay," in Long, *Ellipsis*, 200.

120. Cone, *Spirituals and the Blues*, 90.

traditions, and institutions characterizes the postmodern era, the same affirmation of life heard in the sorrow songs infuses the spirituals, the blues, jazz, and the best of modern black music. This history speaks to the power of music, and this would not be the first time that a "musical experience sets forth an alternative vision to the way things have been, a vision of a new and better time."[121] Still, the idea that Thelonious's stylistics can be imagined as an icon of the kingdom of God and offer insights into theological structure, the substance of theology, and its symbolics may surprise those who think primarily in historicist or rationalistic modes of thought. I will reiterate here what Monk's stylistics anticipate, even more sharply, as a form of theology that advances Barth and Cone from a pneumatological starting point.

First, in keeping with the overall theme and structure of this book, Monk's mode of musical thinking provides the illustrative power to help us reconceptualize and restructure the architectural form often associated with Barth's ordering of the theological topics, *loci theologici*. He moved along a line from creation to reconciliation and ultimately to redemption. Second, Monk's penchant for "improvising on the melody" as the decisive basis and criterion for his composing suggestively reiterates the inner material content heard in a mode of theologizing *from* revelation as the one whole truth *to* partial truths, lights, and voices within the external world of the covenant. Barth's (and Cone's) preservation of the revelation of Christ as the definitive locus for redemption is thus preserved, analogically speaking, in Monk's preoccupation with the melodic foundation or cantus firmus, providing a way for us to rethink the peculiar ordering I use without deprioritizing the revelation of God. Put differently, variations on the melody find their ultimate meaning in the melodic content itself, i.e., from the Word to the words or vice versa, ex-centrically.[122]

When accenting a pneumatological Christology, we can use Monk as an icon of the eschaton and bring more diverse forms of data into the constellation of the melodic center of revelation. The unfamiliar coming from Monk can be interpreted through the Spirit in the Dark. In this way the divine mystery itself liberates us from the impulse to ground our aesthetic imaginations in modern techniques and their limitations. This freedom includes a freedom from what Jürgen Moltmann identified as monarchical patterns (although I believe Barth was concerned with a different order

121. Steckel, "How Can Music," 24.

122. The notion of thinking in an "ex-centric" direction toward reconciliation with Christ as the center is essentially grounded in Barth's view of the covenant as the internal ground of creation. Again, the language of "ex-centric" is borrowed from Jan Lochman, "Reconciliation and Creation," 171–72.

than what Moltmann criticizes).[123] And although it is the tendency of some to understand the pneumatic (spiritual) over against the christic (christological), which includes the human, Monk's music promotes a form of thinking that embraces harmony in the triadic activity of God that includes the Spirit. It is the Spirit that ensures our harmony beyond contradictions. Ideally, we should hear the Trinitarian life of God in a "harmonic cluster."[124] As the redemptorist theologian Francois Durrwell points out, there is an "indestructible unity of the Spirit and Christ . . . [and] an attentive ear can perceive two melodies."[125] Indeed, in the union between pneumatology and Christology, according to Barth, Christ is interpreted through the Spirit of Christ. Monk's musical language of "harmonic cluster," therefore, presents us with a way to think with the harmony and distinction necessary to honor the polyphony of life that resides in the world of God.

This brings me to the third contribution Monk makes as a parable of the eschaton. Monk's insistence on the logistics of building musically on a centering melody or cantus firmus provides a way for theology to break through its shell to an extension to other voices, melodies, or counterpoints that, according to Bonhoeffer, "give life a wholeness and at the same time assure us that nothing calamitous can happen as long as the *cantus firmus* is kept going."[126] Although Bonhoeffer was more proficient in classical music, and he probably did not think about music with the same capaciousness as a jazzman like Monk, the logics are the same. The cantus firmus allows for other melodies, which Bonhoeffer calls "melodies of life," to exist in their complexity and versatility. With even a little bit of imagination Monk's various accents, notes, motives, and melodies come to represent an eschatological symbol of redemption where all sorts of life's conditions are recognizable within the purview of the divine melody.

These melodies of life are akin to Barth's so-called "doctrine of lights,"[127] a theological position that was part of his early beginnings. Barth has, in fact, been criticized for abandoning his early position, which in hindsight has been reconceptualized. While I tend to be sympathetic to Bonhoeffer's masterful interpretations, here it seems clear that he prejudged Barth's

123. See Markus Barth's brief description of what culture means to Barth in his response to Michael Novak at the Karl Barth Colloquium that convened at Union Theological Seminary in 1970: M. Barth, "Response to Novak."

124. Solis's description is perhaps most pertinent among many: "By 'harmonic cluster' I intend to preserve both a sense of the triadic, harmonic, and melodically progressive aspects of these concatenations of pitches." Solis, *Monk's Music*, 211–12.

125. Durrwell, *Holy Spirit of God*, 92.

126. Bonhoeffer, *Letters and Papers*, 303. Emphasis in original.

127. *CD* IV/3.1; see §69.2.

theology based on the Romans commentary and the early beginnings of the *Church Dogmatics*. Jürgen Moltmann reiterates Bonhoeffer's position, contending that Barth "never consistently followed through this beginning of the *Church Dogmatics*," referring to Barth's flirtation with a "kind of public, universal theology."[128] To the contrary, Barth's doctrine of lights can be interpreted to represent the logical turn of his earlier theological beginnings and anticipate his ultimate direction toward embracing the natural world in light of revelation. For this reason, I routinely describe Barth's theology of revelation as inaugurating what I call *a more natural "natural theology"* or a more radical natural theology, a viewpoint that can be discussed as a "theology for nature."[129] This insight aligns me with the position Moltmann describes as a third possible tradition for engaging natural theology, that is, "Christian theology as the true natural theology."[130]

Barth's singular focus on revelation may explain the logic behind his hesitancy to canonize any of the "free communications of the Lord" as being other than extraordinary.[131] Borrowing an apt phrase from Robert Jensen, the Lutheran theologian, it seems that this hesitancy represents Barth's efforts to maintain a "disciplinary grip" in order to avoid slipping into a polymorphous view of creation. Indeed, polymorphous is not polyphonic.

As Eberhard Busch contends, Barth's "sharp nose" and sensitivity to theological danger characterized his outlook, which may have been too cautious.[132] Moreover, despite his profound appreciation for freedom as human responsibility, Barth also sought to avoid any slippage into a kind of nostalgia for previous traditions, especially those that gave way to reification of German institutions and ideological views of humanity. Thus, he maintained a well-earned suspicion of the danger in cultural trends, fashions, and fads

128. Moltmann, *Experiences in Theology*, 75; see Pangritz, *Karl Barth*, 132–47. Pangritz's argument is indispensable for clarifying Bonhoeffer criticism.

129. I am not the first to use the language of a "theology of nature" as opposed to "natural theology." Reformed and Lutheran theologians have used this terminology. Raymond Anderson, for instance, identifies Barth's position as a grace-based "theology of nature," meaning God's grace is *for* nature. R. Anderson, *American Scholar Recalls*, 244–46. Joseph Sittler uses the term "*theology for* nature" even more pointedly to describe the turn of "the revelation of God in the Son to a corollary and further revelation of the Father in nature." Sittler argues, "This is not a 'natural theology' in the sense that God is disclosed in nature without the revelation in the Son; but it is a *theology for* nature in the inevitable sense that the hand of God the Creator, which is the hand of the Son, should be seen, following the Incarnation, also into nature." Sittler, *Essays on Nature and Grace*, 58. Emphasis in original.

130. Moltmann, *Experiences in Theology*, 64, 73–79.

131. *CD* IV/3.1:133.

132. Busch, "Deciding Moments," 55.

that hyphenated Christian faith and in the end substituted themselves for the gospel of Christ, positions that unwittingly qualified Christ's relationship to the world, crudely dismissing the dominant culture. In my thinking, however, the way forward is to listen for the "Spirit in the Dark" and hear not just the soulfulness of Aretha Franklin, who sings this tune, but to hear her testifying to the grounding melody of Christ.[133]

In this mode of listening, we do not merely hear the collaboration between the Father and the Son. We must hear the extension of the cantus firmus in the Spirit's witness in multiple voices, each of which plays the melody in different ways, in different rhythms and harmonics, and in different places, amounting to the polyphonic melody of the Spirit's witness in creation. Consequently, Monk's musical aesthetic makes a grand contribution to theological aesthetics because he helps us reimagine the divine theatre of grace and its relationship to the polyphony of life. His music gestures toward a more natural "natural theology," being a "secular parable" that attunes us to a more kaleidoscopic view of creation. Thus, when Monk is interpreted as a "secular parable," Barth's doctrine of lights or *Lichtenlehre* can be reimagined as a doctrine of melodies, *Melodielehre*, and thus we can hear the Spirit in the Dark.

Spiritual Seculars and Their Playful Versatility[134]

If we follow this renewed vision of the natural world, then Monk's jazz can function as a powerful metaphor for thinking structurally, substantially (around the inner material content of faith), and symbolically as a "spiritual secular," a true word that gestures to the signs, symptoms, indications, and tokens of the kingdom.[135] This way of advancing Monk as an icon builds on Cone and Barth, signifyin(g) on Cone's notion of "secular spirituals" and Barth's concept of "secular parables."[136] This signification throws light on the

133. See Cone, *God of the Oppressed*, 125.

134. The language of "playful versatility" is adopted from Earl, *Dark Symbols, Obscure Signs*, 149–55. Earl sees this type of playfulness in black folk traditions associated with folk characters like the Signifying Monkey and Brer Rabbit, who "never does the 'same trick twice'" (148). In my view, this ethic of versatility, a demonstration of wisdom, is also heard in the music of Art Tatum, Thelonious Monk, and other jazz luminaries who displayed a penchant for playful improvisations, leading them during certain songs to avoid playing the same run twice on the piano.

135. I do not use "symbol" in the Tillichian sense of the term, but more in the tradition of Joachim Wach and others who think of symbols (*di'eikonon*) as the grammar of religious experience. Thus, I use Monk as an icon to point to those symbols designed to address and ritualize certain modes of religious and nonreligious being. See Wach, *Sociology of Religion*, 19–20.

136. For an earlier discussion of this inversion of Barth and Cone, see Carr,

reason I adopted the term "spiritual secular" to signal a radical new openness toward the church, society, and world, beginning with pneumatology. This turn takes seriously both the God of *black experience* and the *God* of black experience—without separating God *from* black experience and without reducing God *to* black experience. In this patterning the astute ear will hear an echo of Chalcedonian Christology.

To employ jazz in this playful way is not to toy with the irreverent but to acknowledge "music as a vehicle for transcendence,"[137] witnessing to truth beyond a particular form. Quincy Jones, the musician and producer, stated that "jazz has a way of transforming darkness into light through comedy or taking the pain away from a bad love relationship or whatever."[138] Jazz, in this respect, signifies a form of power and agency, and this potential in jazz discloses why I have sought to mine the data of one of jazz's most important periods in history, the bebop period, and attend to Monk, a jazz original.

This latter context only partially signals Monk's importance. Because Monk is known as the bebop artist who never really played bebop, he points in another way. To employ Stanley Crouch's phrase again, Monk created "a movement within the movement."[139] On that account he can be interpreted as a revolutionary among revolutionaries. Extending my previous conversation, this means that Monk's revolutionary social horizon and music gesture toward a reality that revolutionizes our revolutions. This is not a movement or "revolution that devours its children" as the saying goes among the French; nor is it the kind of revolution that promises paradise but fails to deliver. On the contrary, Monk's music, heard parabolically, gestures structurally, materially, and symbolically to the revolutionary relationship between Christ, the divine melody, and the melodies or voices that make up the polyphony in our world of grace.

This gesturing is substantial in its import and in its playful self-referentiality; for procedurally, Monk's music functions as a medium to reframe tradition, maintaining both the discordant, anarchic, rule-breaking disorientation of bebop, but simultaneously breaking with the revolution itself and pointing to another world. It is no wonder then that when bop became known as a movement grounded in digital dexterity and virtuosity, Monk became pensive and more calculated in his playing of the piano; when technique became the rage, Monk accented the sound through strangely voiced

---

"Thelonious Monk."

137. Asante, *Afrocentric Idea*, 207–11.

138. Quoted in Rothschild, *Baroness*, 134.

139. Crouch, *Considering Genius*, 88. For the Jazz Baroness's description of bebop that informs this section, see Rothschild, *Baroness*, 134–35.

chords and intervals that highlighted the silence; and when it was touted as a music that did not allow one to dance, Monk became known for dancing in front of the bandstand, (inter)rupting that so-called sacred space.

This (inter)ruption speaks on one hand to a certain kind of self-affirmation and agency that first has its origins in an authority, i.e., a blackness that transcends the categorizations and conditions of the West; and it speaks, on the other hand, to a deeper agency grounded in a history "that materially changes all things and everything in all things."[140] In this respect Monk's mode of composing represents something more fundamental, something redemptively playful that opens up space so other "instruments" can fully participate in God's jazz combo. Recognizing this apt analogue, particularly the dialogical interdependence between performers—who share space and inspire one another—we can further elaborate on our emphasis that the melodic foundation, the basis of God's own composition, or what Dietrich Bonhoeffer called the "great counterpoint" to the polyphony of voices that witness to the kingdom through the Spirit.[141] As I noted above, Bonhoeffer brilliantly drew a correlation between the cantus firmus and other voices within the world. As he surmised, this invention of his signals the dimension of depth heard in the Chalcedonian formula, i.e., "without confusion and without separation." Improvising in this respect is founded on (but not confused with or separated from) the divine melody. This construction, then, echoes the inner material content of the gospel and allows for a "unity in diversity" and "diversity in unity." Bonhoeffer called it "a musical reflection of this Christological fact."[142]

This connection allows me to build on Barth's Mozart, who "heard the whole world of creation enveloped by this light." Barth recognized in

140. *CD* II/1:258. Those familiar with left-wing Barthian thinkers will recognize this passage as a programmatic passage with its play on the words the "Wholly Other" (der Ganz Andere) being linked to the One who in Christ changes everything (der Ganz Ändernde), in *CD* IV/1:316.

141. For an extended discussion on "redemptive play," see Raymond Carr, "Can Work Be Redeemed Through Play," in J. G. Smith and Renslow, *Blessed Are Those*, 25–40. See Bonhoeffer, *Letters and Papers*, 219.

142. See Bonhoeffer, *Letters and Papers*, 303, 305. He used the terms "undivided and yet distinct." Cf. *CD* IV/3.1:113 (§69.2, "The Light of Life"). I should note here that I did not first learn of the cantus firmus from Bonhoeffer, but from Monk, I subsequently discovered Bonhoeffer's invention. With that noted, Bonhoeffer has helped to deepen my christological thinking and may have had an influence on Barth who also refers to the cantus firmus and polyphony in *CD* IV/3.1. For more insights into Dietrich Bonhoeffer, see *Epistrophy* (vol. 1) and *'Round Midnight* (vol. 2) where Bonhoeffer is considered in relation to both my hermeneutical strategy and Barth's development of revelation, respectively.

Mozart an echo of God's providential concern for the world.[143] He imagined being "transported to the threshold of a world which in sunlight and storm, by day and by night, is a good and ordered world."[144] Hence, Mozart captured the goodness of all creation and standing over against everything else echoed God's triumphant yes, which relativizes the shadow unto being less than an ultimate darkness.[145] Life finds its meaning as it assembles in the orbit of this special subject matter (*Sache*). Indeed, according to Barth, everything comes alive. And this is precisely where Monk's emphasis fundamentally complements Mozart's. Monk's vision signals a radical subjectivity. His attention to the melody was not constricted in a way that allowed its totality to overdetermine the subjectivity of the viewing/listening subject. On the contrary, as French critic André Hodier puts it, "his music exhibits an underlying complexity, or strangeness, that does not match up easily with conventional musical thinking,"[146] including the thinking of Barth's beloved Mozart. Monk heard the *particulars* of the world of creation. He certainly heard the negative with the positive like Mozart, for the ludic quality in his music also sounds forth with a joyful yes. But there is more articulated in Monk. His harmonic progressions and melodic variations and rhythmic cadences are an exercise in assembling the familiar in an unfamiliar manner.[147] To speak in the mode of Monk, then, is to identify an unfamiliar way of listening to the familiar. The question is do we have ears to hear Monk's acoustics as an artistic analogue of the world of God?

While Monk did not have religious correspondences in mind, his approach to composition and performance provides the melodic connection for the deeper pattern I use to imagine *why* "true words" exist alongside the one word of God. This connection furnishes the analogy as well for thinking of Christ as the "melody for theology," and it sets up the pneumatological turn to the church that improvises on the melody. As a matter of fact, Monk's musical stylistics teach us the way to accent the center of theology without reducing the possibilities and virtualities on the periphery of faith, without capitulating to provincial categories, and most of all, without eliminating our openness to what some may deem is the alienating center itself—as the way forward.

The melody, the cantus firmus, is the constant here. It is the centering agency, and it grounds the multivocal or multidialogical forms of freedom,

143. *CD* III/3:298.

144. K. Barth, *Wolfgang Amadeus Mozart*, 22.

145. *CD* III/3:298.

146. Van der Bliek, *Thelonious Monk Reader*, 226.

147. Van der Bliek, *Thelonious Monk Reader*, 226.

organizing (without totalizing) the sonic space for the multiplicity of voices that resound throughout creation in their own unique ways. This thematic interplay between centering melody and various dialogical forms includes the polyphonic witness of the churches. This expansion from a centering melody to polyphonic forms of witness suggests a pneumatic eschatological turn. This turning or epistrophe means that the way toward a theology of playful freedom is to think harmoniously in a way where we do not merely move from the melodic center to other modes of being, but where we think ex-centrically. Another way to imagine this is to ask what the black church brings to the melodic center. In my view, the answer to this question sets forth why we must begin, in this "new world," with the improvisations of Cone rather than with the melody like Barth.

Avoiding any return to the failed solutions of neoorthodoxy, a radical interpretation of Barth's theology has a corresponding relationship to the gift of blackness as seen in black religion and black theology. In fact, the harmonious thinking I am suggesting here honors the correspondence between tradition writ large and various traditions that, according to Rabbi Max Kadushin, "may account for its unity and yet allow for the differences of opinion."[148] Moreover, the best interpretations of Cone's theology, *mutatis mutandis*, acknowledge his profound concern for black consciousness as providing "a theology of revolution that 'begins and ends with the man Jesus—his life, death, and resurrection.'"[149]

Cone's contributions must be heard not only within the corresponding relationship between God the Father, who is the great Giver of gifts, or Jesus, the Son who is the perfect Gift of God. It must be heard in relation to the Spirit and the giftedness of the black church. Stated differently, the charismata of the black church are heard in the improvisational gift of blackness; for blackness is the gift of the Spirit. Christian faith must therefore come to terms with what the black experience means in the American church, but it is uncommon, even for black theologians, to wrestle with this problem. As a point of fact, Gayraud Wilmore insightfully addressed this problem when he summed up an ecumenical discussion in view of a common expression of apostolic faith in Richmond, Virginia (1985). He stated that "one can count on the fingers of one hand the number of times in the past two hundred

148. Here again I articulate a "harmonious thinking" that draws on Rabbi Max Kadushin's comments that "the term 'harmonious thinking' puts us in mind immediately of aesthetic harmonies." Kadushin, *Theology of Seder Eliahu*, 20, 29.

149. See Sydney Ahlstrom's cogent analysis of "Black Religion in the Twentieth Century," in Ahlstrom, *Religious History*, 1077. Ahlstrom quotes from Cone but I single out his interpretation as it relates to the gift of the black tradition and its potential contribution to an ecumenism. For Cone, see *Black Theology and Black Power*, 34.

years that black church leaders have met in a conference to promulgate a theological opinion on ecumenism."[150]

This means that the charism the Lord has given the black church is profoundly unique. What is its gift or giftedness? Cornish Rogers points insightfully to one of its contributions during the same conference mentioned above. He believes "the meaning of blackness as a religious symbol contributes to the universal meaning of the Christian faith."[151] The marginalization of black Americans opened the door not only to a new orientation among blacks, but to new ways of living out Christian faith. Thus, it is precisely in the crucible of oppression that God sanctified black experience for use in witnessing to the kingdom.[152] And it is precisely in the turn to the universalism of faith in the natural world that Monk as an icon (i.e., Monk's music in its substance and form) makes his greatest contribution.

As a spiritual secular Monk allows us to (re)imagine the connection between the central melody and the various registers, chords, motives, rhythms, and countermelodies that symbolize the polyphonic world of voices and their vitality around the melody. One can, in other words, truly hear the music around the music. Imagined this way, Barth and Cone represent two counterpoints, a cluster of harmonic possibilities on the pathway to imagining a new kind of theological music, especially when their differences are affirmed without prioritizing distinctions between them. More than this, they represent the objective (Barth) and the subjective (Cone) in faith; which means that through the prism of Monk they can represent a subjectivity within the objectivity of faith, two points "in the circle of its event" along with the people of Israel and other traditions.[153] As the cantus firmus sounds, the counterpoints gather round in a polyphonic chorus—each singing its own melody in response—"as the spirit enables them." Their differences understood ex-centrically, meaning in relation to the center, allow for the various perspectives to bring a dimension of depth to the witness of the gospel. We hear, symphonically, the above and below, the joy and pain, the sunshine and rain, at midnight and noon, where all things are a part of God's refrain.

When hearing the playful versatility in Monk as a "true word," theologies need not flirt with a Pollyannaish return to some idealized vision of church and certainly not engage in some ideological effort to "make America great again" under the auspices of Christian faith for a "Christian nation."

150. Wilmore, "Disturbing Ecumenism," 115.

151. Rogers, "Gift of Blackness," 572.

152. For sociopolitical charisms, refer to Mühlen, *Charismatic Theology*, 157.

153. *CD* II/1:262–63.

We must resist such romanticizing of either the church or the nation and avoid any idealized visions of a future America. Rather, we should embrace the radical realism where churches stand in solidarity with the world. Churches, as the body of Christ, are called to lead the way *or* follow in service while "looking for and identifying with those who are voiceless."[154] This can be the churches' true service to America, and this reveals why we should begin with Cone's theological vision rather than Barth's since Cone accentuated the black *experience* in America. Indeed, found within the theological grammar of black experience in America is a critique of any emerging, grandiose claims about America or its future; moreover, a certain aspect of black religious experience and history anchors this discussion squarely in the American setting and within the matrix of industrial complexes where "structures of evil are camouflaged, the enemy is elusive, and the victim trained to accept the values of the oppressor."[155]

This peculiar American location is one of the reasons the methodologies and metrics of the academy often function as a cipher to maintain whiteness as property in America, even aiding and abetting the inertia that preserves the nation's structural racism. Theology participates in this structure as well and consents to non-inclusive disciplinary spaces in the American academy. This is perilous for African Americans for many black Americans live according to a "metronome sense," a profound sense of rhythm that transcends and resists the prefabricated rhythms of the academy.

Randy Weston, the jazz pianist, goes so far as to argue that "music" was black peoples' first language. The music of God, the music of Mother Nature, that is, the birds, the wind, and the sound of thunder. And no matter what one thinks about Weston's musings, it is true that black Americans, indigenes, and others are epitomized by organic relationships in this world of contingencies. This world was never meant to be a perfect world but a world of flesh and blood, a world filled with angularities, dissonances, deformations, contradictions, and concrete limitations. It is a world where the power of death manifests itself in human and corporate alienations. This is the world *from the beginning*. It is a world with silences, evils, and abominations.

Appealing to Monk's aesthetic sensibility, illuminates this world of dissonances because of the brilliance of his harmonic scheme. Through his music we come to terms with the dissonances of life, life's gritty realism(s), revealed in a dissonance that is analogous to the harmony of God's creation, but we also hear a dissonance in conjunction with Monk's rhythms. According to Nat Hentoff, Monk used rhythm to set his harmonies in

154. Cone, "Introduction to Black Theology," 61. I am thinking of church as a community of witness.

155. Cone, *Black Theology and Black Power*, 105.

relief, choosing dramatic time signatures.[156] These rhythms of creation are echoed in the language about God that comes out of an aesthetic perception of black experience whose meaning, according to Cone, is "found in its style."[157] For that reason, black life is never reducible to the dissonance in the world because black styles of life are expressed in the "surplus" of black aesthetic modes of being, which sound forth in Martin Luther King Jr.'s oratory and B. B. King's tremolo; they are heard in James Cone's blues inflections and Aretha Franklin's tone; in Toni Morrison's characters and Denzel Washington's walk; in Oprah Winfrey's generosity and Keith David's voice; in Michael Jordan's creativity and Mary Lou Williams's touch. Turning to black life in the mode of Monk, then, can give us an aesthetic analogue where we find access to the excess of life's playful versatility that affirms the giftedness of black life, despite its beginning in the crucible that is described by W. E. B. Du Bois as a descent "into Hell; and in the third century they arouse from the dead."[158]

To find hope in such giftedness is to live in the midst of this world, but not be alone in it. For in this world, we do not simply tear down walls; we build coalitions. We create improvised communities. We affirm traditions that incorporate dissonance. We celebrate the past in new ways and embrace the future. And we shall gather at the rendezvous, a place where we will not just partly know, but a place where we will be fully known (1 Cor 13:12). For it is there in the luminous darkness at the noon of night where the Spirit in the Dark leads us in a spirit of playful freedom—the Spirit who secures our victories in the midnight hour. The Spirit who outflanks us and turns life around is the same Spirit who leads us to sound off with Fred Hammond, the gospel singer, who celebrates God's intervening actions when he sings that God turns life around in the midnight hour. For in the noon of night, when we respond as countermelodies to the harmonies and rhythms of the Melody of God,

> we not only turn the world upside down;
> but we turn it inside out and round and round;
> and outside in and right side up
> and around, and around, and around . . .[159]

156. Hentoff, *Jazz Life*, 181.

157. Cone, *Said I Wasn't*, 89–90.

158. Du Bois, *Black Reconstruction*, 727.

159. See a recommended Hammond recording in the listening guide at the end of the coda (164).

CODA

The Beginning as the Way Back

He [Raymond Carr] thinks there is something in Barth and me that can illuminate the theological enterprise when Barth's theology and Cone's theology are seen in relation to each other. I told him I left Barth a long time ago. But he said, "No, you have not." As I said last night . . . "Critics can see things in your work that you do not."
—James H. Cone (Chicago 2012)

IN THIS THEOLOGICAL AESTHETICS, I have drawn from the grand contributions of Karl Barth, James Cone, Charles H. Long, Angela Davis, and many others to proffer what I interpret as a beginning to a constructive theology of playful freedom. Recognizing them as counterpoints in harmony with Christ, I have endeavored to create new pedagogical directions for black theology and theology in general. In this respect, Monk's musical thinking is employed as a functional analogue to structure the architectural harmony of this whole project, to substantiate the mystery of the melodic foundation or inner material content at the heart of the text, and to emphasize the alternating rhythms between God's freedom and black liberation. Moreover, I have attempted to gesture symbolically beyond any parochial vision of a racial aesthetic to the polyphonic nature of creation itself. This required me to affirm the differences between Barth and Cone throughout—by strengthening their arguments in light of my interpretations of their theologies. In this regard, this book represents the culmination of a constructive exercise grounded in Jesus Christ, the "great counterpoint," to use Bonhoeffer's term, who reconciles our differences.

While differences between thinkers like Barth and Cone are often framed disjunctively, playing up the discontinuities or contradictions (in terms of their individual theologies and the traditions that follow), Monk's harmonious thinking has encouraged me to resist such bifurcated thinking and engage in a theological *turning about* (epistrophe). The christological concentration therefore resounds in this project and opens the way, in immensely creative ways, to the playful joy that percolates in the spontaneous interplay suggested throughout this project. Underscoring their correspondence, I believe Barth and Cone belong on the same melodic line in revelation and harmonize in freedom and liberation. Naturally, I not only affirm their differences but also seek to strengthen the differences they affirm, playing in the tensions and contradictions that attend even the shadow side of their relative strengths. Indeed, I have benefited from sustained efforts to hear and rehear these theological giants—without judging one by the other—because their relative strengths have contributed to the sociopolitical context, particularly my location(s) in the American academy and the church.[1]

I close with an overture to the reader. I offer you an invitation to the bandstand—to come up front and hear these two theologians *in the mode of Monk*. On the whole, to think in "Monk mode" is a summons to think counterintuitively to our dominant Western logics; remembering that Monk "was interested in how things struggle with their opposites."[2] And to foster your thinking in this mode, I appeal to the imagination and summarize in broad lines what I have attempted to say in this lengthy project: I first invite you to imagine Karl Barth's *Mozartean* theology and James Cone's *blues-inflected* theology, both "singing a new theological song, a blues song." Imagine them both coalescing here in the aural aesthetics of Monk's jazz.

You can even imagine them juxtaposed above and below, angled like the two Monk silhouettes pictured on the cover of this book. Barth approaches theology "from above," from the perspective of the humanity of God; whereas Cone approaches the discipline primarily "from below," from the perspective of the black oppressed. Hermeneutically, Barth appeals to God above, signifying on the *form*; Cone, however, attends to black humanity below, "dancing with his words," *signifyin(g)* on the form. Christologically, Barth improvises on the *melody*; Cone *improvises* on the melody. Ethically, Barth affirms God's *freedom* for liberation; Cone affirms God's freedom for *liberation*. Their respective sociopolitical situations and locations are indeed rife with implications, filled with potential for harmonic progressions and melodic variations that encourage rhythmic alternation(s)

1. An affirmation of difference, formally understood, is an attempt that "teaches us to see the justification for the other's point of view." See Gadamer, *On Education, Poetry, and History*, 152–53. Gadamer described it as the "soul of hermeneutics."

2. Komunyakaa, "It's Always Night," 52.

between God's freedom and human liberation. Indeed, when heard together in the alternating rhythms of a harmonic cluster, Barth's emphasis on God's freedom animates Cone's involvement in black liberation—similar to the way "redemption is the spiritual ground of creation." Inversely, Cone's involvement in black liberation substantiates Barth's emphasis on God's freedom—similar to the way "creation is the natural ground for redemption."[3] For this reason, rather than abandoning Barth in his subsequent theological development—primarily because of the criticism coming from black theologians—Cone could have freely intensified his engagement with Barth, signifyin(g) on European forms and substantiating the God who loves in freedom as the ground of liberation. Moreover, those who have studiously avoided Cone and his transmutation of Barth's theology have abandoned the charismata of the black experience, the gift of blackness, and they have ignored the "primogenitor," the child of the next generation, of the Reformation in America.

In these harmonies, melodies, and alternating rhythms, the reader should imagine Barth and Cone, even now, as living voices standing together, juxtaposed theologically. Barth emphasizing the *already*; Cone emphasizing the *not yet.* Barth fixing his eyes on *die Sache*, the centrality of Christ; Cone dancing with his words in the black situation—in a form of liberating praxis for his people. Barth moves *from above* to below, *apocalyptic in impulse*, irrupting like a bolt from the blue; Cone sees Barth moving and moves *from below* to above, *cataclysmic in impulse*, erupting like a volcano. When brought together in a form of spontaneous interplay, we encounter two different movements, two modes of revolt, two representatives: Karl Barth hears God's yes to God's order and no to the disorder in the European world order. James Cone hears God's no to white disorder and God's yes to black affirmation in the American world order. As Barth *turns his backside* to the devil in contempt of the world's feigned power, Cone gives the principalities and powers *a dialectical slap* in the name of Black Jesus. Barth, of course, risks reducing Christ to Christomonism. Cone risks relativizing Christ among the revolutions.

Like the dilemma for all theologians, risks of faith involve dangers if we center ourselves on some other melody. But *in the mode of Monk*, even wrong may be right and we are free "where the cantus firmus is clear and plain" to imagine Barth and Cone standing back to back, personified in their theologies. As we stand by the bandstand or sit in the audience, waiting,

3. K. Barth, "Theological Dialogue," 172. Although Barth, especially in terms of a left-wing emphasis, can be interpreted as articulating "*freedom* for liberation," this juxtaposing of Barth with Cone privileges the black experience; thus pitching Barth's theology toward human experience and sociopolitical liberation without forfeiting Barth's notion of the proper order or sequence in a theology of freedom.

listening, "hearing the light," Cone whirls around towards Barth and states, "Now you know racism is anti-human!?!" And Barth peers over his horn-rimmed glasses at Cone and responds, "Yes . . . and it is anti-Christ!"

Listening Guide

If you are new to Monk's jazz, a good place to begin is to listen to Monk, to listen to/watch the following, and to consider various ways his music is presented by others.

Thelonious Monk, "This Is My Story, This is My Song," 1967, https://www.youtube.com/watch?v=FIQ6fj1BJXo

Oscar Peterson "'Round Midnight," 2010, https://www.youtube.com/watch?v=N7yazIH4rAI

Thelonious Monk Quartet with John Coltrane, "Epistrophy" (live at Carnegie Hall, New York), 1957, https://www.youtube.com/watch?v=Xm1A5RYKjJQ

John Coltrane, "Trinkle, Tinkle," 1957, https://www.youtube.com/watch?v=3_dZHmMg4zE

Marvin Gaye, "Symphony," 1985, https://www.youtube.com/watch?v=MFGYiAm3YS4

Clint Holmes, "At the Rendezvous" (featuring Joey DeFrancesco), 2017, https://www.youtube.com/watch?v=mo9wVdi32HQ

Aretha Franklin, "Spirit in the Dark," 1970, https://www.youtube.com/watch?v=SM_cjUXZEQA

Fred Hammond, "We're Blessed," 1991, https://www.youtube.com/watch?v=UYVYM671MGc

Thelonious Monk, "Blue Monk," 1966, https://www.youtube.com/watch?v=yHKloeuhZIo

Glossary[1]

Affirmation of difference	A term used to describe the strengthening of an interlocutor's argument for the purpose of a richer conversation. In this way the disagreement can become in essence a strong counterpoint.
Arpeggio	A chord played with notes separated in rapid succession moving up or down the scale.
Bebop	A genre of jazz style that emerged in the 1940s (c. 1943–53). Also known as re-bop.
Blues	Emerging from the life of black slaves, the blues is a form of United States folk music, including work songs and slave laments. The blues came to a completed form in the nineteenth century.
Cadence	A progression of chords that produces certain effects at the end of musical phrases.
Cantus firmus	A fixed melody played underneath other melodies or voices.
Chord	Simultaneous sounding of two or more notes.
Cluster	A musical chord comprised of at least three adjacent tones in a scale.
Coda	From the Latin term "tail," a coda is the distinct closing section of a musical tune.

1. For further reference to short concise definitions of jazz, visit the Jazz Glossary at the Center for Jazz Studies—Columbia University, https://ccnmtl.columbia.edu/projects/jazzglossary/.

Countermelody	A secondary melody that is played simultaneously with a fixed or lead melody. This melody is played in counterpoint, hence countermelody.
Counterpoint	A musical contribution with several independent melodic voices occurring simultaneously.
Dissonance	The discordant or disjunctive sound that occurs when two or more notes are played together.
Fugue	From Latin, meaning "flight." A musical term in which three or more voices sequentially follow or "fly" after one another in an imitative or non-imitative manner. It is sometimes identified with counterpoint.
Ground tone	The fundamental or first partial tone that is the key component of a complex sound arrangement.
Head	A collective arrangement, often at the beginning of a tune.
Heterophony	Denotes a more sophisticated harmonic and rhythmic independence of individual parts than polyphony.
Improvisation	A manner of playing extemporaneously. It is often interpreted as the key element in jazz.
Jazz	Originating among African American communities in the late nineteenth century, the jazz genre emerged from the blues and ragtime. Jazz has become one of the most influential forms of music, influencing traditional and modern musical expressions.
Locus theologicus	A term used to refer to a place or source for theological knowledge.
Methodus est arbitraria	This is the concept that the method we used in theology is not normative or final but subject to a form of variety based on the predilections of the theologian.
Modulation	A shift from one tonal center to another.
Motive	A motive (or motif) is a melodic idea or phrase that is reproduced throughout a movement or composition.
Pianissimo	A musical movement played very softly.

Polyphony	A Greek term meaning "many voiced" that characterizes a musical structure with two or more independent musical lines.
Polyrhythm	The use of several rhythms simultaneously.
Rent party	An informal party occurring in the 1920s and early 1930s.
Riff	A short harmonic, melodic, or rhythmic pattern repeated often in a jazz composition.
Ring shout	A dance in which dancers move counterclockwise in a ring, often singing in a *call-and-response* form.
Sequence	A musical phrase segment or phrase often repeated at different intervals. The term in this context refers to a peculiar ordering in theology.
Soundscape	Refers to music when considered in a larger group of component sounds.
Stretch out	When one plays as long as one wants. John Coltrane would often stretch out when Monk visited the bar.
Stride piano	A style of pianism that favors a dominant left hand pattern that alternates between base notes and chords. It substitutes as a rhythm section. Stride emerged in the early twentieth century (c. 1917–30).
Subject	The main melodic line in a fugue.
Swing	A genre of American jazz (c. 1935–45) characterized by popular "swing" bands or "big bands" that is often identified as the "swing era." Also a rhythmic element where the emphasis is on beats two and four or on some other rhythmic element.
Tonic	The tonic or tonic chord is the root (or first) chord of the key. The tonic establishes the tonal center and creates resolution.
Vamp	The term used to describe a chord progression or rhythmic figure that is repeated indefinitely into or out of a tune.
Via cognoscendi	A Latin phrase used to identify a "way of knowing."

Bibliography

Abrahams, Roger D. *Deep Down in the Jungle: Negro Narrative Folklore from the Streets of Philadelphia.* Rev. ed. Chicago: Aldine, 1970.

Ahlstrom, Sydney E. *A Religious History of the American People.* New Haven, CT: Yale University Press, 1972.

Anderson, Raymond Kemp. *An American Scholar Recalls Karl Barth's Golden Years as a Teacher (1958–1964): The Mature Theology.* Lewiston, NY: Mellen, 2013.

———. *Karl Barth's Table Talk: Transcripts of Barth's Conversations with His Students at the Bruderholz Restaurant in Basel During the Years 1958–1964.* Lewiston, NY: Mellen, 2014.

———. *New Testament Micro-Ethics: On Trusting Freedom; The First Christians' Genotype for Multicultural Living.* Eugene, OR: Wipf & Stock, 2018.

Anderson, Victor. *Beyond Ontological Blackness: An Essay on African American Religious and Cultural Criticism.* New York: Continuum, 1995.

———. "Flesh-Stuff: The Matter of the Reality of God(s)." *American Religion* 2 (2021) 25–38.

Aquinas, Thomas. *Summa Theologica.* 5 vols. Translated by Fathers of the English Dominican Province. New York: Christian Classics, 1948.

Arendt, Hannah. *On Revolution.* Penguin Classics. Repr., New York: Penguin, 1963.

Asante, Molefi Kete. *The Afrocentric Idea.* Rev. ed. Philadelphia: Temple University Press, 1998.

Baldwin, James. *The Cross of Redemption: Uncollected Writings.* Edited by Randall Kenan. New York: Pantheon, 2010.

Baraka, Imamu Amiri. *Black Music.* New York: Akashic, 1968.

———. *Blues People: Negro Music in White America.* New York: HarperCollins, 1963.

Barth, Karl. *Against the Stream: Shorter Post-War Writings 1942–52.* Edited by Ronald Gregor Smith. London: SCM, 1954.

———. *Barth in Conversation.* 3 vols. Edited by Eberhard Busch et al. Translated by Fellows of Center for Barth Studies. Louisville: Westminster John Knox, 2017–19.

———. *The Christian Life: Lecture Fragments.* Translated by Geoffrey W. Bromiley. Vol. IV/4 of *Church Dogmatics.* T&T Clark Cornerstones. Edinburgh: T&T Clark, 1981.

———. *Church and State*. Translated by G. Ronald Howe. Greenville, SC: Smyth & Helwys, 1991.

———. "Continental vs. Anglo-Saxon Theology: A Preliminary Reply to Reinhold Niebuhr." *ChrCent* (1949) 201–4.

———. *Dogmatics in Outline*. Translated by G. T. Thompson. New York: Harper & Row, 1959.

———. *The Epistle to the Romans*. Translated by Edwyn C. Hoskyns. London: Oxford University Press, 1933.

———. *Ethics*. Translated by Geoffrey W. Bromiley. New York: Seabury, 1981.

———. *Evangelical Theology: An Introduction*. Translated by Grover Foley. Grand Rapids: Eerdmans, 1963.

———. *The Faith of the Church: A Commentary on the Apostle's Creed According to Calvin's Catechism*. Translated by Gabriel Vahanian. New York: Living Age, 1958.

———. *Final Testimonies*. Edited by Eberhard Busch. Translated by Geoffrey W. Bromiley. Grand Rapids: Eerdmans, 1977.

———. *Gespräche: 1959–1962*. Collected Works 25. Zurich: Theologisch, 1995.

———. "The Gift of Freedom." In *The Humanity of God*, translated by John Newton Thomas and Thomas Wieser, 66–96. Philadelphia: Westminster, 1960.

———. *God in Action*. Translated by E. G. Homrighausen and Karl J. Ernst. Manhasset, NY: Round Table, 1963.

———. *The Göttingen Dogmatics: Instruction in the Christian Religion*. Edited by Hannelotte Reiffen. Translated by Geoffrey W. Bromiley. 2 vols. Grand Rapids: Eerdmans, 1990.

———. *The Heidelberg Catechism for Today*. Translated by Shirley C. Guthrie Jr. London: Epworth, 1964.

———. *The Humanity of God*. Translated by John Newton Thomas and Thomas Wieser. Philadelphia: Westminster, 1960.

———. *Karl Barth 1886–1968: How I Changed My Mind*. Edited by John D. Godsey. Edinburgh: Saint Andrew, 1969.

———. *Die Lehre vom Worte Gottes: Prolegomena zur christlichen Dogmatik*. Vol. 1 of *Die christliche Dogmatik im Entwurf*. Munich: Kaiser, 1927.

———. *Letters: 1961–1968*. Edited by Jürgen Fangmeier and Hinrich Stoevesandt. Translated by Geoffrey W. Bromiley. Grand Rapids: Eerdmans, 1981.

———. "Poverty." In *Against the Stream: Shorter Post-War Writings 1942–52*, edited by Ronald Gregor Smith, 241–46. London: SCM, 1954.

———. "Reformation as Decision." In *The Reformation: Basic Interpretations*, edited and translated by Lewis W. Spitz, 153–70. Lexington, MA: Heath & Co., 1972.

———. *Der Römerbrief*. [1st ed.] Collected Works 16. Zurich: Theologisch, 1985.

———. "Schleiermacher." In *Theology and Church: Shorter Writings 1920–1928*, 159–99. New York: Harper & Row, 1962.

———. "Theologians Answer Student Questions." *Student World* 54 (1961) 151–67.

———. "A Theological Dialogue." *Theology Today* 19 (1962) 171–77.

———. *Theology and Church: Shorter Writings 1920–1928*. Translated by Louise P. Smith. New York: Harper & Row, 1962.

———. *The Theology of Schleiermacher: Lectures at Göttingen, Winter Semester of 1923/24*. Translated by Geoffrey W. Bromiley. Grand Rapids: Eerdmans, 1982.

———. *Wolfgang Amadeus Mozart*. Translated by Clarence K. Pott. Eugene, OR: Wipf & Stock, 2003.

Barth, Karl, and Eduard Thurneysen. *Come, Holy Spirit: Sermons.* Translated by G. W. Richards et al. Grand Rapids: Eerdmans, 1978.

———. *Revolutionary Theology in the Making: Barth Thurneysen Correspondence, 1914–1925.* Translated by James D. Smart. Richmond, VA: John Knox, 1964.

Barth, Markus. "Current Discussions on the Political Character of Karl Barth's Theology." In *Footnotes to a Theology: The Karl Barth Colloquium of 1972*, edited by H. Martin Rumscheidt, 77–94. N.p., Can.: Corporation for the Publication of Academic Studies in Religion in Canada, 1974.

———. "Response to Novak." *USQR* 28 (1972) 53–54.

Berkouwer, G. C. *The Triumph of Grace in the Theology of Karl Barth.* Translated by Harry R. Boer. Grand Rapids: Eerdmans, 1956.

Bonhoeffer, Dietrich. *Letters and Papers from Prison.* Edited by Eberhard Bethge. New York: Collier, 1972.

Born, Georgina, et al., eds. *Improvisation and Social Aesthetics.* Durham: Duke University Press, 2017.

Burnett, Gary W. *The Gospel According to the Blues.* Eugene, OR: Cascade, 2014.

Busch, Eberhard. "Deciding Moments in the Life and Work of Barth." *Grail* 2 (1986) 51–67.

———. "God Is God: The Meaning of a Controversial Formula and the Fundamental Problem of Speaking About God." *PSB* 7 (1986) 101–13.

———. *The Great Passion: An Introduction to Barth's Theology.* Translated by Geoffrey W. Bromiley. Grand Rapids: Eerdmans, 2004.

Byrd, Donald. "Music Without Aesthetics: How Some Nonmusical Forces and Institutions Influence Change in Black Music." *Black Scholar* 9 (1978) 2–5.

Carr, Raymond. "Barth and Cone in Dialogue on Revelation and Freedom: An Analysis of James Cone's Critical Appropriation of 'Barthian Theology.'" PhD diss., Graduate Theological Union, 2011.

———. "The Dancing Monk and the Rhythm of Divine Life: Faith, Soul, and All That Jazz." *Harvard Divinity Bulletin*, Autumn/Winter 2023. https://bulletin.hds.harvard.edu/the-dancing-monk-and-the-rhythm-of-divine-life/.

———. *Epistrophy: Historical and Hermeneutical Backgrounds.* Vol. 1 of *Theology in the Mode of Monk: An Aesthetics of Barth and Cone on Revelation and Freedom.* Eugene, OR: Cascade, 2024.

———. "Imagination Lost: The Dancing Monk and the Aesthetic Dimensions of *Theologia Naturalis*." Unpublished manuscript.

———. "Merton and Barth in Dialogue on Faith and Understanding: A Hermeneutics of Freedom and Ambiguity." *Merton Annual* 26 (2013) 181–94.

———. "'A More Certain Sound': King's Prophetic Harmony of the Sacred and the Secular." In *Prophet with a Pencil: The Continuing Significance of the "Letter from Birmingham Jail,"* edited by Arthur Sutherland. Eugene, OR: Cascade, forthcoming.

———. *'Round Midnight: Revelation and Experience in the Theologies of Barth and Cone.* Vol. 2 of *Theology in the Mode of Monk: An Aesthetics of Barth and Cone on Revelation and Freedom.* Eugene, OR: Cascade, 2024.

———. "Thelonious Monk—Icon of the Eschaton: Karl Barth, James Cone and the 'Impossible Possibility' of a Theology of Freedom." In *Karl Barth and Liberation Theology*, edited by Kaitlyn Dugan and Paul Dafydd Jones, 177–93. Explorations in Reformed Theology. London: T&T Clark, 2023.

———. "Theological Response to the 'The Living God and the Context of Idols.'" In *The Cruciform Church: Becoming a Cross-Shaped People in a Secular World*, by C.

Leonard Allen, 125–28. Anniv. ed. Abilene: Abilene Christian University Press, 2016.

———. "Wade in the Water Children: Charles Long, Karl Barth and the (Re)imagination of Matter." *American Religion* 2 (2021) 61–86.

Carter, J. Kameron. *Race: A Theological Account*. Oxford: Oxford University Press, 2008.

Chung, Paul. "Engaging Karl Barth's Missional Church and Hermeneutics: Evangelization, Reconciliation, and *Diakonia*." Lecture, Karl Barth Conference, Princeton Theological Seminary, June 2010.

———."Karl Barth and Inter-Religious Dialogue: An Attempt to Bring Karl Barth to Dialogue with Religious Pluralism." *Asia Journal of Theology* 15 (2001) 232–46.

———. *Karl Barth: God's Word in Action*. Eugene, OR: Cascade, 2008.

Colette, Jacques. "Joy, Pleasure and Anguish: Thoughts on Barth and Mozart." In *Theology of Joy*, edited by Johann Baptist Metz and Jean-Pierre Jossua, 96–104. New York: Herder and Herder, 1974.

Comstock, Gary David. *A Whosoever Church: Welcoming Lesbians and Gay Men into African American Congregations*. Louisville: Westminster John Knox, 2001.

Cone, James H. "Black Consciousness and the Black Church." *Christianity and Crisis* 2 (1970) 244–50.

———. "Black Power, Black Theology, and the Study of Theology and Ethics." *Theological Education* 6 (1970) 202–15.

———. *Black Theology and Black Power*. Maryknoll, NY: Orbis, 1997.

———. "Black Theology and Ideology: A Response to my Respondents." *USQR* 31 (1975) 71–86.

———. "Black Theology: Its Origin, Method, and Relation to Third World Theologies." In *Churches in Struggle: Liberation Theologies and Social Change in North America*, edited by William K. Tabb, 32–45. New York: Monthly Review, 1986.

———. *A Black Theology of Liberation*. 20th anniv. ed. Maryknoll, NY: Orbis, 1990.

———. "Black Worship." In *The Study of Spirituality*, edited by Cheslyn Jones et al., 481–90. New York: Oxford University Press, 1986.

———. "Christianity and Black Power." In *Is Anybody Listening to Black America?*, edited by C. Eric Lincoln, 3–9. New York: Seabury, 1968.

———. "Christian Theology and the Afro-American Revolution." *Christianity and Crisis* 30 (1970) 123–25.

———. "A Conversation with James H. Cone." *Alive Now!* 26 (1996) 18–23.

———. *The Cross and the Lynching Tree*. Maryknoll, NY: Orbis, 2011.

———. "The Dialectic of Theology and Life or Speaking the Truth." *USQR* 29 (1975) 75–89.

———. *For My People: Black Theology and the Black Church*. Maryknoll, NY: Orbis, 1984.

———. "Freedom, History, and Hope." *Journal of the Interdenominational Theological Center* 1 (1973) 55–64.

———. "God Is Black." In *Lift Every Voice: Constructing Christian Theologies from the Underside*, edited by Susan Brooks Thistlethwaite and Mary Potter Engel, 101–14. Rev. ed. Maryknoll, NY: Orbis, 1998.

———. *God of the Oppressed*. Maryknoll, NY: Orbis, 1997.

———. "The Gospel and the Liberation of the Poor." *ChrCent* 98 (1981) 162–66.

———. "An Introduction to Black Theology." *Enquiry: Studies for Christian Laity* 1 (1978) 51–80.

———. "James Cone on *The Cross and the Lynching Tree*." Bill Moyers, Nov. 23, 2007. Interview with Bill Moyers. https://billmoyers.com/content/james-cone-on-the-cross-and-the-lynching-tree/.

———. "Looking Back, Going Forward: Black Theology as Public Theology." In *Black Faith and Public Talk: Critical Essays on James H. Cone's "Black Theology and Black Power,"* edited by Dwight N. Hopkins, 246–59. Maryknoll, NY: Orbis, 1999.

———. *Martin & Malcolm & America: A Dream or a Nightmare*. Maryknoll, NY: Orbis, 1991.

———. *My Soul Looks Back*. Maryknoll, NY: Orbis, 1986.

———. "One Lord: 'Who Is Our Lord?'" In *Proceedings of the 14th World Methodist Conference in July 21–22, 1981*, edited by Joe Hale, 34–42. Honolulu: World Methodist Council, 1981.

———. "Rev. Dr. James H. Cone Responds to 2014 AAR Panel." YouTube, 2014. www.youtube.com/watch?v=bY-vnMtAZFw.

———. *Risks of Faith: The Emergence of a Black Theology of Liberation, 1968–1998*. Boston: Beacon, 1999

———. *Said I Wasn't Gonna Tell Nobody: The Making of a Black Theologian*. Maryknoll, NY: Orbis, 2018.

———. *Speaking the Truth: Ecumenism, Liberation, and Black Theology*. Maryknoll, NY: Orbis, 1986.

———. *The Spirituals and the Blues: An Interpretation*. Maryknoll, NY: Orbis, 1972.

———. "Theology as the Expression of God's Liberating Activity for the Poor." In *The Vocation of the Theologian*, edited by Theodore W. Jennings Jr., 120–34. Philadelphia: Fortress, 1985.

———. "Toward a Black Theology." *Ebony* (1970) 113–16.

———. "Violence: A Response to J. M. Lochman." *Christianity and Crisis* 32 (1972) 166–67.

———. "What Does It Mean to Be Saved?" In *Preaching the Gospel*, edited by Henry Young, 20–24. Philadelphia: Fortress, 1976.

Cone, James H., and William Hordern. "Dialogue on Black Theology." *ChrCent* 88 (1971) 1079–80, 1085.

Cooper, Anna J. *The Voice of Anna Julia Cooper: Including "A Voice from the South" and Other Important Essays, Papers, and Letters*. Edited by Charles Lermert and Esme Bhan. Lanham, MD: Rowman & Littlefield, 1998

Copland, Aaron. *Music and Imagination*. Cambridge, MA: Harvard University Press, 1980.

Cox, Harvey. *The Feast of Fools: A Theological Essay on Festivity and Fantasy*. Cambridge, MA: Harvard University Press, 1969.

Crouch, Stanley. *Considering Genius: Writings on Jazz*. New York: Basic Books, 2006.

Davis, Angela Y. *Abolition Democracy: Beyond Empire, Prisons, and Torture*. Open Media Series. New York: Seven Stories, 2005.

———. *Blues Legacies and Black Feminism: Gertrude "Ma" Rainey, Bessie Smith, and Billie Holiday*. New York: Vintage, 1998.

Del Gandio, Jason. "Neoliberalism and the Academic-Industrial Complex." *Truthout*, Aug. 12, 2010. https://truthout.org/articles/neoliberalism-and-the-academicindustrial-complex/.

Dixie, Quinton Hosford, and Cornel West, eds. *The Courage to Hope: From Black Suffering to Human Redemption*. Boston: Beacon, 1999.

Dochuk, Darren. *From Bible Belt to Sun Belt: Plain-Folk Religion, Grassroots Politics, and the Rise of Evangelical Conservativism*. New York: Norton, 2011.

Douglas, Kelly Brown. *Black Bodies and the Black Church: A Blues Slant*. New York: Palgrave Macmillan, 2012.

Douglass, Frederick. *The Life and Times of Frederick Douglass: His Early Life as a Slave, His Escape from Bondage, and His Complete History*. Mineola, NY: Dover, 2003.

Du Bois, W. E. B. *Black Reconstruction, 1860–1880*. New York: Free Press, 1998.

———. *Writings*. New York: Literary Classics of the United States, 1986.

Dugan, Kaitlyn, and Paul Dafydd Jones, eds. *Karl Barth and Liberation Theology*. Explorations in Reformed Theology. London: T&T Clark, 2023.

Durrwell, François-Xavier. *Holy Spirit of God: An Essay in Biblical Theology*. Translated by Sr. Benedict Davies. Cincinnati: Servant, 2006.

Earl, Riggins R., Jr. *Dark Symbols, Obscure Signs: God, Self, and Community in the Slave Mind*. Maryknoll, NY: Orbis, 1993.

Edgar, William. *A Supreme Love: The Music of Jazz and the Hope of the Gospel*. Downer's Grove, IL: IVP Academic, 2022.

Edwards, Mark James. *Christ Is Time: The Gospel According to Karl Barth (and the Red Hot Chili Peppers)*. Eugene, OR: Cascade, 2022.

Eikelboom, Lexi. *Rhythm: A Theological Category*. Oxford Theology and Religion Monographs. Oxford: Oxford University Press, 2018.

Eppehimer, Trevor. "Victor Anderson's *Beyond Ontological Blackness* and James Cone's *Black Theology*: A Discussion." *Black Theology* 4 (2006) 87–106.

Fanon, Frantz. *Toward the African Revolution: Political Essays*. Translated by Haakon Chevalier. New York: Grove, 1967.

Fitterling, Thomas. *Thelonious Monk: His Life and Music*. Berkeley: Berkeley Hill, 1997.

Fromm, Erich. *The Revolution of Hope: Toward a Humanized Technology*. Minneapolis: Harper & Row, 1970.

Fulbright, J. William. "The War and Its Effects: The Military-Industrial-Academic Complex." In *Super State: Readings in the Military-Industrial Complex*, edited by Herbert I. Schiller and Joseph D. Phillips, 173–78. Urbana: University of Illinois Press, 1970.

Gadamer, Hans-Georg. *Hans-Georg Gadamer on Education, Poetry, and History: Applied Hermeneutics*. Edited by Dieter Misgeld and Graeme Nicholson. Translated by Lawrence Schmidt and Monica Reuss. Albany: State University of New York Press, 1992.

Giroux, Henry A. *The University in Chains: Confronting the Military-Industrial-Academic Complex*. Racial Imagination. Boulder, CO: Paradigm, 2007.

Gitler, Ira. *Swing to Bop: An Oral History of the Transition in Jazz in the 1940s*. New York: Oxford University Press, 1985.

Goba, Bonganjalo. *An Agenda for Black Theology*. Braamfontein, S. Afr.: Skotaville, 1988.

Godsey, John D. "Barth and Bonhoeffer." *Journal of Comment and Criticism* 33 (1982) 3–20.

———, ed. *Karl Barth 1886–1968: How I Changed My Mind*. Edinburgh: Saint Andrew, 1969

———. *Karl Barth's Table Talk*. SJT Occasional Papers 10. Edinburgh: Oliver and Boyd, 1963.

Gollwitzer, Helmut. *The Existence of God as Confessed by Faith*. Translated by James W. Leitch. Philadelphia: Westminster, 1965.

———. "The Kingdom of God and Socialism in the Theology of Karl Barth." In *Karl Barth and Radical Politics*, edited and translated by George Hunsinger, 77–120. Philadelphia: Westminster, 1976.

Gordon, Lewis R. *Her Majesty's Other Children: Sketches of Racism from a Neocolonial Age*. Lanham, MD: Rowman & Littlefield, 1997.

Gorringe, Timothy. *Karl Barth: Against Hegemony*. Christian Theology in Context. Oxford: Oxford University Press, 1999.

Gourse, Leslie. *Straight, No Chaser: The Life and Genius of Thelonious Monk*. New York: Schirmer, 1997.

Greeley, Andrew M. *God in Popular Culture*. Chicago: More, 1988.

———. *Religion: A Secular Theory*. New York: Free Press, 1982.

Green, Clifford, ed. *Karl Barth: Theologian of Freedom*. Making of Modern Theology: Nineteenth- and Twentieth-Century Texts. London: Collins, 1989.

Gunton, Colin. "Mozart the Theologian." *Theology* 94 (1991) 346–49.

Gutiérrez, Gustavo. *The Power of the Poor in History: Selected Writings*. Translated by Robert R. Barr. Maryknoll, NY: Orbis, 1983.

Hammond, Fred, vocalist. "We're Blessed." By Tommie Walker. On *Nothing but the Hits: Fred Hammond*. Verity Gospel Music, 1991.

Harney, Stefano, and Fred Moten. *The Undercommons: Fugitive Planning & Black Study*. New York: Minor Compositions, 2013. https://www.minorcompositions.info/wp-content/uploads/2013/04/undercommons-web.pdf.

Hart, William David. *Afro-Eccentricity: Beyond the Standard Narrative of Black Religion*. New York: Palgrave Macmillan, 2011.

Hartwell, Herbert. Review of *Theologie und Sozialismus: Das Beispiel Karl Barths*, by Friedrich-Wilhelm Marquardt. *SJT* 28 (1975) 63–72.

Highfield, Ron. "Opinion: What Makes a University 'Christian'?" *Pepperdine Beacon*, Apr. 20, 2021. https://pepperdinebeacon.com/opinion-what-makes-a-university-christian.

Heltzel, Peter G. *Resurrection City: A Theology of Improvisation*. Prophetic Christianity. Grand Rapids: Eerdmans, 2012.

Hentoff, Nat. *The Jazz Life*. New York: Dial, 1961.

hooks, bell. *Outlaw Culture: Resisting Representations*. Routledge Classics. New York: Routledge, 1994.

Hopkins, Dwight N. *Black Theology USA and South Africa: Politics, Culture, and Liberation*. Bishop Henry McNeal Turner Studies in North American Black Religion. Maryknoll, NY: Orbis, 1989.

———. *Introducing Black Theology of Liberation*. Maryknoll NY: Orbis, 1999.

Hordern, William. "Barth as Political Thinker." *ChrCent* 86 (1969) 411–13.

Horne, Gerald. *Jazz and Justice: Racism and the Political Economy of the Music*. New York: Monthly Review, 2019.

Hunsinger, George, ed. *Karl Barth and Radical Politics*. Philadelphia: Westminster, 1976.

———. *How to Read Karl Barth: The Shape of His Theology*. New York: Oxford University Press, 1991.

Hyde, Lewis. *Trickster Makes this World: Mischief, Myth and Art*. New York: North Point, 1998.

James, Robison B. "A Tillichian Analysis of James Cone's Black Theology." *Perspectives in Religious Studies* 1 (1974) 16–30.

James, William. "*The Will to Believe" and Other Essays in Popular Philosophy.* New York: Dover, 1956.

Jennings, Brach S. *Transfiguring a Theologia Crucis Through James Cone.* Dogmatik in der Moderne 48. Tübingen: Mohr Siebeck, 2023.

Jennings, Willie James. "The Aesthetic Struggle and Ecclesial Vision." In *Black Practical Theology*, edited by Dale P. Andrews and Robert London Smith Jr., 163–85. Waco: Baylor University Press, 2015.

———. *After Whiteness: An Education in Belonging.* Theological Education Between the Times. Grand Rapids: Eerdmans, 2020.

———. *The Christian Imagination: Theology and the Origins of Race.* New Haven, CT: Yale University Press, 2010.

Johann, Robert O., ed. *Freedom and Value.* New York: Fordham University Press, 1976.

Johnson, James Weldon. "Lift Every Voice and Sing." Poets, 1917. From *Saint Peter Relates an Incident.* https://poets.org/poem/lift-every-voice-and-sing.

Johnson, Keith L. *The Essential Karl Barth: A Reader and Commentary.* Grand Rapids: Baker Academic, 2019.

Johnson, Matthew V. *The Tragic Vision of African American Religion.* New York: Palgrave Macmillan, 2010.

Jüngel, Eberhard. *God as the Mystery of the World: On the Foundation of the Theology of the Crucified One in the Dispute Between Theism and Atheism.* Translated by Darrell L. Guder. Grand Rapids: Eerdmans, 1983.

———. *God's Being Is in Becoming: The Trinitarian Being of God in the Theology of Karl Barth.* Translated by John Webster. Grand Rapids: Eerdmans, 2001.

Kadushin, Max. *Theology of Seder Eliahu: A Study in Organic Thinking.* New York: Bloch, 1932.

Kelley, Robin D. G. *Africa Speaks, America Answers: Modern Jazz in Revolutionary Times.* Nathan I. Huggins Lectures. Cambridge, MA: Harvard University Press, 2012.

———. "Monk's Dance." Lecture-performance, Ovalhalle, Museumsquartier, Vienna, Nov. 2005.

———. "The Secret Life of Thelonious Monk." *Atlantic*, Mar. 29, 2010. Interview by Douglas Gorney. https://www.theatlantic.com/entertainment/archive/2010/03/the-secret-life-of-thelonious-monk/38128/.

———. *Thelonious Monk: The Life and Times of an American Original.* New York: Free Press, 2009.

Kirylo, James D., and James H. Cone. "Paulo Freire, Black Theology of Liberation, and Liberation Theology: A Conversation with James H. Cone." *Counterpoints* 385 (2011) 195–212.

Komunyakaa, Yusef. "It's Always Night." In "A Forum on the Prosody of Thelonious Monk." *Caliban* 4 (1988) 52.

Kraus, H.-J. *Reich Gottes: Reich der Freiheit; Grundriß systematischer Theologie.* Neukirchen-Vluyn, Germ.: Neukirchen, 1975.

Küng, Hans. *Justification: The Doctrine of Karl Barth and a Catholic Reflection.* Translated by Thomas Collins et al. New York: Nelson & Sons, 1964.

Lawrence, John W. "Editorial." *Frontier* 13 (1970) 81–86.

Lee, Felicia R. "Academic Industrial Complex." *New York Times*, Sept. 6, 2003. https://www.nytimes.com/2003/09/06/arts/academic-industrial-complex.html.

Leonard, Neil. *Jazz: Myth and Religion.* New York: Oxford University Press, 1987.

Lincoln, C. Eric, and Lawrence H. Mamiya. "The Religious Dimension." In *The Black Church in the African American Experience*, 1–19. Durham, NC: Duke University, 1990.

Litweiler, John. *The Freedom Principle: Jazz After 1958*. New York: Da Capo, 1984.

Lochman, Jan Milič. "The Church and the Humanization of Society." *USQR* 24 (1969) 131–39.

———. *Encountering Marx: Bonds and Barriers Between Christians and Marxists*. Translated by Edwin H. Robertson. Philadelphia: Fortress, 1977.

———. *Living Roots of Reformation*. Philadelphia: Fortress, 1979.

———. *The Lord's Prayer*. Grand Rapids: Eerdmans, 1990.

———. "Reconciliation and Creation: The Freedom of the World of God." *Communio Viatorum* 13 (1970) 171–75.

———. *Reconciliation and Liberation: Challenging a One-Dimensional View of Salvation*. Translated by David Lewis. Philadelphia: Fortress, 1980.

———. "Toward a Theology of Christological Concentration." In *The Context of Contemporary Theology: Essays in Honor of Paul Lehman*, edited by Alexander J. McKelway and E. David Willis, 209–23. Atlanta: John Knox, 1974.

———. "The Trinity and Human Life." *Theology* 78 (1975) 173–83.

Long, Charles H. "The Chicago School: An Academic Mode of Being." In *Ellipsis . . . : The Collected Works of Charles H. Long*, 89–98. London: Bloomsbury Academic, 2018.

———. *The Codex Charles H. Long Papers Project*. Moses Mesoamerican Archives and Research Project, Westlake, CA, box 1.

———. *Ellipsis . . . : The Collected Works of Charles H. Long*. London: Bloomsbury Academic, 2018.

———. "A New Look at American Religion." *AThR* 7 (1973) 117–25.

———. "New Orleans as an American City: Origins, Exchanges, Materialities and Religion." In *Ellipsis . . . : The Collected Works of Charles H. Long*, 25–38. London: Bloomsbury Academic, 2018.

———. "Passage and Prayer: The Origin of Religion in the Atlantic World." In *The Courage to Hope: From Black Suffering to Human Redemption*, edited by Quinton Hosford Dixie and Cornel West, 11–21. Boston: Beacon, 1999.

———. "Perspectives for a Study of Afro-American Religion in the United States." *HR* 11 (1971) 54–66.

———. *Significations: Signs, Symbols, and Images in the Interpretation of Religion*. Philadelphia: Fortress, 1986.

———. "Signs of Wholeness in the Black Religious Tradition." Lecture, Agenda for the Black Church, Vanderbilt University Divinity School, 1971.

Macchia, Frank D., and Paul S. Chung, eds. *Theology Between East and West: A Radical Legacy; Essays in Honor of Jan Milič Lochman*. Eugene, OR: Cascade, 2002.

Maldonado-Torres, Nelson. *Against War: Views from the Underside of Modernity*. Latin American Otherwise. Durham: Duke University Press, 2008.

Marquardt, Friedrich-Wilhelm. "First Report on Karl Barth's Socialist Speeches." In *Theological Audacities: Selected Essays*, edited by Andreas Pangritz and Paul S. Chung, translated by Don McCord, 103–22. Princeton Theological Monograph Series. Eugene, OR: Pickwick, 2010.

———. "The Idol Totters: The General Attack from the *Epistle to the Romans*." In *Theological Audacities: Selected Essays*, edited by Andreas Pangritz and Paul S.

Chung, translated by Don McCord, 172–89. Princeton Theological Monograph Series. Eugene, OR: Pickwick, 2010.

———. *Theologie and Sozialismus: Das Beispiel Karl Barths.* Munich: Kaiser, 1972.

Maury, Pierre. *Predestination and Other Papers.* Translated by Edwin Hudson. Richmond, VA: John Knox, 1960.

McKelway, Alexander J. "*Magister Dialecticae et Optimarium Partium:* Recollections of Karl Barth as Teacher." *USQR* 28 (1972) 93–97.

———. Review of *The Göttingen Dogmatics: Instruction [in] the Christian Religion*, by Karl Barth." *Int* 47 (1993) 415–18.

———. *The Systematic Theology of Paul Tillich: A Review and Analysis.* Richmond, VA: John Knox, 1964.

McKim, Donald K., ed. *How Karl Barth Changed My Mind.* Grand Rapids: Eerdmans, 1986.

Merton, Thomas. *Opening the Bible.* Collegeville, MN: Liturgical, 1970.

Migliore, Daniel L. *Called to Freedom: Liberation Theology and the Future of Christian Doctrine.* Philadelphia: Westminster, 1980.

Moltmann, Jürgen. *Experiences in Theology: Ways and Forms of Christian Theology.* Translated by Margaret Kohl. Minneapolis: Fortress, 2000.

———. *Religion, Revolution, and the Future.* Translated by Douglas Meeks. New York: Scribner's Sons, 1969.

———. *The Source of Life: The Holy Spirit and the Theology of Life.* Translated by Margaret Kohl. Minneapolis: Fortress, 1997.

Monk, Thelonious. "Interview de Thelonious Monk." YouTube, n.d. https://www.youtube.com/watch?v=oA_XoqoZN8w.

Monson, Ingrid. *Freedom Sounds: Civil Rights Call Out to Jazz and Africa.* Oxford: Oxford University Press, 2007.

———. *Saying Something: Jazz Improvisation and Interaction.* Chicago: University of Chicago Press, 1997.

Mühlen, Heribert. *A Charismatic Theology: Initiation in the Spirit.* New York: Search, 1978.

Niebuhr, Reinhold. *Essays in Applied Christianity: The Church and the New World.* Edited by D. B. Robertson. New York: Meridian, 1959.

———. "We Are Men and Not God." *ChrCent* (1948) 1138–40.

Noel, James A. *Black Religion and the Imagination of Matter in the Atlantic World.* New York: Palgrave Macmillan, 2009.

Pangritz, Andreas. *Karl Barth in the Theology of Dietrich Bonhoeffer.* Translated by Barbara Rumscheidt and Martin Rumscheidt. Grand Rapids: Eerdmans, 1989.

Panikkar, Raimon. *The Rhythm of Being: The Unbroken Trinity.* Gifford Lectures. Maryknoll, NY: Orbis, 2010.

Pederson, Ann. *God, Creation, and All That Jazz: A Process of Composition and Improvisation.* St. Louis: Chalice, 2001.

Pelikan, Jaroslav. *Obedient Rebels: Catholic Substance and Protestant Principle in Luther's Reformation.* New York: Harper & Row, 1964.

Ricoeur, Paul. *Hermeneutics and the Human Sciences.* Edited and translated by John B. Thomson. New York: Cambridge University Press, 1981.

Riedel, Johannes. *Soul Music, Black and White: The Influence of Black Music on the Churches.* Minneapolis: Augsburg, 1975.

Roberts, J. Deotis. "A Critique of James H. Cone's *God of the Oppressed.*" *Journal of the Interdenominational Theological Center* 2 (1974) 60.

Rogers, Cornish. "The Gift of Blackness." *ChrCent* 102 (1985) 572–73.

Rothschild, Hannah. *The Baroness: The Search for Nica, the Rebellious Rothschild.* New York: Knopf, 2013.

Ruether, Rosemary. *Christianity and Social Systems: Historical Constructions and Ethical Challenges.* Lanham, MD: Rowman & Littlefield, 2009.

———. *Liberation Theology: Human Hope Confronts Christian History and American Power.* New York: Paulist, 1972.

Rumscheidt, Martin. *Revelation and Theology: An Analysis of the Barth-Harnack Correspondence of 1923.* New York: Cambridge University Press, 1972.

Schellong, Dieter. "A Theological Critique of the 'Bourgeois World-View.'" *Concilium* 125 (1979) 74–82.

Schiller, Herbert I., and Joseph D. Phillips, eds. *Super State: Readings in the Military-Industrial Complex.* Urbana: University of Illinois Press, 1970

Schuller, Gunther. *Gunther Schuller: A Life in Pursuit of Music and Beauty.* New York: University of Rochester Press, 2011.

Sehgal, Kabir. *Jazzocracy: Jazz, Democracy, and the Creation of a New American Mythology.* Mishawaka, IN: Better World, 2008.

Sims, Angela D. *Lynched: The Power of Memory in a Culture of Terror.* Waco: Baylor University Press, 2016.

Sittler, Joseph. *Essays on Nature and Grace.* Philadelphia: Fortress, 1972.

———. *Gravity and Grace: Reflections and Provocations.* Edited by Linda-Marie Delloff. Minneapolis: Augsburg, 1986.

Smallenburg, Harry. "Monk, Bop, and a New Poetics." In "A Forum on the Prosody of Thelonious Monk." *Caliban* 4 (1988) 36–41.

Smith, J. Goosby and Erin D. Renslow. *Blessed Are Those Who Ask the Questions: What Should We Be Asking About Management, Leadership, Spirituality, and Religion in Organizations?* Charlotte, NC: Information Age, 2021.

Smith, Wadada Leo. *Solo: Reflections and Meditations on Monk.* Liner notes. Helsinki: Tum Records Oy, 2017.

Soelle, Dorothee. *On Earth as in Heaven: A Liberation Spirituality of Sharing.* Translated by Marc Batko. Louisville: Westminster John Knox, 1993.

Solis, Gabriel. "Hearing Monk: History, Memory, and the Making of a 'Jazz Giant.'" *Musical Quarterly* 86 (2002) 82–116.

———. *Monk's Music: Thelonious Monk and Jazz History in the Making.* Berkeley: University of California Press, 2008.

Solomon, Maynard. *Mozart: A Life.* New York: HarperCollins, 1995.

Somers, Steven. "The Rhythm of Thelonious Monk." In "A Forum on the Prosody of Thelonious Monk." *Caliban* 4 (1988) 44–49.

Spencer, Jon Michael. *Theological Music: Introduction to Theomusicology.* Westport, CT: Greenwood, 1991.

———, ed. "The Theology of American Popular Music." Special issue, *Black Sacred Music: Journal of Theomusicology* 2 (1989).

Steckel, Clyde J. "How Can Music Have Theological Significance?" Special issue, *Black Sacred Music: Journal of Theomusicology* 8 (1994) 13–35.

Stewart, Carlyle Fielding, III. *God, Being, and Liberation: A Comparative Analysis of the Theologies and Ethics of James H. Cone and Howard Thurman.* New York: University Press of America, 1989.

———. "The Method of Correlation in the Theology of James H. Cone." *Journal of Religious Thought* 41 (1983) 27–38.

Stoltzfus, Philip E. *Theology as Performance: Music, Aesthetics, and God in Western Thought*. New York: T&T Clark, 2006.

Stringfellow, William. *A Private and Public Faith*. Grand Rapids: Eerdmans, 1962.

Szwed, John F. *Jazz 101: A Complete Guide to Learning and Loving Jazz*. New York: Hyperion, 2000.

Tanner, Kathryn. *God and Creation in Christian Theology: Tyranny or Empowerment?* New York: Basil Blackwell, 1988.

Thornton, L. S. *Revelation and the Modern World: Being the First Part of a Treatise on the Form of the Servant*. London: Dacre, 1950.

Thurman, Howard. *Deep River: The Negro Spiritual Speaks of Life and Death*. Richmond, IN: Friends United, 1975.

Tillich, Paul. *Courage to Be*. New Haven, CT: Yale University Press, 1952.

———. *A History of Christian Thought: From the Judaic and Hellenistic Origins to Existentialism*. Edited by Carl E. Braaten. New York: Simon & Schuster, 1968.

———. *Life and the Spirit; History and the Kingdom of God*. Vol. 3 of *Systematic Theology*. Chicago: University of Chicago Press, 1963.

———. "The Problem of Theological Method." *Journal of Religion* 27 (1947) 16–26.

———. *Reason and Revelation; Being and God*. Vol. 1 of *Systematic Theology*. Chicago: University of Chicago Press, 1951.

———. *Theology of Culture*. Edited by Robert C. Kimball. New York: Oxford, 1959.

Torrance, T. F. *Theology in Reconciliation: Essays Towards Evangelical and Catholic Unity in East and West*. Grand Rapids: Eerdmans, 1975.

Turner, William C. Jr. "The Musicality of Black Preaching: A Phenomenology." *Black Sacred Music* 2 (1988) 21–34.

Vahanian, Gabriel. *Wait Without Idols*. New York: Braziller, 1964.

Van der Bliek, Rob, ed. *The Thelonious Monk Reader*. Readers in American Music. New York: Oxford University Press, 2001.

Van der Leeuw, Gerardus. *Sacred and Profane Beauty: The Holy in Art*. Translated by David E. Green. London: Holt, Rinehart and Winston, 1963.

Van der Post, Laurens. *The Dark Eye in Africa*. New York: Morrow & Co., 1955.

Wach, Joachim. *Sociology of Religion*. Chicago: University of Chicago Press, 1944.

———. *Types of Religious Experience: Christian and Non-Christian*. Chicago: University of Chicago Press, 1951.

Walker, Corey D. G. "'Serious Human Discourse': Charles H. Long and the Challenge of Elliptical Thinking." *Black Theology* 18 (2020) 95–103.

Ware, Frederick L. *African American Theology: An Introduction*. Eugene, OR: Wipf & Stock, 2002.

Washington, Joseph R. *Black Religion: The Negro and Christianity in the United States*. Boston: Beacon, 1964.

West, Cornel. *The Cornel West Reader*. New York: Civitas, 1999.

———. *Democracy Matters: Winning the Fight Against Imperialism*. New York: Penguin, 2004.

———. *Prophetic Reflections: Notes on Race and Power in America*. Vol. 2 of *Beyond Eurocentrism and Multiculturalism*. Monroe, MA: Common Courage, 1993.

———. *Prophetic Thought in Postmodern Times*. Vol. 1 of *Beyond Eurocentrism and Multiculturalism*. Monroe, MA: Common Courage, 1993.

Weston, Randy. *African Rhythms: The Autobiography of Randy Weston*. Edited by Willard Jenkins. Refiguring American Music. Durham: Duke University Press, 2010.

———. "Interview—Randy Weston: Montreux Jazz Festival 2016." YouTube, July 4, 2016. https://www.youtube.com/watch?v=HMGIkzqPSHs.

Wilde, Laurent de. *Monk*. Translated by Jonathan Dickinson. New York: Marlowe, 1997.

Williams, Delores. *Sisters in the Wilderness: The Challenge of Womanist God-Talk*. Maryknoll, NY: Orbis, 1993.

Williams, Martin. "What Kind of Composer Was Thelonious Monk?" *Musical Quarterly* 76 (1992) 433–41.

Wilmore, Gayraud. "The Disturbing Ecumenism of the Black Church in America." *Ecumenical Trends* 14 (1985) 113–15.

———. Review of *A Black Theology of Liberation*, by James Cone. *USQR* 26 (1971) 413–19.

Wilmore, Gayraud S., and James H. Cone. *Black Theology: A Documentary History, 1966–1979*. Maryknoll, NY: Orbis, 1979.

Witvliet, Theo. *A Place in the Sun: An Introduction to Liberation Theology in the Third World*. Translated by John Bowden. Maryknoll, NY: Orbis, 1985.

———. *The Way of the Black Messiah: The Hermeneutical Challenge of Black Theology as a Theology of Liberation*. Translated by John Bowden. Oak Park, IL: Stone, 1987.

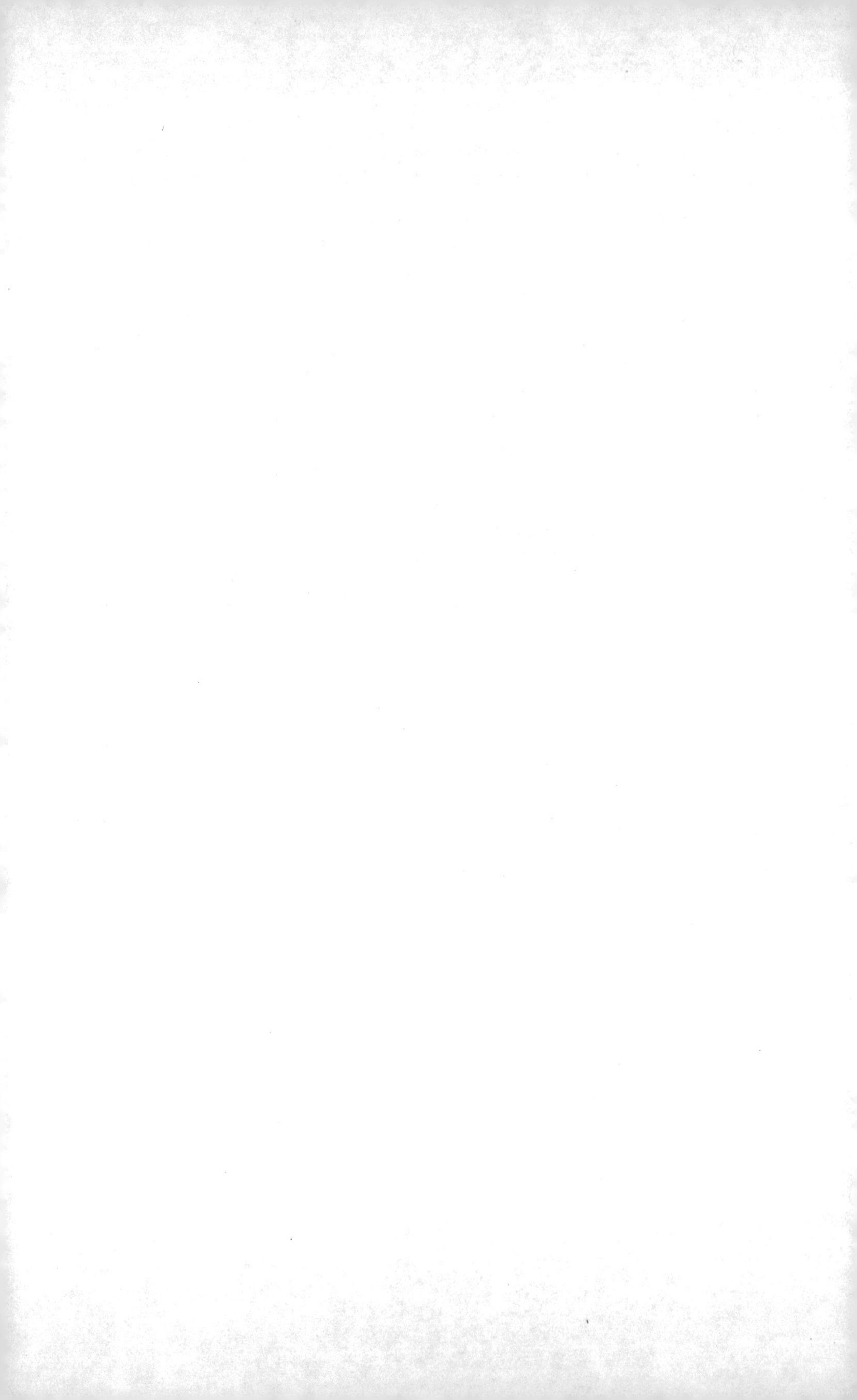

Index

(*)Asterisks signify definitions in the glossary.

www.ingramcontent.com/pod-product-compliance
Lightning Source LLC
LaVergne TN
LVHW091134080826
845145LV00008B/2144
9781666745252